THE JUNGIAN TAROT
AND ITS
ARCHETYPAL IMAGERY

THE
JUNGIAN TAROT
AND ITS
ARCHETYPAL
IMAGERY

Robert Wang

VOLUME II
The Jungian Tarot Trilogy
HISTORICAL STUDIES

U.S. GAMES SYSTEMS, INC.

ACKNOWLEDGMENTS

I wish to sincerely thank those who have made a contribution to this work including F. Sanford Brainard, III and Professor Lucy Bregman of the Department of Religion at Temple University, whose criticism of the manuscript at an early stage was very useful. Sincere appreciation is also due to Dr. Peer Hultberg of the C.G. Jung Institute in Zurich, to that Institute's Director, Dr. Helmut Barz, to Dr. Peter Lynn co-founder and former Dean of the New York Training Institute for Analytical Psychology, to the many analysts and scholars connected with the C.G. Jung Institute in New York whose advice has been of special importance in developing this text, to Princeton University Press for permission to quote from Jung's Collected Works, and to Rev. Laurence Brett for his exceptional help in interpreting some complex Early Christian and biblical texts.

Special appreciation for support and encouragement in this project is owed to Professor Marilyn Demorest, Department of Psychology, University of Maryland, to Professor Gregory Lehne, Department of Psychiatry, the Johns Hopkins University, to Sandra Beach, former Director of the Archive For Research in Archival Symbols of the C.G. Jung Institute in New York, and to Mark Whitehead who assisted in production of this book.

Published by
U.S. Games Systems, Inc.
179 Ludlow Street • Stamford, CT 06902 USA
www.usgamesinc.com

CONTENTS

PREFACE

The Jungian Tarot, which I first published in 1988, is intended to be a visual introduction to Jungian philosophy. The key is the archetypal image encountered through creative visualization or, as Jung called it, "active imagination." It is a process which may, theoretically, lead to discovery of a true Inner Self. Such creative visualization is at the heart of all mystical and religious systems, from those of the ancient world, to the spiritual exercises of Ignatius Loyola, to Hemeticism and Rosicrucianism, to Alchemy, and to the remarkably creative occult exercises of the nineteenth century.

Carl Jung, who brought the overview of a scientist to the age-old question of man's potential for self-knowledge, developed a special vocabulary (to which I loosely ascribe, but by which I do not feel bound). For example, he coined the word "individuation" to describe what tradition has called "enlightenment." Unquestionably spurred on by his own psychic experiences, Jung wanted to understand the nature of consciousness, and—ultimately—to solve the problem which so engaged the Greeks, the relationship between the *one* and the *many.*

The creative visualization which stimulates inner development can be very spontaneous; it can involve little more than clearing one's mind and allowing whatever wells up to become the focus of an inner play. But I personally believe that there is greater utility in a structured assault on the unconscious such as may be achieved through the tarot images. These cards, without reference to any belief system, and even if considered merely arbitrary images, are very powerful stimulus cues to the imagination.

Those familiar with my earlier work *The Qabalistic Tarot*, will be comfortable with an attribution of tarot cards to that central diagram, the *Tree of Life*. I consider this glyph to represent a hierarchy of archetypes and, indeed, a sort of road map of the collective unconscious. Thus one of my main efforts here is to demonstrate parallels between Jungian philosophy and Hermetic Kabbalah, a system which has been essential to Western mysticism since the Italian Renaissance.

I am considering Jung's ideas about regressions from the personal into the collective to be commensurate with the Kabbalistic method of working backwards from the lowest level of the Tree of Life (the material condition), through the upper levels which symbolize not only the enlightened Self, but a condition of nonbeing which transcends all consciousness, personal or collective.

This book also attempts to address a loose correlation of pantheons, under the file categories provided by tarot. It may be argued that ideas which emerge repeatedly across cultural boundaries lend credence to the postulate of archetypes which, in the minds of most people, is merely an interesting and remote theory. I am of the opinion that to rapidly (although admittedly arbitrarily in the present work) skim across ancient concepts of, for example, a mother goddess, is to consider the various faces of the Mother archetype represented in tarot as *The Empress*. And, again, the main reason for making such a comparison is to determine if the "true" nature of an archetype is revealed by those areas where far-removed cultures have deities with similar qualities. In this regard, the earliest mythologies seem to be the most useful.

I must, however, stress that, as an art historian, my amateur incursion into comparative religion is very tentative and my sources are general. I should also admit that as a historian I have a specific bias. History is, to me, something secure against which religious, mythological, and psychological ideologies must be measured, and it bothers me to find so many discussions of the history of tarot predicated upon irresponsible speculation (one of the unfortunate legacies of eighteenth-century romanticism), especially when the historical tracks of the cards are so clear.

In this regard let me say that I have no doubt that the tarot originated in fourteenth-century Italy. And because the earliest extant decks are from royal courts, one must assume that the artists of these decks were professional manuscript painters who would have been subject, in their rare secular pursuits, to a sequence of archetypal images allowing for the most obtuse of psychological interpretations.

Of course interpretation of the tarot in serious psychological terms would have seemed laughable, if not absolutely bizarre to its originators, who developed the cards as a game! It is not entirely clear how, over time, the cards came to be used for telling fortunes. But it was the spurious claim of the eighteenth-century writer Court de Gebelin, that the tarot cards originated in Egypt which sealed their later negative association with the "occult."

It was not until the late nineteenth century that tarot was systematically related to Astrology, to Kabbalah, and to Alchemy. And it was the twentieth century which added an overlay of modern psychological theory. But many supposed changes in tarot interpretation have merely been a change in labels. The terms of the medieval philosophers have been systematically supplanted by a more precise psychological language for the same mental processes and conditions. A man described by the Renaissance as "Born under Saturn" might today be considered to be a manic depressive. In any event, to view the tarot images in psychological terms may serve to amplify our understanding of a whole class of literature previously considered "mystical."

But of course, in contemporary terms, the tarot does address little-understood areas of psychic experience. So the following essays are, by definition, subject to limitations. To approach symbolic structures in an intellectual way tends to avoid the real issue—the inexpressible, irrational, and unconscious materials which the symbols describe. The passion of inner discovery does not communicate easily, if at all. And researchers in these areas are understandably hesitant to express their own feelings and intuitions about what may be deeply buried behind a given symbolic image. This was certainly true of Carl Jung, whose weighty corpus of studies is strikingly different from the description of his own personal experiences with the unconscious as described in his autobiographical *Memories, Dreams, Reflections*.

Finally, let me say that this work, which is predicated on Jung's rather remarkable methodology, is in no way intended to present a belief system. Nothing except the historical facts should be taken at face value. The exercise of dealing with each of the tarot keys as an archetypal image is meant to stimulate thought about the nature of consciousness and about the root causes of the human condition.

The central, and empirically unverifiable, thesis of this book is that it is possible to establish true principles of organization and structure of the archetypes of the collective unconscious by correlating related deities, images, and ideas from historical pantheons under the file categories of the tarot.

R.W.
Washington, D.C.
2001

INTRODUCTION

Jungian Methodology

Few would dispute an assertion that Carl Jung was one of the most original thinkers of the twentieth century. His postulation of the "collective unconscious," and of the denizens of that realm, the "archetypes," has created a school of modern psychological thought which may be pointedly questioned by empirical traditionalists, but which cannot be ignored. It was Sigmund Freud who, immersed in the Jewish mystical tradition, set the stage with his ideas about a personal unconscious. But it was Jung who took the idea to the logical conclusion that the mind of no person is "an island."[1]

At first glance, Jungian psychology may appear painfully complicated—if not unapproachable. Jung's frequent quotes in Latin and in Greek, his obscure references, and, indeed, the very aloofness of his language, tend to set him apart from those whose education was not strictly "classical." Nevertheless, Jung's ideas are not at all difficult. His main point is the resolution, or reconciliation, of *dualities* within the individual.

Dualities, existing in each person, are represented through the most diverse possible of symbols, such as male and female, sun and moon, black and white, gold and silver, conscious and unconscious. Confusion often arises because these opposites in manifestation have been symbolized in so many different forms, including plants, animals, and colors. Also, male can be father, son, or grandfather; female can be mother, daughter, grandmother.

Of course, these attributes are all symbolic of states of consciousness.

Now it should be understood that Jungian thought dovetails quite exactly with the underlying structure of the tarot, and of that Hermetic Kabbalah, which since the fifteenth century has formed the basis of Western mysticism.

The Hermetic Kabbalah, a metaphysical system developed by Italian Renaissance philosophers, combines Jewish mysticism with Neo-Platonism and with ideas then believed to have been drawn from ancient Egyptian religion by a mythical "great adept" named Hermes Trismegistus (Thrice Greatest Hermes).[2] The basic concern of this system—a concern identical to that of the Greek philosophers—is the way in which the one becomes many. Theoretically, the Creator produces an androgenous potential for opposites, a united condition of Mother ("Water") and Father ("Fire"), from which develop truly opposite, though interactive, states of consciousness symbolically described as male and female. Everything else derives from these essential opposites.

Kabbalists symbolize this sequential process, found over and over again at different "levels" of consciousness, through the divine name, YHVH. This name represents the opposites within the Macrocosm ("The Greater Universe") and within the Microcosm ("God in Miniature"). It is produced by the Creator, who is outside of the sequence, and who, theoretically, continuously revitalizes the process: Yod = the Father, Heh = the Mother, Vau = the Son, who is the resolution of conflicting dualities, and Heh final = the Daughter, who is the receptacle in which the activities of the primary three take place. She is the material condition and the physical body.

This symbolism is totally consistent with Jungian psychology, which draws parallel descriptions of the symbolic interaction of father, mother, son, and daughter from mythologies, from religions, and from the alchemists whom Jung described as having created the "forerunner of our modern philosophy of the unconscious." Moreover, Jung agrees with the Hermetic Kabbalistic principle that the reconciliation of these opposites within the individual results in the "loss" of the personality (what has been accepted by waking consciousness as the "self") to a state of consciousness described in metaphysical literature as the "Higher Self."

One of Jung's major contributions was his suggestion that a man has within his unconscious a female personality *(Anima),* and that a woman has within her unconscious a male personality *(Animus).*[3] These are the opposites which one strives to resolve. For a man to know the Anima, his own *contrasexual component* as Jung described it (to resolve the dualities of the self), is to achieve what traditional literature has called "enlightenment," or what Jung called "individuation." Jung said, "I use the term 'individuation' to denote the process by which a person becomes a psychological 'in-dividual,' that is, a separate, indivisible unity or whole."[4] That process (for either a man or a woman) is symbolized by the creation of the Son, who is the Perfected Self in manifestation.

The tarot can be understood as descriptive of the various activities of integral opposites—whatever they are called—*force and form, male and female*—within the Self. Theoretically, *The Fool* (Spirit) creates *The Magician* (the first male), from which emerges *The High Priestess* (the first female). All of the cards are understood to show these opposites in various garbs (at various levels, and in different situations of consciousness).

Eighteenth and nineteenth-century esotericists developed some complicated intellectual systems about the cards, which they expressed in curiously dispassionate terms—often through lengthy charts and complex lists of symbolic forms and colors. Analytical psychology, *per se,* did not exist, and it was up to the individual to recognize the personal implications of the symbols.

Today Jung's methodology points the way toward a direct understanding of the card images as psychological conditions and as personal experiences. Purposeful interaction with what he called "archetypes" can be an overwhelming emotional experience; it can produce unparalleled insights into the Self; it can also be devastating, even dangerous.

Beyond an appreciation of Jung's overview of opposites, his work is easily related to the tarot if his special, and occasionally idiosyncratic, terminology is understood. Jungian psychology depends upon a few underlying principles which, once grasped, will be recognized throughout the psychologist's writing. As his books emerged, it was seen that Jung repeated himself over and over again, defining and redefining the same ideas in ever more precise language.[5]

The Collective Unconscious

At the core of Jung's system is the idea that "the psyche" is a total self divisible into two key parts, the *conscious* and the *unconscious*. The hidden side, an unconscious which is personal to the individual, borders on a greater unconscious which all people share. Jung called this shared unconscious the *collective unconscious*. "My thesis," he wrote, "is as follows: In addition to our immediate consciousness, which is of a thoroughly personal nature and which we believe to be the only empirical psyche (even if we tack on the personal unconscious as an appendix), there exists a second psychic system of a collective, universal, and impersonal nature which is identical in all individuals. This collective unconscious does not develop individually but is inherited. It consists of pre-existent forms, the archetypes, which can only become conscious secondarily and which give definite form to certain psychic contents."[6]

He further stated that "the collective unconscious is a part of the psyche which can be negatively distinguished from a personal unconscious by the fact that it does not, like the latter, owe its existence to personal experience and consequently is not a personal acquisition....Whereas the personal unconscious consists for the most part of *complexes,* the content of the collective unconscious is made up essentially of *archetypes.* "[7] Jung's attempt to define aspects of the total self is not new. The divisions for which Jung developed a psychological language have traditionally been described in the language of mystical symbolism. For example in symbolic literature, wherever *water* appears, it generally refers to the unconscious. And where *planets are* mentioned, it is often to represent psychological types or categories of emotional states.[8]

Jung created new terms to express what visionaries have said for many centuries. The psychologist would certainly have agreed with the poet William Butler Yeats who, in 1912, stated his belief in three doctrines: "(1) That the borders of our mind are ever shifting, and that many minds can flow into one another, as it were, and create or reveal a single mind, a single energy. (2) That the borders of our memories are as shifting, and that our memories are a part of one great memory, the memory of Nature herself." And "(3) That this great mind and great memory can be evoked by symbols."[9]

Archetypes

Jung, whose father was a Protestant minister,[10] and who was well-versed in ancient literature and in the documents of the Early Christian period, discovered the word "archetype" in several works, including those of Philo Judeaus and of Irenaeus. He also referred to the *Corpus Hermeticum,* those supposedly ancient documents which so fascinated Renaissance philosophers.[11]

The term "archetype" has been used since ancient times, though never with the specificity that Jung applied it. Indeed, what Plato termed "archetypes" are "absolute essences," rather than "cultural imprints" as Jung explained them. Jung said that archetypes are "deposits of the constantly repeated experiences of humanity."[12] He called them "primordial images."

The number and form of these archetypes, created by human experience, is limitless. They can appear as specific personalities, such as those suggested in the archetypal images of the tarot cards, personalities which are like dream images with which one can converse in imagination. Or they can be situations, or they can be places.

In the most simple of terms, archetypes are conceived as something deeply buried in each person which *in toto* make up what is called the collective unconscious. When these archetypes enter the individual consciousness, they take on the color and tone of the personality which perceives them. Thus, Jung repeatedly points out that the archetypes are not determined by their content—they are not a kind of unconscious idea. The archetypes are, he says, encountered at first only as *"forms without content,* representing merely the possibility of a certain type of perception and action."[13]

All of this sounds more complicated than it really is. The principle is that each person has within, for example, an idea of "mother," which is not purely individual, but which has been built up for centuries as a socially-determined concept, and to which interaction with the actual mother is related. In tarot the archetypal Mother figure is seen as *The Empress*. She is Hera in Greek mythology; she is the Egyptian Isis; she is Hans Christian Andersen's Snow Queen.

Indeed, archetypes are best seen at work in mythology. The patterns of Greek and Roman gods, those of fairy tales, and of the most imaginative (i.e., apparently irrational) of the noncanonical

Christian gospels are especially instructive. *The Gospel of Thomas,* for example, emphasizes the miraculous, and presents a young Christ who can be a genuinely nasty and vindictive little boy.[14] It would seem that the more miraculous the events described, and the more polar the behavior of the key figures, the closer to the archetypes of the collective unconscious.

Patterns of the Jungian Tarot Deck

Jung never wrote specifically on the tarot. But he said, "If one wants to form a picture of the symbolic process, the series of pictures found in Alchemy are good examples, though the symbols they contain are for the most part traditional despite their often obscure origin and significance. It also seems as if the set of pictures in the tarot cards were distantly descended from the archetypes of transformation."[15]

The psychologist devoted only minimal attention to the tarot; his comments are very casual. Indeed, his own definition of "archetypes of transformation" is hardly consistent with the intense personalities of the Major Arcana and of the Court Cards. He said that these special-category archetypes "are not personalities, but are typical situations, places, ways and means, that symbolize the kind of transformation in question. Like the personalities, these archetypes are true and genuine symbols that cannot be exhaustively interpreted, either as signs or as allegories. They are genuine symbols precisely because they are ambiguous, full of half glimpsed meanings, and in the last resort inexhaustible." And he speaks of "their almost limitless wealth of reference, which makes any unilateral formulation impossible."[16]

What Jung suggests is, actually, a new way of considering the Minor Arcana, those forty numbered cards which have traditionally been considered to represent situations, or what Jung called "transformations."

The application of Jung's ideas to the tarot yields some re-markable insights. Yet however much Jungian psychology points toward a useful, if not revolutionary, overview of the cards, a special deck, one which closely relates to the archetypes, is clearly required. If, as Jung believed, traditional tarot images are only "distantly descended" from the archetypes of the collective un-conscious, how, one must ask, can those images be brought into more exact alignment with the archetypes? The answer appears twofold: first, a recognizable human figure must appear in every card, and second, the images must be worked into a visual story consistent with the patterns of world religions and mythology as reported by Jung.

The Jungian Tarot, unlike any other deck, is an attempt to create a set of truly archetypal images, pictures to which there may be an immediate (and involuntary) intuitive response on the part of the viewer. The figure in each card shows some aspect of male ("force") and female ("form") within the Self. And although one archetype is emphasized, each of the cards represents a mul-titude of archetypes that overlap each other in meditation. The necessity for fluidity of interpretation of these cards cannot be overemphasized. They are not rational. What is represented is not linear and sequential; it is at base irrational, which means that to write about these images, or to talk about them, is to skirt the serious issues that they represent.

Each of the twenty-two major cards incorporates a *mandala* (a word meaning a magic circle used in Lamaism, and in other non-Tibetan forms of Tantric Yoga, as an aid to contemplation).[17] Jung, who dedicated a significant amount of attention to this form, related the circular (meaning "complete" in his terms) mandala to the Self.[18] He explained that "there are innumerable variants...but they are all based on the squaring of the circle. Their basic motif is the premonition of a center of personality, a kind of central point within the psyche to which everything is related....The center is not felt or thought of as the ego but, if one may so express it, as the *Self*....The totality comprises consciousness, first of all, then the personal unconscious, and finally an indefinitely large segment of the collective unconscious whose archetypes are common to all mankind."[19]

So, as mandalas are used in the *Jungian Tarot Deck,* they are intended to represent aspects of the "Self." Indeed, the mandala in each card is another way of showing those same energies symbolized by the archetypal image of the card and its environment.

Notes: *Introduction*

(Page number references appear in normal type; paragraph numbers appear in boldface.)

1. Pursuant to the use here of the term "no person" to represent both man and woman equally, it must be asserted that although this book attempts to avoid terms which could be considered to be sexist, textual flow demands a certain stylistic consistency with quotes from Jung's writings which universally employ the older form in which "he" encompasses both male and female, and which such general terms as "man," "mankind," and "men" are freely used in the general sense.

2. The most important work to appear on this subject is D.P Walker, *Spiritual and Demonic Magic, from Ficino to Campanella,* London, 1958. Other scholarly works of significance in this area include Frances A. Yates, *Giordano Bruno and the Hermetic Tradition,* Chicago, 1964 and Charles G. Nauert, *Agrippa and the Crisis of Renaissance Thought,* Urbana, 1965.

3. Carl Jung, *Civilization in Transition,* Princeton, 1964. **243-244**; *Two Essays on Analytical Psychology,* New York, 1953. **297.** *Anima* is a Latin word meaning the breath of life, or the underlying principle of physical life. It is often considered to be simply the soul. *Animus* is the spiritual, or rational, principle of life. It is often considered to be simply the spirit.

4. Carl Jung, *The Archetypes and the Collective Unconscious,* Princeton, 1977, **275.**

5. Jung's last work, *Mysterium Coniunctionis* is a summation and synthesis of his ideas, considered by many to be his finest work.

6. Jung, *Archetypes,* **43**.

7. Carl Jung, *Aion,* Princeton, 1978, **42.**

8. Frances A. Yates, *Giordano Bruno and the Hermetic Tradition, Chicago, 1964,* 142.

9. William Butler Yeats, *Essays,* New York, 1912,33.

10. See Jung's autobiography, *Memories, Dreams, Reflections,* New York 1963. This is a work of special interest when measured against Jung's very cautious scholarly texts. It suggests, among other things, the emotional and spiritual intensity of his own encounter with the ar-

chetypes.

11. The so-called *Corpus Hermeticum* attracted the attention of Cosimo de' Medici, a powerful Renaissance prince who instructed thehead of his Platonic Academy, Marsilio Ficino, to translate these documents even before he worked on Plato's *Republic* or on his *Symposium*. It was believed that these books had been handed down from ancient Egypt and held key to all knowledge and to all of the mysteries of the human condition. This idea was discredited in the early seventeenth century, although the documents remain significant in the history of metaphysics. An English translation of the collection was reprinted with very scholarly commentaries by Walter Scott as: *Hermetica,* Oxford, 1924-36. 4 vols. Philo Judeaus (c.20 B.C.E.-C.E.c.50) was a mystic and an eclectic who (following Plato) introduced the idea of *Logos* as intermediary between God and the world. Irenaeus (c.125-c.202) was one of the Greek Fathers of the Church. His most important work was *Against Heresies* which attacked Gnosticism. Jung mentions that he was influenced by Philo Judeaus, by Irenaeus, by Dionysius the Areopagite, by Augustine, by the *Hermetica,* and by Plato. See: *Archetypes,* **4.**

12. Carl Jung, *Alchemical Studies,* Princeton, 1976, **237.**

13. Jung, A*rchetypes,* **48**.

14. Montague Rhodes James, *The Apocryphal New Testament,* Oxford, 1969, 49-65.

15. Jung, *Archetypes,* **81.**

16. Ibid., **81** and **38.**

17. Carl Jung, *Psychology and Alchemy,* Princeton, 1968, **95.**

18. Ibid.,**174**

19. Jung *Archetypes,* **357**

1 / THE FOOL

Archetype of Creative Emptiness

The Fool, although its place at the beginning of the trumps has become traditional, was not the first card of the deck in the very earliest versions of the tarot. And speculation about the original order of the cards goes hand-in-hand with the question of the original meanings intended for the trumps. In her pioneering 1966 study of the earliest-known deck, the *Visconti-Sforza Tarot,* Gertrude Moakley concluded that these cards were used for a game called *Triumphs* based on a poem by Petrarch. One particular game used twenty-one triumphs ("trumps" in English) and a *Fool.* A "Triumph" referred also to a triumphal parade modeled on those of the Romans, and Moakley suggests that each card was intended to represent a symbolic participant in the parade of Carnival. *The Fool*, she says, was not a part of the procession, but played an adversarial role. He was the ragged personification of Lent, reminding the party-makers that their frivolous parade must soon come to an end.

But eventually *The Fool* took over the place of the Juggler (*Magician*) as the King of Carnival and was thus placed at the beginning of the deck (leading the parade).[2] It is a theory which seems extremely probable on the basis of the evidence which Moakley gathered. As an archetypal image, *a fool* has most easily been interpreted to mean "foolish man" on the road of life, passing sequentially from the experience of one card to the other. And the very fact that the keys had such a clear underlying sequential plan helps to date their invention. The tarot, like the morality plays of the same period, undoubtedly emerged during the mid or late 1300s when there was renewed interest in the works of Aristotle with his emphasis on intellectual clarity and classifications of all sorts.[3]

In any event, six hundred years of fascination with the seventy-eight tarot pictures have transformed the tarot first from a simple game into an allegorical device, and then into a receptacle for some very complicated metaphysical principles. The fact that the tarot cards were not originally intended to carry the meanings that they do today in no way detracts from the utility of the cards as archetypal images. Thus, *The Fool*, the first card of the modern tarot deck, may legitimately be viewed as the principle of universal *becoming* and the source of all that is known. It is symbolic of the very creation of the universe.

The "Unmanifest"

Theoretically, *The Fool* is a separation out from what Qabalists call an *Unmanifest*. It is the No Thing to which all mythologies refer in some way.[4] The Fool is a sort of "Grandfather of the gods." And, in one of its key aspects, it is the *Archetype of Spirit*. But fool represents more than Spirit. It is the One which emerges from an Unmanifest, and from which the many derive. Yet the One does not exist; it is all potential. The course of creation, a divine thought rather than an act, is described by the first five cards of the Tarot: *The Fool, The Magician, The High Priestess, The Empress,* and *The Emperor*. These are the generative figures of Mt. Olympus. They also refer to spiritual steps in return to the Godhead. For the individual, two cards represent completed stages. First is *The Lover*, which means true Self-consciousness (what St. John of the Cross called "recollection') and the perfect balance of opposites. The second stage is *The Magician*, which is union with God and the willful dissolution of the recollected Self. As stated by that great alchemical text, *Splendor Solis:* "the whole work of this Art ends in two Operations hanging very close together, so that when the one is complete, the other may begin and finish, this perfecting the whole Mastery."[5] Beyond this "mastery" is absorption into the creative emptiness of *The Fool* and then into the ultimate emptiness of the Unmanifest (the *Ain Soph)*

Creation Myths

The story of creation most common to Western society is that of *Genesis*, the first book of The Bible. The text describes a sequential creation of the world out of a void. But, as the history of this document demonstrates, there is little in any creation myth which can be taken for granted.

Until a century or so ago the text of Genesis was accepted as revealed doctrine and, over the centuries, it was the basis of some extremely complicated interpretations—such as the idea that the original work represented a cryptogram, a complicated code based on numbers assigned to Hebrew letters. But in the year 1876 the archaeologist George Smith published the fragmentary work, which he called *The Chaldean Account of Genesis.* This was an earlier and different version of the text which he painstakingly assembled from thousands of small broken pieces of clay tablets written in cuneiform.[6] His discovery changed Bible studies forever. More recent scholarship makes it clear that what is known as the book of Genesis is actually a compendium of texts, carefully edited to exclude unacceptable tenets of earlier religions, such as polytheism or the primacy of a female deity.[7] It is not even clear what *"tohu and bohu,"* (translated as "without form and void") originally meant.[8] Indeed, there appear to be few stories which have not been in some way modified from their original text. A good example is the story of Noah, shown by scholars to have been based originally on the Zeus myth, wherein that god castrated his father, Kronos, and became King of Heaven. In the traditionally accepted text of Genesis, the castration of Noah has been omitted. It states that Noah awoke from a drunken sleep and "learnt what his youngest son had done to him."[9] This is watered down in Genesis to having seen his father naked,[10] for which we are to believe a son might be sentenced to a lifetime of servitude. The editing presumably represents an attempt to distance the Noah story from its Greek roots.

Thus it is clear that creation commentaries in the Judaeo-Christian tradition cannot be taken at face value. They have, among other things, suppressed a widespread emphasis on the female goddess. In *The Babylonian Epic of Creation (Enuma elish),* the Moon is created before the Sun whereas the opposite order, Sun and then Moon, is given in the Judeo-Christian version. The same order was found in the earlier Sumerian cosmology. Sumerian mythology considered the Moon, known as either Sin or Nanna, to be the son of the primary deity, Enlil, god of air.[11] The primitive emphasis on the moon may be of particular interest in that the Greek religion followed precisely the same pattern of evolution, first emphasizing the Moon, and later the Sun. As Robert Graves reports, "the Sun's subordination to the Moon, until Apollo usurped Helios'place and made an intellectual deity of him, is a remarkable feature of early Greek myth."[12]

Whatever the sequence, a creative progression of evolving deities was the essence of the earliest creation myths. In his *Theogony,* the Greek writer Hesiod, for example, describes an elaborate developmental order of early gods out of *Chaos,*[13] a condition which is probably commensurate with that of *The Fool.* But there is little consensus among ancient Greek philosophers about the order and process of manifestation, or even about the meaning of Chaos, which some say emerged from darkness; others say that darkness emerged from Chaos. What is most interesting in this debate is a tacit agreement that *darkness precedes light.*

The Western esoteric tradition states that the entire realm of the upper gods is pure darkness and that light does not reveal, rather it obscures. In these terms, it may be said that *The Fool* exists in darkness and is obscured to normal waking consciousness by the light.

There are stories about a God of All Things who suddenly emerges within Chaos, or about a Goddess of All Things, Eurynome, who, rising naked from Chaos, divides the sky from the seas so that she can dance upon the waves. In the Olympian creation myth, it is Mother Earth who comes out of Chaos to create the gods.[14]

The Egyptians made reference to companies of creator gods, usually in four pairs of male gods, and their female consorts. All of these are described by Budge as "personifications of aspects, or phases, or properties of primeval matter." Nu was the first among equals, as the god of the watery mass of the sky from which the heavens and the earth emerged.[15]

The earliest known cosmology, that of Sumer—as it has been pieced together by scholars (there is no known Sumerian cosmogony)—is disarmingly simple and primitively logical. At first there is a primeval sea within which a cosmic mountain of a united Heaven and Earth emerged. Heaven (male) and Earth (female) gave birth to Enlil, the air god who separated Heaven and Earth. Creation began with the union of Enlil and his mother, Earth.[16] And although the Sumerians believed the primeval sea to be a "first cause," their religion never speculated about the source of that first cause. It never went so far as to postulate a condition of unmanifest, or of "negative existence."[17] The question about where the gods come from and where they go seems typical of a much later thought pattern.

In any event, a comparison of the earliest known creation myths yields general agreement that something comes out of nothing and begins to multiply. These early mythologies, which are very simplistic and, if one may say so, less culturally determined than later versions, bear a remarkable similarity to the cosmology of the tarot cards in their emphasis on the importance of the female goddess and of water. In tarot *The Fool* and *The Magician* both represent aspects of Spirit, and thus of air. From these two comes the moon (a lesson identical to that of the Sumerian cosmology), who is *The High Priestess* and who will influence the waters of consciousness of *The Empress*, the fertile source of life.

The Fool as Point of Origin

The young man in the Jungian Tarot Deck represents a beginning which is pure potential, the birth of No Thing from an "unmanifest." He is shown, as has become traditional, about to step over a precipice. His impending act of walking into the Star-filled night sky is the act of creation commensurate with the separation out of elements chronicled by Sumerian, Greek, and Egyptian religions. He is the god who creates the possibility of the heavens, and of all other gods. Above his head is a crown referring to the title given by Qabalists to the ultimate source of the universe. Reference is to the first of ten centers of energy (Sephirot) on that metaphysical diagram called the "Tree of Life."[18] These centers, which may be related symbolically to the Minor Arcana, are considered to be objective, as opposed to the twenty-two images of the Major Arcana, which are subjective, and relate to "Paths" connecting those objective centers of energy on the Tree. This complicated system of Hermetic Kabbalah may appear to be remote and clinical, but it is remarkably useful when applied to daily life.

The cards represent human experience at a variety of levels and under all kinds of conditions. *The Fool* initiates the sequence and symbolizes a special creative aspect of the individual. This is beyond even what has been called *the Monad,*[19] the indivisible Self, the ultimate being from which contradictions arise, and within which opposites are resolved.

In his hand the youth holds a rose in flames. This is intended to suggest the principle that *Cosmic Fire is carried by Spirit;* they are not one and the same. The Cosmic Fire (sometimes called *Kundalini)* is that which, coming out of Chaos, continuously replenishes and maintains the order of the universe. Perhaps the most important principle here, relative to tarot, is that creation is a continuous process; each of the tarot keys represents transition.

Now although creation is considered to be continuous and cyclic, something like the figure eight on its side (the *Leminscate)* the pattern is theoretically described as becoming ever tighter, until the universe itself becomes the dense point, the ultimate "One" symbolized by the card of *The Fool*. The inevitable return to this condition, the destruction of *all that is* into No Thing, is suggested by the black leopard, one of the most cunningly dangerous of all animals. Its lethal attack is direct and, presumably, not negotiable.

This return to a primal point has been symbolized in many ways over the centuries. The crocodile, as destroyer, found in ancient Egyptian religion, raises some very significant issues. In Egyptian mythology, both the crocodile and the hippopotamus had dual natures—the crocodile being particularly aggressive in its destructive aspect.[20] Of course, the Egyptians did not venerate animals; rather, they considered them to be *abodes of the gods.*[21] Moreover, Egyptian religion was understood (at least by the nobility) to be ultimately monotheistic—all of the gods being aspects of one creator deity. And, in fact, the Egyptian pantheon provides one of the best, if not the most logically-structured, pattern of archetypes of any historical society. Jungian psychology reinforces the principle of Egyptian thought that every god (archetype) is bipolar, having a positive and a negative side. And as the innocent, virgin, aspect of Spirit is represented by the youth, the malicious, arbitrary, and very unpleasant aspects of Spirit are symbolized by the large cat. Here there may appear to be a contradiction in terms since, on the one hand, *The Fool* is described as unity, and, on the other hand, as having two opposite natures. The answer has to do with the nature of mind and of thought, and is not easily explained. One way to approach what is really a *koan* is to suggest that *The Magician* is the source of what the Buddhists call *mindfulness,* a special kind of mental attention. The egg at the right of the card is the *Orphic Egg*, symbol of the ancient Orphic Mysteries, meaning the embryonic cosmos encircled by the creative Cosmic Fire.[22] Symbolically, the egg is that from which the universe will emerge. It also suggests the birth of that which, through an evolutionary process, is to become consciousness.

The mandala at the left implies first motion and may be related to the *swastika,* one of the oldest known of symbols also known as the *gammadian* (being composed of four Greek gammas), or as the *fylfot cross.*[23] The swastika has been variously interpreted, but Jung views it as a rotating mandala, "a projection of an unconscious collective attempt at the formation of a compensating unified personality."[24] This idea adds a dimension to the possible interpretation of the mandala of *The Fool*, for it suggests that the desire for return to the source, to the condition of creative emptiness, is implicit in the projection of opposites.

Spirit

The tarot deck contains no image representing the Unmanifest, or those "waters"[25] from which *The Fool* may be said to emerge. The first of the philosophic elements, related to *The Fool* by Hermetic Qabalistic tradition, as in the Sumerian tradition, is *air*.[26] Jung also stressed the importance of air, and commented on the original wind nature of Spirit. Spirit is, he said, winged and "swift moving.[27] It is also defined as the essential principle opposed to matter. While matter is inert and static, Spirit is a dynamic, stimulating principle.[28] It is "the totality of primary forms from which the archetypal images come. In this world of the collective unconscious, Spirit appears as an archetype which is expressed through the figure of the divine Hero, whose counterpart in the West is Christ."[29]

Relative also to the relationship which we have mentioned between *The Fool* and *The Hermit*, Jung commented that "Graybeard and Boy belong together. The pair of them play a considerable role in Alchemy as symbols of Mercurius."[30] However, what is called *Mercurius* is, as will be shown, more appropriately related to *The Magician* than to *The Fool*

The interaction of the *Young Boy* and the *Old Man*, two aspects of the archetype of *Spirit*, is an especially magical theme when it appears in fairy tales and in folk myths. It is Merlin who guides and teaches the young Arthur. The archetype of Spirit appears as a *Deus ex Machina* (the God of medieval theater lowered onto stage with a rope) to save the hero, when all else fails. However, at the most profound symbolic level, this may be seen as the Spiritual Self[31] guiding and protecting the emerging self-consciousness. Here it should be noted that *The Hermit* is but one aspect of Spirit's activities, whereas the totality of Spirit is but one aspect of *The Fool*.

Notes: *The Fool*

1. Gertrude Moakley, *The Tarot Cards Painted by Bonifacio Bembo for the Visconti-Sforza Family,* New York, 1966, 46.

2. Moakley, 113.

3. Aristotle assumed major authority when Thomas Aquinas applied his point of view to Christianity. But the early influence of Aristotle has often been overstated. His works were not accepted blindly and, in the thirteenth century, there was a definite movement to discredit his work. Ironically, some of the first scientific experiments were a product of this attempt.

4. The idea of an "Unmanifest," the "Ain Soph," meaning that which is limitless and uncharacterizable, is emphasized in the essential Kabbalistic text *The Zohar.* This is a mid-thirteenth century work interpreting Genesis to represent various degrees of creative power. In the Soncino version the translators comment that it cannot be stated with certainly that such a doctrine was originally intended in Genesis. (See: *The Zohar,* Sperling and Simon Translation, v. 1, London 1934, 380.) Scholem explains that the term was invented by early Kabbalists of Provence and Spain and that its meaning was not originally clear. He defines it as "the absolute perfection in which there are no distinctions and no differentiations, and according to some no volition. It does not reveal itself in a way that makes knowledge of its nature possible, and it is not accessible even to the innermost thought of the contemplative." He mentions also, what he calls an "extreme thesis" which proposes that neither the Bible nor oral law referred to Ain Soph, and that only the mystics knew something about it. Gershom Scholem, *Kabbalah,* New York. 1978, 88-89.

5. Solomon Trismosin , *Splendor Solis,* London , Kegan Paul, Trench, Trubner & Co., Ltd. undated, 21.

6. George Smith, *The Chaldean Account of Genesis,* photographic reproduction of the original edition, Minneapolis 1977. Passim. This work is today more commonly referred to as *The Epic of Creation* or *The Babylonian Genesis.*

7. Robert Graves and Raphael Patai, *The Hebrew Myths: the Book of Genesis,* New York, 1964, 26. This is the companion book to Robert Graves, *The Greek Myths,* New York, 1957.

8. Graves, *Hebrew Myths,* 31.

9. Genesis, 9:24.

10. Graves, *Hebrew Myths*, 15.

11. Samuel Noah Kramer, *History Begins at Sumer,* London 1961, 139.

12. Graves, *Greek Myths, 156.*

13. Hesiod was one of the oldest known Greek poets, often contrasted with Homer. From the fifth century B.C. on there were disputes about which man came first. The *Theogony* is a long poem describing the origin of the gods and the powers born (in two separate lines) from Chaos and Earth. The best English translation and commentary to date is that of M.L. West: *Hesiod, Theogony; Works and Days,* Oxford 1988.

14. For a summary of Greek creation myths see: Graves, *The Greek Myths,* 27-34.

15. E.A. Wallis Budge *The Gods of the Egyptians,* New York, 1969 (Original Edition London, 1904), vol.I, 283.

16. Kramer, 138. Kramer bases this cosmology on a number of sources, relying primarily on the preface to the Akkadian poem which he calls "Gilgamesh, Enkidu, and the Netherworld."

17. Kramer, 120.

18. Extensive information on The Tree of Life and summaries of the Hermetic-Kabbalistic system will be found in Dion Fortune, *The Mystical Qabalah,* London 1935, and in Gareth Knight, *A Practical Guide to Kabbalistic Symbolism,* Cheltenham, 1965. The special relationship of Qabalah and tarot is addressed by Robert Wang in *The Qabalistic Taint,* York Beach, 1983.

19. The idea of a *monad,* meaning a 'Unit" or a "one," goes back to Pythagorus. The monad is the one from which all numbers derive. Plato applied the Pythagorean term to forms and to ideas; Neoplatonists and Christian Platonists later interpreted "Monad" to mean an irreducible entity which is the source of all being. Later philosophers to espouse some form of monadology included Leibnitz and Immanuel Kant. See: "Monad and *Monadology,*" Encyclopedia of Philosophy, New York, 1967, vol. 5, 361-363.

20. H.R. Hayes, *In the Beginnings,* New York, 1963, 255.

21. Budge, *Gods of the Egyptians,* vol. I, 2 note.

22. Manley Palmer Hall, *The Secret Teachings of All Ages: An Encyclopedic Outline of Qabbalistic and Rosicrucian Symbolic Phil-*

osophy, Los Angeles, 1975 (original, 1928), XX. Few books have stood the test of time as has this enormous compilation of facts about mystery religions and occultism.

23. Goblet D'Alviella, *The Migration of Symbols,* Wellingborough, Northamptonshire,1979 (Original, Paris 1892), 32-83. The word "swastica" is from the Hindu words "Su,"meaning *well* and "Asti," meaning *it is.* D'Alviella states that the symbol originated in Troy about the thirteenth century B.C., where it was transported" to Mycenae and to Greece. Eventually it reached Rome, Germany, England, Africa, and even Iceland. He asserts also that the symbol is not found either in Egypt or in Mesopotamia, which is incorrect. There are many Sumerian and Assyro-Babylonian examples of crosses and figures (as early as the 5th millennium B.C.) with wave lines indicating turning motion. See, for example, André Parrot, Sumer; *the Dawn of Art,* New York, 1961 figures 60 and 61, facing p.44. The figure has been interpreted to represent prosperity, fecundity, running water, a lightning storm, and the god of air. D'Alviella concludes that it is ultimately a solar symbol.

24. Jung, *The Symbolic Life,* Princeton 1980, **1332.**

25. Some confusion may exist because of the rather loose ways in which elements, i.e., fire, water, air, and earth have been applied. "primeval waters" should not be confused with the element of water—traditionally interpreted to mean consciousness—related to the Moon, as fire is related to the Sun.

26. Robert Wang, *Qabalistic Tarot,* 245-250.

27. Carl Jung, *The Archetypes and the Collective Unconscious,* Princeton, 1977, **210.**

28. Jung, *Archetypes,* **208.**

29. Jung, *Symbols of Transformation,* Princeton, 1976, **413.**

30. Jung, *Archetypes,* **215.**

31. The Spiritual Self, beyond the Higher Self and the Ego, is not a postulate of Jungian psychology but is one of Qabalistic doctrine. It assumes that an even higher principle stands behind that of the recollected Self, which is the object of Jung's methodology.

2 / THE MAGICIAN

Archetypes of First Matter
and of Animus

This card has acquired some very remarkable attributes over the centuries. If originally intended to be the frivolous King of Carnival, what is now called "The Magician" would have been the first card of the game of Triumphs. So it appears that an amusing figure, commensurate with the Juggler who entertained the royal courts, has been transformed into a sort of celestial Merlin on the one hand, and into one of the essential components of the creation of the Macrocosm on the other.

The Magician is, as the first phase of creation, an exceptionally complex card to which many archetypes relate. The card shares qualities of *The Fool* and is, in fact, another aspect of the archetype of Spirit. Yet whereas *The Fool* exists, but is No Thing, *The Magician* is the First Matter, or First Principle, which medieval alchemists called *Mercurius*. This concept may be explained by analogy to the artist, who thinks his work into existence before actually translating that thought onto canvas. In the same way, it may be said that *The Magician* is the creative thought of *The Fool*, something that has not yet been brought into manifestation, but which exists completely.

In ancient pantheons there is no god which is exactly equivalent, but the activities of *The Magician* are similar to those of the creator sky gods of every primitive society—powers long forgotten which continue to exist in shadowy and fragmentary references on stone and papyrus.

Tracks of the ancient sky gods, deities which were universally superseded by other religious forms, are found around the world, from Africa to Australia. The underlying pattern agreed upon was a primordial pair, sky (male) and earth (female), which produced everything else,[1] as was seen in Sumerian mythology where the air god Enlil is the product of Heaven and Earth. The Greek poet Hesiod also describes the creative connection of Heaven and Earth in the activities of the now obscure *Ouranos* (sky) and *Gaia* (earth).

This widespread belief in Sky Gods among early societies, and particularly in the generative relationship between sky and earth, is a rather rare area of cross-cultural agreement which maybe of special interest to those seeking cultural parallels that are legitimately "archetypal."

It is in this context that *The Magician* may be understood.

He may be profitably related to an ancient sky god ruling over a Heaven and Earth produced simultaneously out of chaos (as in the first "day" in Genesis) by *The Fool* wherein a "big bang" produces the thought conditions of the apparent separation of man and God. Then evolution fills in everything in between, which is the substance of creation on which man must act: *The Magician* creates the environment of the sky—the air (winds), the water (rains), and the fire (lightning). And then he creates those things which exist in the sky: the moon, the sun, and the stars.

What the primitive religions suggest about this process is that creation is a cooperative effort between man and god, earth and sky. It suggests that everything which exists between the two, all created things, are expressive of the relationship between the Creator (the one) and the created (the many), between the collective unconscious and the individual consciousness. Creation may be considered to be a dialogue between man and God about the perfectly balanced dual nature of *The Magician,* which is man united with God. Theoretically, *The Magician* is at once that which transmits and that which is transmitted. Expressed in another way, *The Magician* is both the subject of the dialogue of life and the dialogue itself.

All tarot cards except *The Fool* are implicit in *The Magician*. He is the totality of the tarot, which explains why the qualities of this card are so widely divergent—from the most sanctified and godlike, to the most capriciously human. *The Magician* is a role model, some might say a Christ or Buddha figure, for the reintegration of opposites, for the dissolution of the personality self. *Magician* is also, insofar as he is Animus and Anima, the antagonist to the personality. It must be explained here that it does not matter if one pursues Anima or Animus; both are Mercurius, both are the Self. Animus is the male aspect of *The Magician*; Anima (separated out as the *High*

Priestess, like Eve from the rib of Adam) is its female aspect. The reconciliation of dualities results in the same condition of wholeness—what is represented by *The Magician*.

The Magician can be variously described: he is the al-chemical *Mercurius;* he is the ultimate Spiritual Self united with God, far beyond the totality of conscious and unconscious. He is the *Macrocosmic* Adam; he is the Son who creates the Mother and Father; he is the androgynous origin of archetypal Sun and Moon; he is the *Philosopher's Stone*. All of these dif-ferent terms describe aspects of the same irrational principle and can, obviously, be very confusing in their diversity.

Magician as Initiator

As the second and final stage of spiritual awakening, living union with God, *The Magician* is God which acts upon the recollected-Self and, as the alchemists literally and accurately described what happens to the ego (the lower aspect of Self-con-sciousness), *dissolves* it. In the design of The Jungian Tarot, *The Magician* is shown as the celestial alchemist who directs the process of final union.

In the earlier passage, it is *The Lover* who represents a terri-fying first encounter with the unreality of the personality and the demand for wilful surrender (*The Hanged Man*) of per-sonal identity. This is a more common experience for the East-erner whose culture and priestly support-systems have con-ditioned him to accept such a change of perspective. But for a Westerner, faced with the unexpected idea that one does not exist separately, the proposition can trigger an emotional up-heaval beyond explanation. As the Buddhist Theologian Nyanaponika Thera said, "the deepest and most obstinate de-lusion in man is belief in a self, a soul, or an eternal substance of any description."[2]

There is absolutely nothing benign about the perception of personality being dissolved away. There are no words to describe the terror, the intense inner pain, and the total isolation of this condition for the unprepared Westerner. And in his *Dark Night of the Soul,* Saint John of the Cross warns that the "dark nights" come over and over again, and that they are relentless.[3] The fact that intense contemplation can produce such powerful inner experience must be emphasized. The symbol systems being discussed here are neither static nor sterile.

"Above and Below"

It is *The Magician* who introduces the seeker to the gods above "Heaven") and to those below ("the Underworlds"), what Jung refers to as the *cythonic* realm.[4] *The Magician* is thus related to Hermes, who was unique among Greek gods in that as the "guide of souls,"[5] Hermes functioned in both the heavens and in the underworld. He was also a god of fertility.[6] As messenger of the gods, he is usually shown in the guise of a traveler, with broad-brimmed hat, sandals, and caduceus wand. He is also occasionally shown carrying another sort of wand, that of the magician. Thus the attribution of Hermes to this card is especially fitting. He is magician; he is messenger. Of the gods, he alone travels both above and below. Dualities and their reconciliation are implicit here.

Sun and Moon

No symbolism throughout history is so widely encountered as that of Sun and Moon. Ideas about the worship of Sun and Moon have been indelibly etched into our culture by ancient societies such as those of Egypt, Greece, Rome, and the Middle

East.

Concepts about Sun and Moon were more or less grafted onto early Christianity as a transformation of the cult symbols of Helios and of Selene in the late antique period. Sun was explained as Christ. Moon was said to mean the Church, as well as the Mother Mary.[7] Perhaps the most consistent symbolism of Sun and Moon, found throughout the ancient and medieval world, is that of Moon as silver and Sun as gold. The alchemists took this idea a step further. Gold meant Sun, but it also meant the Philosopher's Stone. Jung, who believed that the alchemists were describing psychological processes,[8] made an even more pointed analogy: Sun means Self; Sun also means conscious, and Moon means unconscious.

In tarot, *The Magician* represents the perfect balance and source of the symbolic Sun and Moon. In this regard Jung quotes an Alchemical treatise which says that "As blood is the origin of flesh, so is Mercurius the origin of Sol...and thus Mercurius is Sol and Sol is Mercurius." Jung further points out that "Sol is therefore Father and Son at once, and his feminine counterpart is Mother and Daughter in one person; furthermore Sol and Luna are merely aspects of the same substance that is simultaneously the cause and the product of both, namely Mercurius duplex, of whom the philosophers say that he contains everything that is sought by the wise."[9]

There are two cards in particular which duplicate the functions of *The Magician* at a lower level, and which are also androgynous (meaning representative of resolved dualities). These are *The Lover* and *The Sun*. Both, like *The Magician*, symbolize the True Self and are Christ/Buddha figures. *The Lover* is the microcosmic magician; *The Sun* is magician as Child and the beginning of personal Self-recollection.

This idea of Christ as Perfected Self runs throughout Jung's work. It is, in fact, impossible to appreciate Jung's thought without reference to Christianity. He was a scientist whose intellectual roots were deeply buried in Christian tradition, despite his overt hostility toward Catholicism.[10] But, it may be argued that his idea of Christ as Self has more in common with Buddhism than with traditional Christian thought. Jung's work is populated with intriguing contradictions as was, apparently, the man himself.

Negative Aspects of the Archetypes

One of the problems with archetypes, to be encountered first with *The Magician*, is that their behavior is so polar and changeable, if not impossible to predict under given circumstances. They can be good or they can be bad. They can be kind or they can be insufferable. The Messenger of the Gods, the "father of language," is also the Trickster, the very source of deception. Jung explains that Mercurius, the Trickster, may appear as a rogue. He underscores the archetype's "fondness for sly jokes and malicious pranks, his powers as a shape-shifter, his dual nature, half animal, half divine, his exposure to all sorts of tortures, and—last but not least—his approximation to a figure of a saviour."[11] It will be observed, also, that past commentators have tended to minimize negative and irrational qualities of the tarot. The cards as archetypes do not represent only sweetness and light. In every card where beauty is shown, there is an ugly, if not vicious, obverse condition that is inevitably encountered in meditation. But here an important point of this philosophy must be reiterated: *the archetypes do not ultimately exist.* They are cultural imprints; they are collective projections of the human condition. They are the gods which have been described as "creations of the created."

Potential vs. Actual

One of the more elusive facts of interpretation of the tarot is that some cards represent potential, while others represent the actual. This expresses a differentiation between qualities of the *Macrocosm* and the *Microcosm.* As will be seen, the characteristics which are potential in the Magician become actual in the card of *The Lover.* Conceptually, there is a separation of creative qualities from what happens in manifestation. The principle is most easily described by the traditional terms "Heaven and Earth," or as "Above and Below."

The Magician, *The High Priestess*, *The Empress*, and *The Emperor* are all "gods above" who take different forms as they appear to the individual consciousness. And here one may well repeat Jung's very precise observation that "differentiation is the essence of consciousness,"[12] which is really another way of saying that none of these things make sense to the waking mind. To deal effectively with the archetypes of the collective unconscious, using the images of the tarot as an intermediary, requires a way of mental functioning which may, at first, seem very foreign and uncomfortable. It is a sort of giving up to nonsense; it involves learning to watch without reaction in thought or feeling.

Animus, Male Aspect of The Magician

According to Jungian theory, the unconscious of a man is different from that of a woman, Animus being, however, somewhat more difficult to describe than Anima. The archetype of Animus, the "antagonist" of every woman, covers a broad spectrum of ideas and of principles, none of which is easily defined. It is, as Jung said: "a purely empirical concept, whose sole purpose is to give a name to a group of related or analogous psychic phenomena."[13]

In Jung's essay "Anima and Animus,"[14] he explains Animus as "the deposit...of all woman's ancestral experiences of man." This male aspect of the female has a very distinct personality. It is argumentative, self-assertive, and tending to criticism for its own sake. It involves all of the polarities that a woman's individual and unconscious racial experience would attribute to father, brother, son, etc., and whereas Anima is usually viewed as a single figure, Animus can be a collection of figures, a set of father-like judges. Animus often appears in dreams as a hero figure, a traveler, an explorer of some sort. In her daily activities a woman draws upon the personality of Animus in the same way that a man draws upon the personality of Anima, and it is possible for the contrasexual component to overshadow or to "possess," as Jung calls it. A woman whose Animus is overbearing is in danger of losing her femininity. A very good example of such a pattern is found among women who attempt to compete in traditionally male professions. In order to succeed in the business world, until very recently in the West, a woman had to dress in a mannish way and actively suppress the expression of emotions which might be considered feminine and weak.

Jung states that to come to terms with the Animus a woman must "learn to criticize and hold her opinions at a distance: not in order to repress them, but, by investigating their origins, to penetrate more deeply into the background, where she will then encounter the primordial images."[15] Basically the encounter of Animus or Anima is not a philosophical exercise. It is intensely practical, involving the deepest feelings and the most sensitive interpersonal relationships. In working with Animus, a woman may heal unresolved conflicts with her own father or with some

other important male figure—a figure which helped to determine her attitudes about the masculine component of herself.
And once the personal aspects, a relationship to the individual
father have been resolved, it is possible to approach the deeper,
racial, unconscious imprints of the male figure called by Jung
Animus.

In its Animus aspect, *The Magician* represents a very powerful and changeable, Mercury-like personality. It is swift, elusive, devious, intellectual, and highly opinionated. Imaginary
conversation with the figure as Animus may lead to conversation with Father, Son, Grandfather, or any significant male
archetype. *The Magician* is all male figures of the tarot. In
fact, it cannot be repeated too frequently that the tarot images
are all Anima and Animus in one form or another. The idea
that man is son, father and grandfather, and that a woman is
daughter, mother, and grandmother has to do with life's natural passages.

Notes: *The Magician*

1. Mircea Eliade, *Patterns in Comparative Religion,* New York 1974, 38ff.

2. Nyanaponika Thera, *The Heart of Buddhist Meditation,* New York 1965, 51

3. There are two unique books which describe this condition. They are by Bernadette Roberts, *The Experience of No-Self,* Boston and London 1982 and *The Path to No-Self,* Boston and London 1985. In these works Roberts explains her own experiences, and gives some valuable advice on what may be expected to result psychologically and physically from contemplative exercises. The condition of "No-Self," and the process by which it happens has been explained primarily in Buddhist texts. The fact that the mechanics of this most difficult but normal condition of spiritual growth (appreciating that most know the term "Dark Night") is virtually unknown to clerics in the West, has to do with the emphasis of the Judeo-Christian tradition on perfection of the self. A book addressing this issue is *The Buddhist Nirvana and Its Western Interpreters,* Chicago, 1968, in which Guy Richard Welbon traces the widely divergent responses of Westerners to the encounter of such Eastern ideas.

4. In Greek mythology Hera, wife of Zeus, was originally considered to be cythonic: the father of the gods ruled the sky and the mother of the gods ruled the underworld, exactly as Sumerian myth equated male with heaven and female with earth.

5. Hermes was so viewed from the time of Homer on.

6. As a god of fertility, Hermes is usually represented as a "Herm," an upright slab with a head on top and a phallus at the center. See: *Oxford Classical Dictionary,* "Hermes," 502-503.

7. Hugo J. Rahner, *Greek Myths* and *Christian Mysteries,* London 1963, 89ff. Chapter IV of this work, "The Christian Mystery of Sun and Moon," must be considered to be Christian iconography's classic study of the subject.

8. In an introduction to a contemporary translation of Solomon Trismosin's *Splendor Solis* (London, undated), the writer, identifed only as "J.K."states that the title of the work was intended to mean "Gold Splendour" as well as "Soul Splendour" and that the illustrations refer both to physical conditions, and to states of consciousness. "J.K." also suggests a relationship between the tarot keys and the twenty-two illus-

trations of this manuscript. However neither he, nor any other who has proposed this, offer persuasive evidence or arguments in support of such a theory

9. Carl Jung. *Mysterium Coniunctionis*, Princeton, 1976, **121.**

10. Jung made some extremely vitriolic comments about the Catholic church. He called the *transubstantiation,* the "event" believed by Catholics to be the mysterious essence of the mass, "a showpiece for every collection of human aberrations." He also stated that "to the modern mind this dogma must appear simply absurd." Jung, *Psychological Types,* Princeton 1977, **38.**

11. Carl Jung, *The Archetypes and the Collective Unconscious,* Princeton, 1977, "On the Psychology of the Trickster Figure," **456.**

12. Carl Jung, Two *Essays on Analytical Psychology,* New York, 1953, 329. Ibid, **328-331.**

13. Jung, *Archetypes,* **114**

14. Jung, *Two Essays,* **296-341.**

15. Ibid., **356.**

3 / HIGH PRIESTESS

Archetypes of First Matter and of Anima

It should be obvious that the so-called "High Priestess" does not fit into any logical category of a royal court. She is quite out of step with an Emperor, an Empress, a Bishop (Hier-ophant), and even a Juggler (Magician) whose role is the keep the court amused. So there has been a great deal of spec-ulation about this female figure who is, in the *Visconti-Sforza* deck, a "Popess." As will later be shown, the historical roots of the *High Priestess* are to be found in the medieval iconography of the seven *Virtues.* This will be considered in chapter nine, which is devoted to the first Virtue card of the tarot, *Strength*.

The Anima Principle

In theory, *The High Priestess* and *The Magician* are beyond all archetypes; they are also beyond the collective unconscious. Insofar as they are Animus and Anima or other archetypes, their function happens within the context of *The Empress*, whose fruition is made possible by the continuous impregnations of *The Emperor*, her co-ruler. It is in her most general sense that *The Empress* is Mother-Water, the totality of the collective unconscious. Here the root principle is that *everything is mind*. But the mind principle of *The Magician* and of *The High Priestess* are totally impersonal. Their essence is reflected (literally mirrored) into the collective unconscious, in which context its richly varied activities are archetypal and maybe perceived by the self.

The High Priestess is a cold and calculating point of formulation of undifferentiated consciousness from which collective perception develops. *The Empress* is the Mother of Self which must return through her (as the collective unconscious) in order for it to lose its Self-perspective and to ultimately "dissolve" into the No-Self condition of *The High Priestess* and of *The Magician*. Understanding of Anima/Animus within the (enclosed) framework of *The Empress* confers Self-consciousness. To completely overcome the Anima/Animus aspect of the *High Priestess-Magician* may ultimately lead one past the perspective of the collective unconscious and into the condition of No-Thing of *The Fool*.

The principle of No-Self refutes the idea of an immortal soul and some of the most basic tenets of Christianity and of other religions. It also conflicts with the very idea of a "Creator" God. Indeed, the Creator God is, like all other archetypes, "a creation of the created." The archetypes of Creator and of "creation," exist only within the collective unconscious kingdom of *The Empress*.

Virgin Birth

What is most demanded from those who seek to find a glimmer of order through corresponding systems, is objective discrimination. On the one hand, the ancient world has bequeathed volumes of stories about miraculous impregnations and virgin births. Such tales are generally explained as having been handed down from a faraway primitive and dark society which was childishly ignorant about the true nature of childbirth.

Yet one must ask, on the other hand: did primitive man attempt to symbolize some inner principle lost to the scientific mind? The question is important to tarot because, over the centuries, *The High Priestess*, now interpreted to mean virgin consciousness, a blank slate of mind, has been related to the Virgin Mary and to a variety of virgin goddesses, including Nana, mother of Attis, console of the goddess, Cybele. In that story, the androgynous god Agditis (and note here a parallel to the Androgyny of *The Magician*) was castrated by other gods, and from the severed male parts an almond tree grew, the fruit of which impregnated Nana, and Attis was born.[1] Among those gods whose birth was miraculous were Hermes, Perseus, and Mythra. In fact, Juno, wife of Jupiter, was said to become a virgin each year and, in that state, supposedly bore Cybele, Demeter, Leo, and Vulcan.[2]

And there is the very fanciful story of the birth of the Buddha. In a dream a childless woman of forty-five, Maya (which means *illusion),* saw a small white elephant enter her womb. This was interpreted by the sixty-four Brahmans to mean the birth of a great emperor or sage. And it came to pass that the Buddha was miraculously born out of her side, undefiled and fully aware.[3] These stories all predate Christianity. And scholars have shown the ways in which many of the attributes of earlier goddesses, especially the Egyptian Isis, were taken over in descriptions of the Virgin Mary.[4]

Such tales of the creation of Gods are really like little mystery plays and are quite different from the claims of divine origin made for the Egyptian Pharaohs, for Alexander the Great, for Julius Caesar, for Augustus, or even for Plato who, in some narratives, was said to be the son of Apollo.[5] These are culturally-determined stories as are many myths and folk legends which seem truly to have been generated by ignorance about the nature of childbirth.

But the philosophical principle of virgin birth described in myth cannot be wholly explained as the result of sexual naiveté.The important principle related to *The High Priestess* is that the virgin who gives birth remains virgin and unchanged before, during, and after giving birth. *The High Priestess* remains "ever virgin" as does, also, *The Magician.*

Moon and Sun

The archetypal nature of the tarot is underscored by the extent to which its patterns are consistent with primitive religions and mythologies. Here, following the most ancient tradition, the Moon as *The High Priestess* precedes the Sun in the order of creation. This figure is the first female of the tarot and is, in fact, the first specific card of expressed gender—*The Magician* being androgynous.

The question of the gender of gods in various pantheons, or in the tarot cards, is not as simple as it may appear because, relative to the collective unconscious, maleness and femaleness do not represent static and polar qualities of the physical condition. In fact, although the Moon has come to be understood as female, this was not universally the case in early societies.

It has been seen, for example, that the Moon was male in the Sumerian pantheon as it was much later in some South American mythologies characterizing the Moon as reptile.[6] And in certain primitive Asian myths, as well as in Eskimo myth, the moon is male and the sun female.[7] One very ancient Australian story describes Sun and Moon both as male offspring of the sky god, Baiame.[8] So agreement that the Moon is female appears to be a later development of Western societies.

Presumably, the eventual, generalized agreement of the moon as a female quality relates to its rulership of fluctuations, and to its attachment to the menstrual cycle of a woman. The most important attributes of *The High Priestess* are her fluidity and her relationship to the structuring concept of time, which is of the greatest significance in the kingdom of *The Empress* as the core structure of the Macrocosm.

Indeed, *The High Priestess, The Empress*, and *The Emperor* are all aspects of *The Magician* as Macrocosm. They describe what is required for the final stage of spiritual awakening, dissolution of the recollected-Self and union with God. What Jung called individuation is the initial stage of spiritual awakening, that full realization of Self represented by *The Lover*. All cards below *The Emperor*, from *The Hierophant* through *The World*, and the archetypes which they represent, are aspects of *The Lover*. They show, collectively, the experience that is required to produce Self-consciousness.

Common to both the initial and the final stage of awakening

is an idea which cannot be overstressed and which, once understood, makes Jungian interpretation of the tarot cards more ap-
proachable: The whole tarot describes what happens to the
"male" and '"female" aspects of consciousness (not to be confused with sexual differentiation) under various conditions.

To pursue this idea, calling upon the four symbolic elements
(also considered to be the four letters of the *Tetragrammaton,*
the *YHVH)*[9] may help to clarify the Kabbalistic theory of spiritual dualities. In those terms every tarot card shows something
about fire or about water. In Father or Mother cards, they are
separate, whereas Son cards symbolize the total unity of fire/
water, Male/Female, which is symbolic air. Air is the resolution of the dualities of fire and water; It is the resolution of
male and female or, in Jungian terms, it is the resolution of
conscious and unconscious. The fourth element, earth, is the
vessel within which the commingling of fire and water takes
place. At one level this means the human body in which the
various aspects of consciousness are grounded. It should be
clear that the female (*Empress*) plays two roles: Her primary
role is that of water, the unconscious (the Cosmic Mother); her
secondary role is one of nurturing and enclosing the growing
Self-awareness, in which capacity she is Mother Earth.[10]

To express all of this in another way: *There is nothing in
manifestation but male/fire and female/water.* They are either
opposed to each other or they are unified, in which case they
are called "air." And "earth" could be whimsically characterized as water in disguise. Kabbalistic philosophers, who devoted more attention than any others to the problem of the *quaternity,*[11] understood this meaning in the YHVH. The Heh-final
is not different from the first Heh.

Thus, it will be seen that *The High Priestess* (pure and still
Water) embodies the potential for all phases of the female principle. She is the crystalline-clear root substance of the uncon-

scious, devoid of archetypes, which will become *The Empress* and which will, upon the stimulation of the male, express all of the rich phases of consciousness. On the path of the Self's return, she, as Empress, will turn back upon herself; and she will enclose the developing unity of male and female principle, the emerging God-awareness, often making torturous demands on the individual (what Jung called The Son). This is the role of female as nurturing earth.

There are three phases of woman: *The High Priestess*, who is ever-virgin; *The Empress*, who is the Fertile Mother; and *The Moon* (Hecate), who is the Decaying Earth Mother. To expand this analogy: the pure virgin unconscious becomes the womb (the fertile Earth Mother) for the consciousness which inseminates it and produces something new, the completed Self. Once this activity has occurred, the Fertile Mother (formative principle) decays, i.e., her potential for formative activity ceases.

The Earth Mother is existent only insofar as she nurtures the resolution of male and female principles. The pure female remains unchanged, the ever virgin *High Priestess*. Earth, the crucible for this process "dies" and will be reborn as the process repeats itself.

Characteristics of the Anima

The concept of Anima sums up all of the potential of woman. Implicit in *The High Priestess* are all of the other female figures in the tarot deck. Now this particular archetype, which is at the very core of Jungian psychology, tends to be described in two separate ways. First, Anima is viewed somewhat dispassionately, if not historically, as the woman of myth. Jung refers to that lengthy novel, *She* as descriptive of the phases of

Anima.[12] Anima is the Eternal Woman, the Eternal Queen. In the terms of the ancient world, she can be Hera, Diana, Hecate; she can be virgin, loving mother, hag, or whore and is seen in all of these roles on different tarot cards.

Christianity related to Anima as the Virgin Mary, endowing the mother of Christ with the most noble attributes of ancient deities as they did with Jesus Christ himself, whose iconography drew upon that of Apollo in the earliest church.[13] The great failure of Christianity in this regard is that its divine figures tend to be simplistically polar. The Virgin Mary shows only the innocent phase of *The High Priestess* and none of her arbitrary, vicious, even dangerous, characteristics.

In meditation with the card of *The High Priestess* Anima may appear as a real person with whom one may converse in "active imagination." She may be resplendently robed and aloof or she may appear simple and warmly outgoing. In fact, the initial appearance of such archetypal images will usually reflect a person's expectations and, always, each person's own cultural predispositions. One who relates to an inner female figure as the Virgin Mary will tend, at first, to deal with the archetype through the meek and mild personality proposed for her by Christianity.

But Jung warns about Anima's dark and moody side, especially if one becomes "possessed" by the figure. In Jungian studies this means the emergence of an unconscious focus of energy into a conscious environment—in other words, the archetypes brought out of their natural environment through some aberration of conscious attention to them. What happens in this case is that a man overwhelmed by Anima displays feminine traits, whereas a woman relating to Animus shows more masculine characteristics.[14]

As Jung says: "in the state of possession both figures [Anima and Animus] lose their charm and their values; they retain them

only when they are turned away from the world, in the intro-
verted state, when they serve as bridges to the unconscious.
Turned toward the world, the Anima is fickle, capricious,
moody, uncontrolled and emotional, sometimes gifted with
demonic intuitions, ruthless, malicious, untruthful, bitchy,
double-faced and mystical. The Animus is obstinate, harping
on principles, laying down the law, dogmatic, world-reforming,
theoretic, word-mongering, argumentative and domineering.
Both alike have bad taste: the Anima surrounds herself with
inferior people, and the Animus lets himself be taken in by
second-rate thinking."[15]

Jung offers some very clear and remarkably specific warn-
ings about the dangers of identification with any archetype
which is, again, the possibility of pathological emergence of
unconscious materials into the conscious mind. And, whether
he intended to do so or not, he expressed in psychological terms
those problems which have caused the most difficulties to stu-
dents of the mysteries over the centuries and which have been
lumped under the general category of "dangers of the work."

The Inner and the Outer Personalities

Jungian psychology explains that each individual has a hidden inner personality as well as an outer personality which is a
"mask" shown to the world. The hidden personality is Anima
or Animus and the outer one is the archetype of *Persona,* the
mask, which will be discussed at length with the card of *The
World.*

In general terms it may be said that the person who has an
outward appearance, a Persona, of reason and intellectuality
will usually have an inner personality which is quite the opposite, one which may be quite irrational and emotional.[16]

The psychological implications of this are very profound, for to address Anima is to deal with aspects of the Self which may be the very opposite of the ideal presented to the world. The unconscious can be a Pandora's Box of deeply repressed materials which may be dangerous to the stability of the waking personality if abruptly encountered.

Through Anima one may discover, for example, tremendous buried (and previously unrecognized) hostility toward a mother or other significant female figure which must somehow be resolved. And many will be forced to a reassessment of the nature of their own sexuality. One may discover unknown great strengths, but also a previously unrecognized capacity for savage and irrational behavior that is suppressed by normal persons functioning in civilized society. There are many such polarities of behavior implicit in *The High Priestess* as Anima.

Notes: *The High Priestess*

1. The Oxford Classical Dictionary, "Attis," Oxford, 1978, 146.

2. There is a lively discussion of this in Homer W. Smith, *Man and His Gods,* Boston, 1952, 182. The book includes an introduction by Albert Einstein.

3. A reliable general source for all of these myths is *The New Larousse Encyclopedia of Mythology,* New York 1987. Buddhist legends are discussed p.348ff.

4. E.A.Wallis Budge, *The Gods of the Egyptians,* New York, 1969, v.2, 218.

5. Smith, 183. This undoubtedly symbolic claim made by Plato's nephew Speusippus, as well as by Aristotle's pupil Klearchus, was promulgated by the writers Anaxilides and Diogenes Laertus among others. Plato's actual parents were two distinguished Athenians, Ariston and Perictione. *Oxford Classical Dictionary,* 839.

6. Mircea Eliade, *Patterns in Comparative Religion,* New York, 1958, 167.

7. American Indian Myths and Legends, Ed. Richard Erdoes and Alfonso Ortiz, New York, 1984, 161.

8. Eliade, *Patterns,* pp 43,41.

9. See Robert Wang, *The Qabalistic Tarot,* York Beach, 1983, 39 et passim

10. Gershom G. Scholem, *Major Trends in Jewish Mysticism,* New York 1977, 111ff. Scholem states that the Shekinah is "almost defined as the Logos," 116.

11. A discussion of the significance of the "quaternity," meaning a fourfold pattern, runs throughout Jung's work. In terms of the statement that there is only male and female, the quaternity has to do with the esoteric idea that within every energy is its own opposite.

12. This is a book of dubious literary value by H. Rider Haggard which, originally published in 1886, gained enormous popularity for its fanciful and romantic plot. The "She" is a woman of legend who has lived for centuries,and for whom the hero searches and, after terrible trials, eventually finds. She dies. He lives.

13. The ways in which the image of Christ was, in the earliest centuries of Christianity, based on the Roman god Apollo are discussed extensively in almost any general text on Early Christian Art. The Apollo-like Christ, who was blond and non-bearded, was superseded in

art by the dark-haired, bearded, Syrian type.

14. Such a psychic condition is not to be equated with homosexuality. It is, rather, a pathological state in which the normal psychosexual structure of the individual is overridden

15. Carl Jung, *The Archetypes and the Collective Unconscious*, Princeton, *1977,* **223.**

16. Carl Jung, *Psychological Types,* Princeton, *1977,* **804.**

4 / THE EMPRESS

Archetype of the Mother

The illogical position of *The Empress* before *The Emperor* in the traditional tarot deck lends support to Moakey's arguments about the origins of the tarot. It is her contention that in the Triumphal parade which the cards represent, the order was originally: The Juggler (*The Emperor*), the suit of Cups, *The Empress*, and then *The Emperor*.[1]

Fruition

One of the particular advantages of tarot symbolism is the way in which it compartmentalizes various aspects of universal male and female energies. The distinction between *water* as it relates to *The High Priestess* and to *The Empress* is a good example. *The High Priestess* can be described as crystal-cold, still water, which is without life, but which is the primitive source of all consciousness. *The Empress*, on the other hand, may be thought of symbolically as active, rushing water, filled with plants, animals, and other life forms. *The High Priestess* is absolute simplicity, *The Empress* is the utmost complexity to which four different sets of symbolism are applied: 1) She is the collective unconscious personified, the essence of Creative Water as it is described in almost every known pantheon. But the water which creates also dissolves—immersion into the watery realm of the collective unconscious leads to the total dissolution of the Self, which is the ultimate condition of the *Magician/High Priestess*. 2) She is (to quantify her activities as collective unconscious) the Cosmic Mother, the Mother of the Gods. 3) *The Empress* is also the eternally fertile Mother Earth, ruler of the cythonic realm who acts in concert with the god of air. 4) And, finally, she is the archetypal model of the personal mother. All of these aspects of the Mother archetype are skillfully addressed by Jung, who recognized early that the path to No-Self and ultimately to union with the "Divine Emptiness," is through the Mother. In this regard he did some clever amplification on the work of Sigmund Freud, his friend and colleague in the early psychoanalytic movement.

It was Freud who proposed the Latin word *libido,* meaning *strong desire,* or *lust,* as a descriptive term to mean "sexual instinct, usually directed at an outside object."[2] Jung, however, taking a very broad philosophical overview, called libido a *general psychic energy.* We must consider, he said, "every striving, every desire, including hunger and instinct however understood, as equally a phenomenon of energy."[3] Without explicitly so stating, Jung equated libido with what Schopenhauer spoke of as *will which is a thing in itself, without subject or object.*[4] It is an energy within each person which transcends the Self, and which can be known through the Mother. As a creative energy the Mother is the libido, an idea which Jung attempted to place in perspective when he cryptically wrote that "Mother-libido must be sacrificed in order to create the world; here the world is destroyed by renewed sacrifice of the same libido which once belonged to the mother and then passed into the world."[5]

In the tarot card *The Empress* is shown seated on a throne surrounded by lush foliage, holding a golden chalice as a symbol of the generative yoni. At her right foot is the white dove of Venus, and at her left is a passageway leading to the subterranean kingdom which she rules. The dragon represents the most unpleasant aspects of the Mother archetype which has, as do all archetypes, a dual nature. Although *The Empress* may be kind, loving, nurturing, and creative of vast beauty, she can be "not only the mother of all abominations, but the receptacle of all that is wicked and unclean."[6] The aspect of the Mother as the Terrible and Deadly Mother will be dealt with in the card of *The Moon.*

Anima as the Great Mother

The Great Mother, who is the expression of time and of dimensions, freely moves backwards or forwards into the transformation of maiden or witch. As Jung expressed it, "Anima is bipolar, one moment negative, then positive...now young, now old, now mother, now maiden, now a good fairy, now a witch, now a saint, now a whore."[7]

A key principle of Jungian thought is that the Mother, or at least, aspects of the Mother must be overcome. Of the Logos, for example, Jung states that "its first creative act of liberation is matricide."[8] He explains this point of view in his essay "The Battle for Deliverance from the Mother,"[9] wherein he discusses the mother Hera as the "Mistress Soul," who imposes extraordinary labors on her favorite child (Hero) to "spur him on to his highest achievement." The aim of the repeated and often brutal tests on the Child (*The Sun*, who is the early striving toward the Self recollection of *The Lover*) is absorption of the Self into the Mother and reunification with the Source.[10] In this process Jung explains that "The assimilation of contrasexual tendencies then becomes a task that must be fulfilled....The task consists in integrating the unconscious in bringing together 'conscious' and 'unconscious'....At this stage the Mother symbol no longer connects back to the beginnings, but points towards the unconscious as the creative matrix of the future. Entry into the 'Mother' then means establishing a relationship between the ego and the unconscious."[11] This is the descent into the underworld ruled by one aspect of the Mother.

Jung's conclusion that interaction with the contrasexual component is a process universal to enlightenment may well be his most important contribution, next to his postulation of the very existence of the archetypes. And, indeed, history supports his conclusions. It may be noted, for example, that the devotions of medieval monks to the Virgin Mary (their "bride"), or of nuns to Christ (their "groom"), had the practical effect of being an attempt to absorb, meaning to "overcome," the contrasexual component.

For a man to deal with Anima he must encounter his own contrasexual component under a variety of archetypal conditions of woman (all admirably symbolized in the tarot) from Maiden through Fertile Mother, to Crone. Thus, the interaction of mother and daughter normally foreign to a man assumes special significance, as does the interaction of father and son to a woman.

Jung devoted a long essay to the problem of the relationship of Mother and Daughter archetypes, referring them to the corn goddess Demeter and to her daughter-in-law Kore (known as Persephone in the underworld). Demeter is the Earth Mother, whereas Kore is a goddess of the underworld. Both are related to the moon. The psychologist offers an important distinction here relative to Anima. Although Anima expresses herself in Demeter-Kore, "she is of a wholly different nature. She is in the highest degree *femme à homme*, whereas Demeter-Kore exists on the plane of mother-daughter experience, which is alien to man and shuts him out. In fact the psychology of the Demeter cult bears all of the features of a matriarchal order of society, where the man is an indispensable but on the whole disturbing factor."[12]

And, far from being a vestigial thought from the ancient past, the idea of the man's superfluity is being expressed today by some highly literate proponents of feminism. One popular book states that "In the beginning...was a very female sea." The authors go on to assert that as "a fundamental and recurring pattern in nature: Life is a female environment in which the male appears, often periodically, and is created by the female, to perform highly specialized tasks related to species reproduction and to a more complex evolution."[13]

This idea is consistent with Hesiod's description of the root causes of creation. That Greek poet, who claims that his story was a spiritual revelation,[14] states that the female Earth is really the principal creator. According to his *Theogony,* chaos (which actually means "chasm" and does not imply disorder or confusion) first appeared, and then came the principle identical to Jung's definition of libido.[15] Hesiod called this Eros the "dissolver of flesh, who overcomes the reason and purpose in the breasts of all gods and all men."[16]

Eros, considered to be the libido which goes forth and then

returns to the Mother, is that which causes the dissolution of the perception of matter *("flesh")* and of the very thoughts *("reason")* and desires *("purpose")* not only of the individual, but ultimately of the collective unconscious *("the gods")* itself. Parenthetically, one might note that this is the same essence of *The Magician*, which has been earlier described as both "that which transmits and that which is transmitted."

Hesiod continues to explain how Earth (Cosmic Mother) bore "one equal to herself [The Father], starry Heaven, so that he should cover her all about, to be a secure seat forever for the blessed gods."[17] As spiritual principle, divorced from the realm of social polemics, there is some agreement about a universe in which a "fiery" male element is produced by a "watery" female. Certainly, this is the order of the tarot, where the male *Emperor* is secondary to *The Empress*. And, in this regard a very specific formula may be proposed: It may be said that: The path to Self is through the Father; the path to No Self is through the Mother, although it must also be understood that neither Mother nor Father are attained states of consciousness. Rather, they are transitional conditions along the way. All persons as spiritual beings (whether male of female because Son= Daughter) are symbolized in their quest by the Son whose learning experiences are guided by his parents. Stages of attainment are represented by the Son in different environments.

As this is expressed in tarot symbolism, the experiences of *The Sun* (Child) lead to the Self-recollection of *The Lover*. The Self then initiates a process of wilful and purposeful "sacrifice" (*The Hanged Man*) back into the generalized and Self-less condition of the Mother, who is *The Empress*. To conquer the denizens of the Mother as collective unconscious is to undergo complete absorption, meaning dissolution, of the Self and to reattain the condition of the *Magician/High Priestess*. Finally, beyond life and incarnation, there is the ultimate union with the No Thing, the Divine Emptiness, the Ineffable Silence, of *The Fool.*

These steps, real and powerful emotional and intellectual experiences which, as a new age dawns, are becoming increasingly common (although few Westerners, because their culture isolates them from such ideas, understand what is happening to them), are coherently described in Buddhist doctrine as the *meditative absorptions.* Of the first step which can be equated with the card of *The Sun*, the *Pali Canon* says that a person "detached from sense objects, detached from the unsalutary ideas, enters into the *first absorption* that is born of detachment accompanied by thought-conception and discursive thinking, and filled with rapture and joy." And with *The Lover* one "gains the inner tranquility and harmony of the *second absorption* that is free of thought-conception and discursive thinking, born of concentration and filled with rapture and joy." Then, after passing through the trials of *The Empress*, the rapture fades and is replaced by the "equanimity," the "mindfulness" and the "clear awareness" of the *third absorption* of *The Magician* into which one passes before that living union with the No Thing of *The Fool* "which is beyond pleasure and pain."[18]

Such ideas, although more or less anathema to accepted Christian dogma, are implicit in Gnosticism, which believed in a God the Mother (who in a male-dominated religious society conveniently became the " Holy Ghost").[19] Some Gnostics also read the story of Adam and Eve "as an account of what takes place within a person who is engaged in the process of Self-discovery."[20] Such theologians considered Eve to represent the real Spiritual Self hidden within Adam.

Now, in this regard, a principle must be restated: The Mother who is water is also the Mother who is earth. In the Kabbalistic formula, YHVH, the first Heh and the last Heh are identical;

they are only perceived to be different. Expressed in another way The waters of consciousness are the same as the earthy qualities of manifestation. The physical condition is, in reality, pure consciousness.

The Cosmic Mother and the Earth Mother

The inner "water" may be conceived as a deep pool containing the seeds of creation. It is at once all potential being and it is the actual and present condition of what is called "existence." This condition of group consciousness maintains structure; it purifies and heals. As the Cosmic Mother it is rather concisely personified by the Egyptian goddess Isis, especially insofar as she is a goddess of Wisdom. She was held by the Egyptians in a position of respect very different from any other goddess, as the pioneering Egyptologist Wallis Budge explained: "Isis was the great and beneficent goddess and mother, whose influence and love pervaded all Heaven and Earth, and the abode of the dead, and she was the personification of the great female, creative power which conceived, and brought forth every living creature and thing, from the gods in Heaven, to man on the earth."[21] Another ancient goddess who fits this description is the Phoenician *Asherat-of-the Sea,* who was called "Mother of the Gods" as well as "Creator of the Gods."

In historical terms, it has been observed by Eliade that the Cosmic Mother is an earlier phase of the Earth Mother theme. He asserts that "What makes it quite certain that the hierophany of the earth was cosmic in form before being truly cythonian (which it became only with the appearance of agriculture) is the history of the beliefs as to the origin of children."[22]

The cult of Cosmic Mother appeared at a time in history when children were thought to be implanted into women by magical trees and by vines and by streams. Men had no role as fathers, no part in creation. Birth was understood as a partnership between woman and *every place*. As Eliade expresses it: "what we would call the 'divinities of the earth' were really 'divinities of the place' in the sense of cosmic surroundings."[23] The earth was the totality of a cosmic environment. It was the Cosmic Mother. When later the true origin of children became clear, the principle of motherhood became attached to the earth and to the cythonic realms.

It would appear that at the most primitive stage of historical development mankind functioned within the Cosmic Mother, which we understand to mean the "waters" of the collective unconscious. And in some cosmologies, such as that of the Karaja Indians of Brazil, there remains, even today, a reference to a time when "they still lived in the waters."[24]

Something about that condition of fluid thought may be gleaned from the folk tales of primitive peoples. Even fairly recent tales from Africa, for example, have a totally different feel and quality than do tales from other societies. They are often expressive of a "watery" flow of consciousness unimpeded by linear thought, or by rationality. In a remarkable story (one recalling the Mother and Daughter archetypal interaction of Demeter and Persephone) called "Mother Come Back," the daughter is repeatedly protected from outside forces by a mother who descends from the sky, and who at one point rescues the young girl from the earth into which her body has entirely sunk.[25] The simplicity and innocence of such tales, the dreamlike and magical reality which they express, seems to support the idea of a historical evolution of human consciousness from a phase when it existed *within* a Cosmic Water Mother to a time when it perceived an Earth Mother *without,* as most people do today.

One might speculate that ancient literary references to a "fall" may be symbolic of a change in human consciousness, such as has been suggested by scientists in the development of a bi-cameral mind. In any event, the worship of an Earth Mother who is no longer the Cosmic Mother, the Mother to the Gods, but is specific to crops, to childbirth, and to the underworld, maybe argued to be a response to separation of the individual consciousness from the collective.

Notes: *The Empress*

1. The suit of Cups represented Cupid and the Triumph of Love. Moakley claims that the tarot cards are based upon three Triumphs—those of Cupid, Death, and Eternity. See: Gertrude Moakley, *The Tarot Cards Painted by Bonifacio Bembo,* New York, 1966, 51.

2. Sigmund Freud, *Three Contributions to the Theory of Sex,* "The Libido Theory." This book is found in *The Basic Writings of Sigmund Freud,* New York, 1938, 610. In this article Freud defines the Libido and discusses what he considers to be the chemical basis of sexual excitement.

3. Carl Jung, *Symbols of Transformation,* Princeton, 1956, "The Concept of Libido," **196.**

4. At the time in history when Jung began to write, the ideas of Schopenhauer (1788-1860) were tremendously influential to German intellectuals. Schopenhauer, whose underlying pessimism was certainly reflected in German society of the early twentieth century, expressed the opinion that man can know the reality that underlies his existence. The philosopher placed great emphasis on art as the path to understanding. It involved, he believed, a form of "aesthetic contemplation," resulting in unique mystical perceptions. See The Encyclopedia of Philosophy, V.7, 325-332.

5. Jung, *Symbols,* **658.**

6. Jung, *Symbols,* **315.**

7. Carl Jung, *The Archetypes and the Collective Unconscious,* Princeton, 1977, **356.**

8. Jung, *Archetypes,* **96.**

9. Jung, *Symbols,* **459**.

10. Although very little has been written in the West about this experience, (with the exception of writings by Saint John of the Cross and, most recently, of Bernadette Roberts), those who have actually gone through this agree on a number of points. Many report, for example, that serious progress begins when the student is turned over to a woman teacher, either in real life or in the inner mind. See: Monica Sjeo and Barbara Mor, *The Great Cosmic Mother; Rediscovering the Religion of the Earth,* San Francisco, 1987, *covering the Religion of the Earth,* San Francisco, 1987, 2. It is then that the aphorism "The Father forgives, but

the Mother does not" becomes clear.

11. Jung, *Symbols,* **459.**

12. Jung, *Archetypes,* **383.**

13.Sjeo and Mor, Op.cit., 4.

14. Hesiod, *Theogony* translated by M.L. West, Oxford, 1988, 4. West asserts his belief that this poem predates Homer (viii). He also notes that Hesiod's description of the divine succession is based on the Babylonian *Epic of Creation (xii).*

15. Jung discusses Hesiod in his article defining libido, *Symbols,* **198.**

16. Hesiod, 6.

17. Ibid., 6.

18. Nyanaponika Thera, *The Heart of Buddhist Meditation,* New York 1979, 159-160. In discussing mindfulness Thera points out that this is not a mystical state: "In its elementary manifestation, known under the term 'attention,' it is one of the cardinal functions of consciousness without which there cannot be perception of any object at all," 24. The correspondence between libido and Eros is clear.

19. Elaine Pagels, *The Gnostic Gospels,* New York 1979, 48ff.

20. Elaine Pagels, *Adam, Eve, and The Serpent,* New York, 1988, 66 et passim. This book traces the development of attitudes toward sexuality in the early Christian church.

21. E.A. Wallis Budge, *The Gods of the Egyptians,* New York, 1969, v.2, 203.

22. Mircea Eliade, *Patterns in Comparative Religion,* New York 1956, 403.

23. Eliade, 243.

24. Ibid., 191

25. Roger D. Abrahams, *African Folk tales,* New York, 1983, 316-320.

5 / THE EMPEROR

Archetype of the Father

Although people today tend to think of an emperor as something of a fairy tale figure, the emperor was a very real presence in the late medieval society which created tarot. It was in the year 800 that, in an effort to unite the Church and secular power, the Pope crowned a rather obscure Frankish King, *Charlemagne,* Holy Roman Emperor. The mid-fourteenth century heir to this title was Frederick III, a cousin by marriage to Francesco Sforza, who commissioned the painting of what is now known as the *Visconti-Sforza Tarot.*

The point is that the world of the earliest tarot cards was not invented, but was a reflection of contemporary society. It was the final phase of the Middle Ages in which the formalities of chivalry and knighthood were in their last flowering. It is important to see the original tarot in the context of the society which produced it, because the very distance from that society and a misunderstanding of the original meanings of the cards, has stimulated a fortunate richness of interpretation that has developed over the centuries. One result is today's theory that the cards are truly a sequence of archetypes. And in fact, to the fourteenth-century peasant, the real emperor must have seemed a distant and powerful presence expressing some of the qualities of the archetypal Father.

The Old Man of Eternity

Among the most evocative of all archetypes is that of the Father as a solitary and Wise Old Man who decides to produce something out of nothing. Almost every culture has some variant on this story, handed down from the dark recesses of man's beginnings.

In the Teutonic myths, for example, a huge gap suddenly appeared in the midst of nothingness. And from this gap all things emerged. And within this gap "time first dawned. And in the perpetual twilight was All-Father, who governs every realm and sways all things great and small."[1] As the course of creation progressed, there appeared a great giant, Ymer, from whose left armpit sprung the first man and woman.

In another version of the same myth, life developed from "burning ice and from biting flame," at the farthest edge of which sat the Terrible Father, "Black Surt brandishing a flaming sword" and "already waiting for the end when he will rise and savage the gods and whelm the whole world with fire"[2]

Eventually the ruling place of Black Surt was assumed by the god Odin, who was the very model of Father/Wise Old Man: "He was tall and old, and his aspect was wise and reverend. White was his beard and long, and he seemed ever to brood deeply over the mysteries of life and death."[3] It was Odin who determined the laws that governed human activities, which is a key role of the Father archetype. Moreover, the quality of intellectual brooding, the mind acting upon a created idea, is another pivotal behavior of the Father.

The extent to which the *force* of the Father is archetypal may be seen in creation myths so remote as those of the American Indian. These myths are almost ideal in the search for archetypal patterns because their distance from the Asian and European mainstream makes it unlikely that cultural intercourse occurred. In some Indian myths the wind (Father-Spirit) broods over the primeval ocean in the form of a bird.[4] In most Indian stories the world is produced by an All-Father Sun, "who thickens the clouds into water which becomes the sea."[5] Thus the Father produces the Mother-Water in a way which is mysterious, and for reasons which are almost never given.

But in one delightful variant the All-Father-God whose name is "Old Man Coyote," produces a woman because, as he said 'We are alone. It's boring.'"[6]

As has been suggested, however, the idea of the All-Father appears to be a later development, a mythology predicated on the cultural supremacy of the male. The earliest creation stories, which scholars have been able to piece together, involve a mother goddess, a watery mass which is understood to be maternal, or an androgynous figure, from which the Father somehow emerges.

In Search of the Father God

There is no certainty about man's earliest beliefs. The discovery of numerous "Venus" figures across Europe, dating from as early as 15,000 B.C.E. and generally considered to be fertility symbols, has generated much speculation among archaeologists about a prehistoric matriarchal society. However, it has been persuasively argued that in an early hunting society, fertility and the production of large numbers of children which had to be fed, was undesirable. A mother-oriented community was more likely to have appeared in the later agricultural society, where the woman assumed special importance in managing the home during the dark winter months.[7]

It also appears likely that there was an equal emphasis on the sexes in prehistoric times. By analyzing Paleolithic rock paintings, one researcher has discovered that sexual values were attributed to certain animals, and that they were paired. Another scientist, working in Siberia, discovered a small symbolic "village" whose houses were divided into two halves. The right half contained male-oriented images, and the left contained female statuettes.[8]

Such data are subject to broad interpretation, and there remains no definite evidence about man's earliest religious convictions. However about 8000 B.C.E. a great Ice Age ended and humanity changed radically. Between 9000 and 7000 B.C.E. what has been called the "Neolithic revolution," involving the cultivation of plants and the domestication of animals, began. At this time the role of mother was emphasized due to the importance of planting cycles and the fertility of the earth.

One may thus reasonably speculate on the course of man's beliefs. It seems probable that the earliest mythologies did involve an almost archetypal equality of the sexes, and that with the dawn of agriculture, the Earth Mother emerged as the primary deity, later to be superseded by the Father God.

Myths about a solitary All-Father who creates the world link the Father archetype to Spirit, and are the wellspring of ideas about the Wise Old Man. However, a distinction must be made between the role of *The Emperor* as Father archetype, and that of Father of the Gods.

The Emperor is Zeus/Odin, recipient of the blessings of The All-Father who creates the Gods. *The Emperor* is also counsellor, teacher, and guide (Wise Old Man, *The Hermit*) to the Child-Hero. The Solitary All-Father of myth is the primary creator who is called, in tarot, *The Fool*.

The Mother Overthrown

In Sumerian cosmology, the Father was clearly subordinate to the Creative Mother. But in the Babylonian version, this matriarchy was overthrown, the Father began his supreme rule, and the stage was set for the Judeo-Christian tradition. There, the role of God the Mother has been virtually eliminated, although one easily recognizes the tracks of the Divine Mother in the mystical documents of these religions. (In fact much of "revealed," or "secret" doctrine involves aspects of earlier religions which have been suppressed for socio-political reasons.)

In this regard the "traditional" tarot sequence of *The Emperor* following *The Empress* is remarkable in its conceptual similarity to the earliest myth, and may suggest an archetypal relationship which transcends culture. In tarot, as in Sumerian mythology, the Father has come to play a role that is distinctly secondary to that of the Mother, unlike the divine patriarchy established with the destruction of the Mother Goddess, Tiamat, in the Babylonian *Epic of Creation*.[9]

In that story Apsu, the consort of Tiamat, became unhappy with their children and planned to destroy them. But Ea (one of the great divinities of the Sumerian triad) caused Apsu to fall into a deep sleep and killed him.

Then, responding violently to the murder of her husband, Tiamat created monsters, and snakes, and demons, and gave supreme power to her son Kingu to battle the young gods. Marduk alone was willing to accept the challenge of Tiamat, and only on condition that he be exalted as the greatest of gods.[10]

In the ensuing battle, as Tiamat opened her mouth to swallow her opponent, Marduk hurled the raging winds into her, and she was ripped to pieces.[11] Jung evaluates this myth as representing the overthrow of the primordial matriarchal world by that of the Father. He views it also as "a historical shift in the world's consciousness toward the masculine."[12]

The same shift of primacy from Mother to Father has been observed symbolically in the relative positions of sun and moon in the early pantheons. The Sun takes over the position of the Moon very early in history, so much so that the primacy of the female Mother-Moon has been all but forgotten.

Sun gods and Father gods reflected a culture where the man was in control, where his role in the family was one of provider and protector. Hesiod describes Zeus in this position as "father of gods and men," variously as having a "great mind," as being "loud thundering," and the "greatest in power." He is the "Aegis Bearer" (meaning that he holds the shield of protection), He is "King in Heaven," and is stronger than his father, Kronos, whom he defeated.

According to the ancient poet, Zeus overcame his "crooked schemer," and cruel Father with the complicity and encouragement of his mother, Earth. To her Zeus said "Mother, I would undertake this task and accomplish it—I am not afraid of our unspeakable father. After all, he began it with his ugly behavior." The Mother then handed Zeus a sickle with a long row of sharp teeth with which he "quickly cut of this father's genitals, and flung them behind him to fly where they might."[13] They landed on the sea and from them emerged Aphrodite. For psychological interpretation, this a remarkable story The Mother schemes to place the Son in the role of the Father whose severed male parts (his essential power) produces a daughter.

As an archetypal progression, the Son actually assumes the place of the Father and, in fact, becomes the Father. But always it is understood that the Father is himself the Son in the process of enlightenment. Jung comments brilliantly on this condition, relating it to the birth of Christ which tells us "that a content of the unconscious ('Child') has come into existence without the natural help of a human father (i.e. consciousness)." It says that "some god has begotten the Son and further that the Son is identical with the Father which in psychological language means that a central archetype, the God-image, has renewed itself ('been reborn') and become "incarnates in a way perceptible to consciousness."[14]

And Jung adds, rather passionately, that: "One comes to the conclusion that creation is imperfect—nay more, that the creator has not done his job properly, that the goodness and almightiness of the Father cannot be the sole principle of the cosmos. Hence the One has to be supplemented by the Other, with the result that the world of the Father is fundamentally altered and is superseded by the world of the Son."[15]

When considered in terms of real parenthood, it may appear that the father is of less importance than is the mother. But this is true only insofar as the mother is a more immediate presence to the child than is the father. As consciousness grows in the child, the father assumes greater and greater importance. The Father archetype, Jung says, "determines our relations to man, to the law and to the state, to reason and the spirit and the dynamism of nature...he is that which moves in the world, like the wind; the guide and creator of invisible thoughts and airy images. He is the creative wind-breath, pneuma, Atman."[16]

It is with the Father, as with the Mother, necessary to separate the complex attributes of the archetype from the more mundane reality of interaction with a parent. There can be no question that Jung's definition of the Father as representative of the "world of moral commands and prohibitions,"[17] as "the sum of conventional opinions"[18] and as one who is "eternally right,"[19] relates to the difficult relationship with his own father as well as to the European society in which he lived. The role of mother and father were clearly defined; they were more polar than they are today: the mother was ideally nurturing, and the father-provider was the maker of rules.

Nevertheless, Father and Mother archetypes are ultimately cross-cultural. They reduce (actually, not symbolically), to *form and force*. The Mother creates the matrix, the structure within which experience takes place; the Father sets the archetypes in motion.[20]

Father is Animus, and he is the Wise Old Man who is the teacher. He is Spirit, but he is also a craftsman; often, as the Father of the Hero, he is a master carpenter or some sort of artisan.[21] And although he is the protector, he can be dangerous to the Son and is, in some aspects, the consort of the Deadly Mother represented in the tarot card of *The Moon*. As Jung explained this principle "the dangers come from both parents: from the Father because he apparently makes regression impossible, and from the Mother because she absorbs the regressing libido and keeps it to herself so that he who sought rebirth finds only death."[22] Indeed, the Son does not always escape the parents. The quest for Self is not always successful, as was demonstrated by the hero Gilgamesh who lost his battle for immortality.

Father and Daughter, Father and Son

To the Daughter, Father as Animus and as the Wise Old Man is "the sum of conventional opinions."[23] His influence increases her intellectuality. The Father brings what Jung calls *Logos* to bear on his Daughter, as the Mother brings *Eros* to bear on the Son.[24] This is really another way of expressing the effect of Anima on a man, and of Animus on a woman. There is always, in fact, a sexual balance, if not tension, between the (opposites) Father and Daughter, and between the Mother and Son. However, to reiterate a principle: Mother and Daughter are of the same essential substance, as are Father (*Emperor*) and Son (*Lover*).

The Emperor is the Father who protects and guides the Son,[25] (the emerging Self-consciousness of *The Lover*) within the manifest world. The Father, as intellect, presides over the condition of Self-recollection, which begins within the context of waking consciousness. Self-awareness, however, is not an end in itself. Rather, it is a recognition of the true nature of the Self and of its relationship to the created universe. To ultimately conquer the Father (and to assume his God-qualities) is to conquer reason. To conquer the Mother is to transcend the collective unconscious and the illusion of an Ego or of a self which is immortal.

Now although the purposeful encounter of the Mother and of the Father may sound remote and symbolic, it is very practical. What are called Mother and Father are part of a built-in system for Self-recollection. And in this regard, visionaries over the centuries have suggested that each person is endowed with exactly that which is required for self-understanding, the combined capacities of intellect, emotion, and spirit. Nothing more is needed—no religious conviction, no specific pattern of behavior, no outside influence, no laying on of hands, no teacher.

Moreover, Kabbalist philosophers stress that it is a cardinal fallacy to believe that the pursuit of Self involves anything "outside," or that some buttons are pushed and a light magically descends. It is said that each person moves continuously in and out of the condition of nothingness symbolized by *The Fool*. This is a sort of wave action where attention is captured by the illusion of matter, and then sinks back into the source only to be again brought to focus on the physical condition. But this truth is hidden from the waking consciousness, because its recognition must destroy the conception of a separate Ego.

The intellect and strength of the Father, who represents security in this material condition, helps to prepare each person for the frightening insecurity of the journey toward what has been described as "No Self." To express this in another way, it may be said that one of the roles of the Father is to lead the Child gently to the edge of the unknown, to the borders of the often wonderful and often terrifying Kingdom of the Mother. The principle here is that although the parents protect and guide, they force the Child into danger and trial which, when overcome, brings absolute independence.

Notes: *The Emperor*

1. Donald A. MacKenzie, *German Myths and Legends,* New York, 1985,1.

2. Kevin Crossley-Holland, *The Norse Myths,* New York, 1980, 3.

3. MacKenzie, *German Myths,* 21.

4. Lewis Spence, *North American Indians,* London, 1985, 107.

5. Ibid., 106.

6. Richard Erdoes and Alfonso Ortiz, A*merican Indian Myths and Legends,* New York, 1984, 88.

7. H.R. Hayes, In *The Beginnings,* New York 1963, 43-44.

8. Mircea Eliade, *History of Religious Ideas,* Chicago, 1978, v.1, 20-21.

9. Alexander Heidel, *The Babylonian Genesis,* Chicago, 1967, 40. This remains the best translation of the Babylonian story of creation, the *Enuma elish*—meaning "when above," words taken from the opening line of the poem. The work is of special importance because its parallels with the Old Testament suggest that it is a source of Genesis.

10. In Babylonian texts, Marduk takes the place of Enlil in the earlier Sumerian pantheon.

11. Eliade, *History of Religious Ideas,* v.I,70-71. The relationship of wind to water is an essentially archetypal one. These elements interact as Father and Mother in a wide range of creation myths.

12. Carl Jung, *Psychology* and A*lchemy,* Princeton, 1968, **26.**

13. Hesiod, *Theogony,* Oxford 1988, 3-8.

14. Carl Jung, *Symbols of Transformation,* Princeton, 1976, **497.**

15. Carl Jung, *Psychology and Religion: East and West,* Princeton, 1977, **201.**

16. Carl Jung, *Civilization in Transition,* Princeton, 1978, 65.

17. Jung, *Symbols,* **396.**

18. Carl Jung, *Aion,* Princeton, 1978, **29.**

19. Ibid., **32.**

20. Carl Jung, *The Archetypes and the Collective Unconscious,* Princeton, 1977, **187.**

21. It is at least possible that the craftsman profession of the Hero's father is intended as an obtuse reference to him as the Demiurge.

22. Jung, *Symbols,* **511.**

23. Jung, *Aion,* **29.**

24. Jung said: "I use Eros and Logos merely as conceptual aids to describethe fact that woman's consciousness is characterized more by the cognitive quality of Eros than by the discrimination and cognition associated with Logos." (lines 3-4) Ibid.

25. It should be reiterated that *Son, Child, Hero,* etc. refer to the emerging Self-consciousness of either a man or a woman.

6 / THE HIEROPHANT

Archetype of the Lesser Creator

This is the tarot card which represented the power of the Church in the Middle Ages. And although the figure on the card is obviously the Pope, he is ultimately anyone who administers by virtue of power given from above. But the power is not always perfectly administered, and may not necessarily always be used for good. Thus it ideally represents the Demiurge.

The Principle of Demiurge

The Hierophant is of cardinal philosophic significance in that it separates the Above from the Below and is said to be "hanging from spirit."[1] It is the "Lesser Creator," a somewhat fluid concept described throughout history by the word "Demiurge." This term has been applied to mean any creator other than God the Ultimate Father. But by definition more or less agreed-upon today (following the Gnostics), a Demiurge is considered to be a false god, one who ensnares the unsuspecting into his worship and into a belief that he is the true creator of the universe.

Yet the Greek word "demiurge" did not originally have this meaning. It was first used by Plato in his *Timaeus*[3] a very cryptic book which has exercised considerable influence on the history of ideas since the fourth century B.C.E.[4] In this book the philosopher refers to the Demiurge as a *craftsman,* a secondary father who produced man and his visible world. Plato says that "He was good" and "desiring then that all things should be good....the god took over all that is visible—not at rest—but in discordant and unordered motion—and brought it from disorder to order."[5]

The Demiurge is necessary to creation, and although he is not the essential creator, he is in no way a negatively "false" god (as the term Demiurge was later applied). Plato's Demiurge had the task of reducing elements of chaos to order and to reason. His Lessor Creator produces a visible universe,[6] which he calls *singular,* a "living creature with soul and reason."[7]

In the late antique period, a point in history when scores of different groups now called "oriental mystery religions" appeared, the Demiurge was described in surprisingly disparate ways. As architect of the material condition he was related to Saturn, to Kronos, and to the Hebrew God, Jahweh.[8] But he was also described by some mystics as the Logos, as the Demiurgic Christ, as the Higher Adam, as the Nous, and as the Serpent. He was even called the younger brother of Christ. Most of these meanings are better related, in terms of tarot imagery, to *The Magician*. *The Hierophant* is the Demiurge as creator of the material condition and of the illusory structure of the universe. In this regard, the Demiurge deserves his title of "Ruler of the Zodiac."

Number Symbolism

As Lesser Creator, *The Hierophant* represents the fourth point of a philosophic quaternity that, although occasionally considered to be evil, is the means by which the other three are expressed. Jung points out that many of the earliest gods had a triadic nature, citing a three-headed Hermes, a three-headed Mercurius, the three-bodied Typhon, and the three-faced Hecate.[10] However, the idea of trinity is far more elegantly expressed as Father, Mother, and Son. The fourth part is sometimes described as the bride of the Son—by which the Son becomes Father, and the process of creation repeats itself. This is the exact principle of the Kabbalistic YHVH.

So the number four expresses the nature of the material condition. Indeed, in Hermetic-Kabbalistic cosmology, the fourth Sephira, Chesed, is the Demiurge. The godhead, Kether, creates all that is above the Abyss (beyond the collective unconscious); Chesed (related to Jupiter), primary formative energy of the Microcosm and of the manifest universe, creates the visible universe in a way that is remarkably similar to Plato's description of the Demiurge.[11]

The other number which may be related to *The Hierophant/*Demiurge, is eight—or double four—the *ogdoad*.[12] The ogdoad is the essence of the cube which, in the Eleusian mysteries of

Greece, was called "the little holy number."[13]

About Gnosticism

Gnosticism, (from the Greek word *gnosis* meaning "knowledge") is not a single school of thought. The term sums up a wide variety of religious teachings, Christian, Jewish and "pagan" from the first centuries C.E. The Gnostic writers of the late antique-early Christian period deeply affected the development of metaphysical ideas up to the present day. In fact, many of these early writers were influenced by Plato's ideas which, although often misunderstood, have been a wellspring of Western thought. It is certainly paradoxical that one man could be the source of principles underlying schools of thought which so entirely disagreed, such as the Neo-Platonic system of Plotinus and Augustine's form of Christianity.

What is called Gnosticism covers a wide spread of ideas, but the schools of Valentinus and of Mani represent the two most important types which emerged.[14]

The philosophy of Mani, *Manichaeism,* is characterized by dualism.[15] Good and evil do not come from the same source; both darkness and light have their own independent realms. God and matter are opposed, as are darkness and light, truth and error. The world in which we live is considered to be a perverted mixture of both good and evil, and it is the purpose of the Manichean (who has recognized the light) to assist in separating these qualities.

On the other hand, there is the Valentinian philosophy which postulates that "evil" is the result of a "fall" which occurred before the emergence of the visible universe.[16] Valentinus (who was highly respected by some of the early Church Fathers[17]), spoke of a Primal Father who produced an "Abyss." And from that

Abyss came Silence, which was the thought of the Primal Father. And from the Primal Father and Silence emerged a series of aeons which form the divine realm, the *Pleroma.* This signifies the totality of the spiritual universe which is the ultimate abode of God which, in Kabbalistic terms, is the "Supernal Triangle. Valentinus taught that the Demiurge existed between the Pleroma," the world of ultimate reality, and the *Kenoma,* the phenomenal universe.[18]

From the Creative Logos (as opposed to the Solar Logos, which is the True Self) emerged the Demiurge. Valentinians believed that this point of energy proceeded to create six more lords ("archons"), exactly as Chesed created the six lower Sephirot on the Tree of Life.[19] Moreover, these Gnostics said that the Supernal Mother rules the Demiurge. The theory holds that the last of the aeons (and the farthest from the original source) was Sophia. In the Kabbalah this means Binah, the Supernal Mother who completes the Supernal Triangle and who could appropriately be called "Sophia."

According to Valentinian teaching, Sophia was guilty of a grave fault and therefore gave rise to a monstrous child, which had to be banished from the Divine Realm. Having "fallen" beneath the Pleroma, the monstrous offspring produced a Demiurge whose task it was to create a perverse copy of the Divine Realm.

The early centuries after Christ were a melting pot of conflicting ideas from which Christianity emerged the victor when, in 313 C.E., it was declared the official religion of the empire and at the ultimate baptism (perhaps on his deathbed[20]) of the Roman Emperor Constantine. And although the development of Western civilization has been integrally linked to Christianity, much of Gnostic thought has, ironically, been preserved by Christian writers wishing to dispute its "heresies."

For example, one of the most important sources of information about Gnostic belief was the Bishop of Lyon, Irenaeus, a

Greek Father of the Church who lived from about 125 C.E. to 202. The bishop, in writings unalterably opposed to Gnosticism, provides some of the best information about that movement. His work *Against Heresies* (a work expanded upon by his student Hippolytus as The *Refutation of all Heresies*)[21] makes it clear that the Gnostics represented a threat to the temporal authority of the bishops. If the Demiurge were a false god who should be defied, then obviously one should not recognize the authority of his bishops.

And whereas Plato wrote of a fairly benign Lesser Creator who was part of the plan of creation established by God the Father, the principle of Demiurge became an intellectual weapon with which to combat Judaism. To Gnostics such as Valentinus the Demiurge was the God of the Old Testament. He was a figure who could be arrogant and malevolent, and who was entirely ignorant of his own origins.[22]

Pagels explains: "What this secret tradition reveals is that the one whom most Christians naively worship as creator, God, and Father, is, in reality, only the image of the True God." The Demiurge is a "lesser divine being who serves as the instrument of the higher powers. It is not God...but the Demiurge who reigns as king and lord, who acts as a military commander, who gives the law and judges those who violate it—in short, he is the God of Israel. And through initiation into the Gnostic school of Valentinus "the candidate learns to reject the creator's authority and all his demands as foolishness. What Gnostics know is that the creator makes false claims to power ('I am God, and there is no other') that derive from his own ignorance. Achieving *gnosis* involves coming to recognize the true source of divine power."[23]

To Valentinus, the Demiurge was actually the monstrous lord of the nether powers, brought into being by the fall. The story says that he found himself outside of the Pleroma and, while retaining the powers which he had inherited from his mother, he remained ignorant of the divine worlds above him. Believing himself to be the one true creator, he produced creatures for the satisfaction of his own ambition and vanity, and for his desire to dominate. He produced six lower lords and established them in six heavens. He himself resided in the seventh heaven above them all.[24] This was the beginning of the cosmic order, which was completed jointly by the seven lords.[25]

Of course, in Hermetic-Kabbalistic principle, *The Hierophant* is not ignorant. It knows its roots and wishes to help seekers of the path of return. It is light, but implicit in it is the way across the terrible Abyss,[26] the path into the virgin darkness. It is the benevolent King, a view held by those Gnostics perhaps less hostile to the material condition than was Valentinus. Many Gnostics treated the figure of the Demiurge more kindly than did Valentinus. Jung, in fact, quotes a Gnostic text which suggests that the Demiurge offers a means of redemption.

In commenting on the *Visions of Zosimos,* an alchemist and gnostic of the third century C.E., Jung emphasizes the references to a "bowl shaped altar." It was, he said "unquestionably related to the *krater of Poimandres.* This was the vessel which the demiurge sent down to earth filled with Nous, so that those who were striving for higher consciousness could baptize themselves in it....I do not think there can be any doubt that the heater of Zosimos is closely related to the vessel of Poimandres in the *Corpus Hermeticum.* The Hermetic vessel, too, is a uterus of spiritual renewal or rebirth."[27]

The Hierophant as Demiurge

The primary characteristic of *The Hierophant* is a rigidity of structure (the Zodiac sign of Taurus is assigned to it), often symbolically called "government," or the "outer Church." But to describe *The Hierophant* as Demiurge adds a special dimension to the card's interpretation in that it may be taken to mean any god figure which is secondary in a progression of creation. A reference to this card as the Demiurge seems also to have been one of the "secrets" conveyed to members by some rather theatrical late nineteenth-century occult groups, such as the Hermetic Order of the Golden Dawn.

One of that group's members, A.E. Waite, very cautiously described *The Hierophant* as "the ruling power of external religion...the order and the head of the recognized hierarchy, which is the reflection of another and greater hierarchic order; but it may happen that the pontiff forgets the significance of this his symbolic state and acts as if he contained within his power all that his sign signifies or his symbol seeks to show forth."[28] Waite managed to straddle the Gnostic fence since his Demiurge knows its roots but occasionally forgets. The question is, however, an interesting one. If *The Hierophant* knows his roots, then he is an attribute of the Divine Will. But considered as an archetype (a creation of the created) can he truly know his own source?

Comparing tarot and Greek mythology, Kronos is both *The Fool* and *The Magician*, whereas one aspect of Zeus (as ruler of the pantheon of a belief system) is *The Hierophant*. Such categorization forces one to look back again to the very roots of creation to understand this figure's role. It may be argued that human consciousness is too fragile to deal with the concept of No Thing and that humanity has, collectively, generated god-archetypes (intermediaries) that serve to protect the perception of individual consciousness and of an "immortal soul."

The principle here are that the No Thing is not God. God, and the gods, are actually archetypal projections of mankind upon the shared and impersonal experience which Jung called the "collective unconscious." This collective embodies the concept of God formulated by man; it is the gods as postulated by all societies. And it is by definition a "false god," although this is not to be understood in any negative sense. To Plato the Demiurge was that which is "always becoming and is never real," as opposed to that which is "always real and has no becoming."[29]

Nevertheless, it is explained by advocates of this system that life experience within the unconscious kingdom of *The Hierophant* can be manipulated through prayer, through "magic," or through certain meditative exercises. And even the most die-hard materialist might agree that some evidence (such as that collected by parapsychologists) for the existence of "miracles" is difficult to entirely ignore. Yet, assuming that such magic actually takes place, it is, theoretically, the result of a manipulation of the perception of "reality" within a manifest condition defined as an illusory condition of consciousness.

This card describes something entirely new, the plan and order of the creator of that illusory condition, a physical universe populated by the archetypal original man and woman, Adam and Eve, in their mythical point of origin, the Garden of Eden. Thus the *Jungian Tarot Deck* attempts to make clear the philosophical sequence of manifestation, and the work of *The Hierophant* as Demiurge.

It will be understood that *The Magician* is Original Man. But until there is a world, a manifest universe, Adam exists only potentially. So one result of *The Hierophant*'s emergence across the Abyss and his creation of a new kingdom (the evolution of *The One Thing* from darkness to light) is that the potential Original Man becomes actual. In this card *The Hierophant* holds a small figure of a man in his right hand and a globe of earth in his left. (The golden cross above the earth-orb is a reference to Venus, *The Empress* who is the mother of *The Hierophant/ Demiurge*.)

The fullest expression of the Original Man archetype is *The*

Lover, but Original Man appears again as the center of the Zodiac in *The Wheel of Fortune.* The underlying principle is very carefully laid out by Jung: Original Man is Self. He is also a circle which is recreated in the Zodiac and thus relates to time. It is this (lower) Original Man who is brought into the world by the Creator/*Hierophant.*

Traps of the Hierophant

Jung raises a profound question in commenting that the arguments of the Gnostics were "very much influenced by psychic experience."[30] In other words, he said that the Gnostics were not merely accepting the tenets of a given system; they were codifying the results of their own personal religious encounters (as, undoubtedly, had Plato before them). And clearly the personal experience of these mystics was often an uneasy mesh with Christianity.

There may be no encounter as difficult as direct spiritual experience which refutes important principles of a belief system. Certainly, in the case of such challenges, psychologists agree that something has to give. And as Gnostic literature demonstrates, there was an early attempt to Christianize a profoundly felt experience of the organizing principle represented in tarot by *The Hierophant.* The attempt at reconciling inner experience with the outer belief structure of a socio-politically created cultus, such as Christianity, has resulted in a plethora of supposedly "revealed" texts, which are often quite confusing and self-contradictory.

Now *The Hierophant* presents two serious obstacles to true spiritual growth. The first, is the emphasis on religious structure. The Organizing Principle of Form is pleased to arrange for Anima to appear to a Catholic mystic dressed as the Virgin Mary, or to a Hindu as Sarasvati,[31] thus reinforcing and deepening the belief.

So the Demiurge may be viewed as an ultimately nonexistent being to whom many so-called "devout" persons mindlessly abrogate responsibility for their lives.

The second, and more subtle trap of *The Hierophant*, is that the contemplative may luxuriate in a resultant sense of joy, compassion, and oneness. The Inner Light can be overwhelming as visionaries such at Saint Theresa have attested. But ecstasy is not an end in itself. Intense feelings belong to the personality and may actually mask a more meaningful experience which is beyond all feeling, and which is beyond the individual Self.

Finally, it may be said that *The Hierophant* principle may be deemed responsible for the spiritual experience of the personality-self in any case where that experience involves a subject-object perspective.[32]

Notes: *The Hierophant*

1. G.R.S. Mead, *Fragments of a Faith Forgotten,* New York 1960, 307-308.

2. See Renford Bambrough, "Demiurge," Encyclopedia *of Philosophy,* v.II, New York, 1967, 337-338.

3. Especially recommended is the work of Francis MacDonald Cornford: *Plato's Cosmology: The Timaeus of Plato translated with a running commentary,* London, 1966.

4. As a point of reference, the Parthenon was about a hundred years old when Plato wrote.

5. Plato, *Timaeus* 29E.

6. F.M. Cornford, *Plato's Cosmology,* London, 1966, 35, 197.

7. Plato, *Timanus,* 30B.C.E.

8. Carl Jung, *Psychology and Religion: East and West,* Princeton, 1977, **350,**

9. Carl Jung, *Aion,* Princeton, 1978, 233 n.**101.**

10. Carl Jung, *Alchemical Studies,* Princeton, 1976, **270.**

11. Hermetic Kabbalah must be understood to be a system different from that of the Hebrew Kabbalah.. However, Gershom Scholem mentions the appearance of God the Creator as the Demiurge in terms of Merkabah mysticism and relative to Ezekiel's vision of a "primordial man" on the throne. *Major Trends in Jewish Mysticism,* New York, 1977, 65.

Belief in an actual Demiurge may be ascribed to the medieval German Hasidim who based their ideas on those of Philo, who said that the Laws, the divine word, acted as intermediary in the process of creation. The German Hasidim taught that God did not create the world directly, but acted through an angelic Demiurge. *Major Trends,* 114.

12. Hippolytus, *Refutation of all Heresies,* Edinburgh, 1877, 263. Hippolytus writes about "The Demiurge of the Supernal Ogdoad." He says that whereas this Ogdoad is eternal, the Demiurge is not. His discussion of the Ogdoad, and of the evolution of the many from the Monad, is very confusing. Here one might suspect that he is blindly reciting some number principles picked up by the Gnostics from the Pythagoreans, and that the confusion may be that of the amanuensis rather than being intrinsic to the system of ideas in question.

13. The earliest codification of number symbolism appears to have been the work of Pythagorus, whose secret society taught that the person who understood the harmony of numerical ratios would become divine. The group, which settled in Crotona, off the Italian coast, was composed of three hundred wealthy aristocrats (men and women) whose motto was "Number Rules the Universe." Both the words "arithmetic" and "mathematics" were first used by the Pythagoreans. (See: Vivian Shaw Groza, *A Survey of Mathematics: Elementary Concepts and their Historical Development,* New York, 1968, 97). The Ogdoad was of special importance. It was the end of a four point geometric sequence: 1) The Point, 2) the Line, 3) the Square, and 4) The Cube. In Kabbalistic terms, undoubtedly also based on the work of Pythagorus, the fourth is Chesed to which, as the "Father of Manifestation," the cube is attributed as the first three-dimensional form. A somewhat more complex explanation was given by Manley Palmer Hall: "The ogdoad—8—was sacred because it was the number of the first cube, which form had eight corners, and was the only "evenly-even" number under 10 (1-2-4-8-4-2-1). Thus the 8 is divided into two 4's, each 4 is divided into two 2's, and each 2 is divided into two 1's, thus reestablishing the monad." *The Secret Teachings of All Ages,* LXIII.

14. Hans Jonas, "Gnosticism," *Encyclopedia of Philosophy,* v. III, New York, 1967, 336-342. This article is an extremely clear and well-written introduction to Gnostic ideas.

15. See: Montague Rhodes James, *The Apocryphal New Testament,* Oxford 1969, 228-438. There are four books which form the key texts of the Manichaean movement: *The Acts of John, The Acts of Paul, The Acts of Andrew, and The Acts of Thomas,* which were substituted for the canonical acts.

16. For a generally Valentinian discussion of the Demiurge, see: "The Tripartite Tractate," I,5, 105, a Gnostic fragment from *The Nag Hammadi Library,* New York 1977. This is the most extensive library of Gnostic documents ever to be unearthed.

17. Eusebius (263-339 C.E.), who has been called the "Father of Ecclesiastical History," referred with great deference to Irenaeus throughout his *History of the Church.*

18. Hippolytus and Irenaeus were the primary sources on Gnosticism available to Jung. Both writers were unalterably opposed to the Gnostic "heresy," and their descriptions of Gnostic beliefs and prac-

tices must be considered discriminatively. See: Mead, 307-308.

19. The similarities between the Kabbalistic principle of Chesed and that of Valentinus' Demiurge, especially as each of them produces six further energies, are sufficiently pointed that one might believe this to be a truly archetypal pattern. On the other hand, the Kabbalah had its roots in exactly this period in history and was clearly influenced by various expressions of Gnosticism, as well as by Neo-Platonism and by Neo-Pythagoreanism.

20. *The Cambridge Medieval History,* Cambridge, 1967, 10. In the early church there was an argument as to whether or not sins could be forgiven after baptism. Those who believed that sins would be forgiven only once, waited until the very last moment to be baptized. Constantine's is believed to be of this nature, what is called a "clinical" baptism.

21. The works of Irenaeus and Hippolytus are in a very direct line from the days of Christ: Hippolytus was the disciple of Irenaeus, Iraneaus was the disciple of Polycarp (Noted by Eusebius in, *History of the Church,* New York, 1965, G.A. Williamson translation, 208), and Polycarp was the disciple of St. John. See: translator's introduction to Hippolytus, *Refutation of All Heresies,* Edinburgh, 1877, 21.

22. Hippolytus made quite a point of finding "Valentinus convicted of plagiarisms from the Platonic and Pythagoric philosophy." He called Valentinus the disciple of Plato and of Pythagorus, and claimed that Valentinus agreed with the 'heresy that "the original cause of the universe is a Monad, unbegotten, imperishable, incomprehensible, inconceivable, productive, and a cause of the generation of all existent things." *Refutation of all Heresies,* 224.

23. Elaine Pagels, *The Gnostic Gospels,* New York 1979, **37.**

24. Jonas, *Gnosticism,* 338.

25. Ibid., 338.

26. This abyss may be equated with the terror of annihilation which must be overcome before wilful absorption into the Godhead.

27. Jung, *Alchemical Studies,* **96.** See: *The Divine Pymander of Hermes,* "The Twelfth Book of Hermes Trismegistus: His Crater or Monas," English translation of 1650, San Diego, 1978, 82. Hermes says: "Dip and wash thyself, thou that art able in this Cup or Bowl: Thou that believeth that thou shalt return to him that sent this Cup; Thou that acknowledges" whereunto thou wert made. As many, therefore, as un-

derstood the Proclamation, and were baptized, or dowsed into the Mind, these were made partakers of knowledge, and became perfect men, receiving the Mind."

28. Arthur Edward Waite, *The Pictorial Key to the Tarot,* New York 1959, 91.

29. Plato, *Timanus,* 27D-28.

30. Jung, A*ion,* **75.**

31. Goddess of learning and of the arts who is the consort of Brahma, the creator God.

32. This means a creator and a created, a God and a loving subject, one who prays, and one to whom the prayer is addressed, the creator God. a "self" and something beyond that self, an "I" and a "You."

7 / THE LOVER

Archetype of Original Man

Interpretation of *The Lover* of the Jungian deck is a baroque philosophical exercise compared to that of the early designs, which showed no more or less than human love. *The Lover* has become a key player in the creation drama which, as "Original Man," cannot be separated from *The Magician*. Original (created) Man and Lesser Creator are interdependent concepts:

Original Man functions in the world of the Lessor Creator, and indeed is its "King." But the symbolism is extremely complicated, and the terms involved, such as anthropos, logos, quaternity, etc., are confusing because they have been so loosely and so variously applied over the centuries.

Through the personality self-sacrifice aspect of *The Hanged Man, The Lover* has seen that he is Original Man. But *The Lover* is "that which is pursued, and that which pursues." He is also the archetype of the Hero who, like Gilgamesh, seeks immortality. As a "downward" surge toward incarnation, *The Lover* is the expression of opposites in the individual personality, in an "upward" path of return, he is the means for reintegration of those opposites—a cyclic "event" symbolized by the birth, death, and rebirth of the Hero. He is *The Magician* incarnate, the true ruler over manifestation whom, as opposed to the Demiurge, each person must seek out to discover.

The Lover is the very principle of Self-recollection, whereby, as Jung described it, one "gathers together what is scattered and multifarious, and exalts it to the original form of the One, the Primordial Man. In this way our existences as separate beings, our former ego nature, is abolished, the circle of consciousness is widened, and because the paradoxes have been made conscious, the sources of conflict are dried up."[2]

The Lover is the Self which knows that it does not ultimately exist. It is a condition of earthly existence without individual being, in which a person lives normally and appears to be no different than anyone else.

To discuss this type of consciousness, in terms of tarot, it is necessary to conceptually separate *The Magician* from *The Lover* by calling the latter "The Second Adam." As Original Man for an illusory universe, his significance may appear to be microcosmic (that is, relevant to ourselves alone). But there can be no true experience of the Microcosm ("below") without equally experiencing the Macrocosm ("above").

And in applying to *The Lover* this important principle of "As above, so below," it is understood that he, like *The Magi-*

cian is Mercurius, about whose natural duplicity Jung explained that: *"the unconscious tends to regard spirit and matter not only as equivalent, but as actually identical* [author's italics], and this in flagrant contrast to the intellectual one-sidedness of consciousness which would sometimes like to spiritualize matter and at other times to materialize spirit."[3]

And, summarizing the attributes of Mercurius in his *Alchemical Studies,* Jung could well have been describing symbolism of *The Lover* which:

> (1) consists of all conceivable opposites. He is thus quite obviously a duality, but is named a unity in spite of the fact that his innumerable inner contradictions can dramatically fly apart into an equal number of disparate and apparently independent figures. (2) is both material and spiritual. (3) is the process by which the lower and material is transformed into the higher and spiritual, and vice versa. (4) is the devil, a redeeming psychopomp, an evasive trickster, and God's reflection in physical nature. (5) is also the reflection of a mystical experience of the artifex that coincides with the *opus alchymicum.* (6) As such, he represents on the one hand the Self and on the other the individuation process and, because of the limitless number of his names, also the collective unconscious.[4]

Adam, Eve, and Androgyny

The card depicts the completion of Self-recollection where the central androgynous figure has reconciled the dualities of human nature. The smaller figures are Adam and Eve; they are the "parents" which *The Lover* himself, created.

Insofar as *The Lover* is *The Magician* on a lower arc, Adam and Eve are the *Magician* and the *High Priestess* in manifestation. They derive from the state of unity of *The Lover* The principle is one of self-fertilization by Mercurius, the Prima Materia.[5] This is a thought-event wherein "the God splits himself into his masculine and feminine halves."[6]

As shown, the male and female figures are in the Garden of Eden. They exist in unity with the Creative Spirit. But a taste of the material condition, of the seductive realm of the Demiurge will cause them to separate, to lose consciousness of their roots, and to "fall" into the illusion of matter.

Jung comments on the process of this fall into dualities. Referring to the theory of world creation in the *Clementine Homilies*, he says that "God unfolds himself in the world in the form of syzygies (paired opposites), such as Heaven/Earth, day/night, male/female. The last term of the first series is the Adam/Eve syzygy. At the end of this fragmentation process there follows the return to the beginning, the consummation of the universe through purification and annihilation."[7] It may be parenthetically added that "annihilation" into the No Self is implicit in Jung's thought because this is the logical consequence of passing beyond the collective unconscious. Moreover, there are subtle hints in his writing that this was a condition of which he was, personally, well aware.

Logos/Lover

As *The Lover* is Original Man, he is also the Logos. "Logos," a word which in classical Greek meant both "word" and "reason,"[8] has assumed some obtuse philosophical proportions because it has been applied in so many different ways. Its use to mean something metaphysical may have begun with Heraclitus, and certainly relates to the Stoics, for whom Logos was the rational principle of the universe; it was the source of law and of morality. Plato and Aristotle explained a similar principle, which they called "Nous," and which was equated with Logos by later commentators. The idea also occurs in the Old Testament, and the Hebrew word "Dabhar" meaning *word event*, is regularly translated into Greek by the word Logos.

The Lover, as Logos, is also Christ, an idea perhaps suggested by Saint John, whose gospel opens: "When all things began, the Word already was. The Word dwelt with God, and what God was, the Word was. The Word, then, was with God at the beginning, and through him all things came to be; no single thing was created without him"[9] This passage became the basis for generations of heated theological argument because in it many, including Saint Augustine, found the essential principles of Heraclitus, of Plato, and of the Stoics—demonstrating, supposedly, that Christian principles (which one might call archetypal) existed long before Christ.[10]

Language and Limitations

It should be constantly borne in mind that what is called "Anthropos," or "Original Man," is a state of consciousness, although it maybe encountered as an (anthropomorphized) archetypal imprint. To accept the idea of "Original Man" at face value is tantamount to the belief that there is a blissful kingdom somewhere called ''Heaven," ruled over by an elderly bearded gentleman who answers to the name "God."

Perhaps the twentieth century is the first which can begin to view anthropomorphic symbolism of the past in terms of real consciousness. A contemporary attuned to psychology may be prepared to accept an archetype such as Anthropos as, to quote Jung: "One of the names that human speculation has given to that collective preconscious state from which the individual arose."[11]

Jung called Anthropos, "Man's wholeness...the conception of a unitary being who existed before men and at the same time represents man's goal."[12] And as *The Lover*/Anthropos card represents a condition of consciousness, so do the relationships described between the Hero and his Father and Mother. The often-mentioned symbolic "entry into the Mother" is a case in point. In ancient Persian mythology Mithras sacrifices the bull in a dark cave, in the presence of the Sun and Moon.[13] This cave is the Mother who is entered by the Hero in his search for immortality. "The dark cave" says Jung, "corresponds to the vessel containing the warring opposites."[14] And, translating this symbolism into psychological terms, he explains that this entry into the mother means to establish a relationship between the ego and the unconscious.[15]

In this regard, Jung found references to "Mother" and "Father" as archetypal conditions of consciousness in many early works. He quotes, for example, the seventeenth-century Kabbalist, Knorr von Rosenroth, who said that "the Mother is nothing more than the inclination of the Father for the lower."[16]

Lover and Christian Context

It is logical that *The Lover*, as Perfected Self, should be equated with Anthropos as Christ, whom Jung describes as androgynous, and whom he calls "a total personality transcending consciousness"[17] But this raises, once more, a question about the doctrine of immortality of the individual soul, in which most Christians believe. In the earliest church, visionaries seem to have been telling quite a different story. Although they stress the ultimate divinity of the soul (as do the Hebrew mystics), they do not flatly state that it functions independently.[18]

In agreement with mystics of all times, the early Church Fathers seem to have taught that *psyche,* the most preciously guarded possession of the individual, only *appears* to exist independently, and that illusory "life" must be sacrificed to a higher principle. Immortality is possible only within the communal context of the "Mystical Body of Christ."[19] As St. Mark wrote that Christ said "The man who tries to save his life [independent consciousness] will lose it; it is the man who loses his life for my sake that will save it."[20]

And although one may argue the original meaning of such statements, it is clear that the earliest Christians thought very differently than did the organized Church after the pivotal Council of Nicaea.[21] Early Christianity was intensely mystical, secretive, and permissive of individual inquiry and beliefs. It was truly a "mystery religion,"[22] as opposed to its later development as a political force in society. Those searching for cross-cultural, archetypal, patterns within Christianity will find them most clearly in the literature of the first and second centuries.

One discovers, between the lines of the earliest Christian writers, a difficult and sincere quest for Self-recollection in which each person must face the deadly challenge of taking free will to its ultimate conclusion. Undoubtedly these people would have agreed with Jung that "Self-recollection...is about the hardest and most repellent thing there is for man, who is predominantly unconscious. Human nature has an invincible dread of becoming more conscious of itself. What nevertheless drives us to it is the Self, which demands sacrifice by sacrificing itself to us. Conscious realization or the bringing together of the scattered parts is in one sense an act of the ego's will, but in another sense it is a spontaneous manifestation of the Self, which was always there."[23]

And, indeed the literature describing this process has also, almost always been there. One of the intellectual markers on the road toward Self-recollection is the discovery that vast numbers of "enlightened" writers have, for centuries, been saying precisely the same thing. For example, one of the principles of Buddhism is that desire binds a person to the condition of matter and that illumination may appear when wanting ceases. And this idea is not limited to the East; it is repeated in the work of Western visionaries, such as the sixteenth-century mystic, Jacob Boehme, who says that all life and growth arise from free will and from desire, which he calls a "hunger."[24]

So in these terms, it may be said that the condition of recollected Self-consciousness of *The Lover* means that one is no longer bound by the fluctuations of matter, of intellect, and of emotions. It confers an absence of desire beyond that required for the most basic maintenance of the physical vehicle.

Hero—The Divine Quest

As generally understood, the "Hero" is a superman. Heroes abound. Some are imaginary and others are amplifications of real persons who lived and who were revered for their exploits. And although Homer used the Greek word for hero to mean simply "gentleman or noble,"[25] in some early cultures the Hero was worshipped as a god.

As an archetype, the Hero is commensurate with the personality, the "I" which is mutable and which, although it may strive passionately for immortality, must ultimately "sacrifice" itself to a greater principle. And Jung observed provocatively that "man as an individual is a very suspicious phenomenon whose right to exist could be questioned by the biologist, since from that point of view he is significant only as a collective creature, or as a particle of the mass. The cultural point of view gives man a meaning apart from the mass, and this in the course of centuries led to the development of personality and the cult of the hero."[26]

The Hero is a great archetypal personality, such as the Sumerian Gilgamesh, whose exploits were recorded on scores of clay tablets written in cuneiform. He is the ideal human being, a king who is stronger, more intelligent, and more handsome than others around him, and who embarks on a perilous journey in search of immortality. But the Hero ultimately fails in his quest! He is forced to recognize that his sense of individuality, of personality separation, is illusory and that although he may act upon himself to regenerate, to be "reborn" over and over again, either symbolically or actually, his soul is not separately immortal.

As the Hero who has reached the end of the road, *The Lover* is the condition of living in the world with full knowledge of the significance of the Self and its relationship to the greater reality which has been called "creative emptiness." How is one to behave after experiencing the truth? Perhaps the best advice is that given to Gilgamesh by his companion, Enkidu: "The Father of the Gods has given you kingship. Such is your destiny. Everlasting life is not your destiny. Because of this do not be sad at heart, do not be grieved or oppressed. He has given you power to bind and to loose, to be the darkness and the light of mankind."[27]

Notes: *The Lover*

1. It is also noted that *The Magician* is both that which transmits and that which is transmitted. Both *Lover* and *Magician*—as Mercurius—act upon themselves. They are the end and the means of that end's accomplishment.

2. Carl Jung, *Psychology and Religion: East and West,* Princeton, 1977, **401.**

3. Carl Jung, *The Archetypes and the Collective Unconscious,* Princeton, 1977, **555**

4. Carl Jung, *Alchemical Studies,* Princeton, 1976, **284.**

5. The early alchemists frequently referred to Adam as the Prima Materia, and as the quaternary. The most ancient Latin treatise, states that: "out of four elements our father Adam and his sons were created, that is, of fire, air, water, and likewise earth." *Turba Philosophorum,* New York 1976, 13. Jung puts this into psychological terms: "The four are the four orienting functions of consciousness, two of them perceptive (irrational) and two discriminate (rational.)" He adds that "Adam stands not only for the psyche, but for its totality, he is a symbol of the self, and hence a visualization of the "irrepresentable Godhead." Carl Jung, *Mysterium Conianctionis,* Princeton, 1976, **55-558.**

6. Carl Jung, *Aion,* Princeton, 1978, **322.**

7. Jung, *Aion,* **400.**

8. "Logos," *Dictionary of the Bible,* ed. James Hastings, New York, 1963, 589.

9. *John,* 1:1-3.

10. It is increasingly being argued that the real influence on Saint John may have been the Hebrew Scholar, Philo Judeaus (c.30 B.C.E.-C.E. 45), who discusses the Logos as intermediary between man and God. G. B. Kerferd, "Logos," *Encyclopedia of Philosophy,* New York, 1972, 83-84.

11. Jung, *Alchemical Studies,* **210.**

12. Ibid.

13. Mircea Eliade, *A History of Religious Ideas,* v.2, 323. One story tells of the birth of Mithra from a rock which appears to explain the emphasis on cave symbolism in this religious system. See also Franz Cumont, *The Oriental Religions in Roman Paganism,* New York, 1956 (Reprint of 1911 Original), 135ff. Most of our information about the mysteries of Mithra (Mithraism) comes from ancient works of art.

14. Carl Jung, *Psychology and Alchemy,* Princeton 1977, **186.**

15. Carl Jung, *Symbols of Transformation,* Princeton 1977, **459**

16. Jung, *Mysterium Coniunctionis,* 592. Von Rosenroth's major contribution was his Latin translation of a key part of *The Zohar,* which he called the *Kabbala Denudata.*

17. Jung, *Psychology and Religion,* **414.**

18. The descriptions of "soul" are not equivalent in the Old and New Testaments, In Hebrew Scripture the word *nephesh* was used to mean variously "soul," 'life," or "self." In the New Testament the word psyche has somewhat the same meaning, but it is much more the center of vital choices than is the nephesh.

The assertion that the immortal soul is individual, rather than collective, is often a matter of textual interpretation. A good example is a passage in the *Bhagavad Gita* which says, "That which pervades the entire body is indestructible. No one is able to destroy the imperishable soul." One modern commentator states unequivocally that this passage means that "every body contains an individual soul, and the symptom of the soul's presence is perceived as individual consciousness." A.C. Bhaktivedanta Swami Prabhupada, *The Bhagavad Gita As It Is,* 26.). In fact, as in so many mystical documents, these lines can equally well be interpreted to mean a communal soul which pervades the individual body, or that the "entire body" in question is the collective unconscious.

19. Much of this present study deals with Jung's "translation" of the language of Alchemy, of early religions and of mythologies into the terms of modern psychology. However, as a descriptive term, "mystical body" is really as good, or better than "collective unconscious." 20. Mark 8: 35-37.

21. The first ecumenical (worldwide) council of the Church was called at Nicaea, in Asia Minor, by the Emperor Constantine, in 325. It was to settle a controversy created in Alexandria between a priest, Arius, who claimed that Christ was of a different substance from God, and the Bishop Alexander, who supported the doctrine that they were of the same substance. The Council agreed with Alexander. *Cambridge Medieval History,* Cambridge, 1967, v.I, 13-14. This is not the sort of question which would have concerned Christians of the first and early second centuries, and underscores a mentality totally different from that of the original, and very loosely organized, Church.

22. The Roman Empire was more tolerant of religious diversity

than perhaps any other society in history. But Judaism and Christianity stood apart because their demands were so totally uncompromising. Judaism could be tolerated, however, because it did not threaten the established economic order as did Christianity. Christians were persecuted for two reasons: First—they interfered with the economic patterns of the Roman religions. For example, the dealers in feed for sacred temple animals were outraged at their loss of business. And silversmiths at Ephesus caused a riot against St. Paul because his preaching was opposed to the idol worship of Diana. Second—the Christians, whose rites were secret, but were rumored to include a communion in which they consumed the body and blood of Christ, were believed to be cannibals who sacrificed small children at their altars, and who committed incest in the darkness of their ceremony." Marjorie Strachey, *The Fathers Without Theology,* New York, 1958, 42.

23. Jung, *Psychology and Religion,* **400.**

24. Jacob Boehme, *The Signature of All Things,* Cambridge, 1969, 43. In the Catholic tradition one may also cite the Carthusians who contrast *cupiditas* and *caritas.* To them, there can be no motion without the initial cupiditas. And much the same ideas can be found in Hegel, whose reading of history is that nothing happens without desire (passion) and who can certainly be interpreted to have suggested that desire was the root cause (the surge) toward manifestation.

25. "Hero Cult," *Oxford Classical Dictionary,* Oxford, 1978, 505.

26. Jung, *Symbols of Transformation,* **259.**

27. *The Epic of Gilgamesh,* N.K. Sandars translation, Harmondsworth, 1964, 68

8 / THE CHARIOT

Archetype of Spirit Below

There can be no question that the design of this card was originally a reference to the *Triumph*,[1] a ceremonial parade recreated from Roman times.[2] However, an appreciation of the card's political and historical roots does not detract from the utility of viewing it as an important archetypal image. Indeed, by the eighteenth century, the political implications of the classical Triumph recreated by the Renaissance had been forgotten, and the card—which had become something of a curiosity—was increasingly explained by reference to mystical and mythical programs.

An Illusion of the Hero Trapped

In the iconography of the Jungian Tarot the key to *The Chariot* is *The Hierophant*, who believes himself to be the true creator, but who is, in fact, only the architect of the manifest condition in which the Hero seems trapped. Of course, this trap is only apparent.

The first man, Adam, may not have known it, but at his right hand had always been the means of redemption, the means for return to the pristine and unified state of consciousness from which he and Eve "fell." In philosophical principle, the Holy Spirit is forever with the Self, ready to impart knowledge directly, and to offer redemption from the fall into the kingdom of the Demiurge—for a terrible price—the willing sacrifice of individual existence. This spirit is symbolized by *The Chariot*, a card which describes the relationship of the Higher Self to the True Creator. Interaction between the pure Non-Being and the Self takes place without reference to the collective unconscious or to any man-made, structured, system of philosophy, of mythology, or of religion. It may be stated that the recollected Self of *The Lover* exists only by reference to its Creator.

The Chariot goes where it wills, and, as the projection of God the Creator, is subject to no power but its own. It is the unified Spirit of the Pleroma. It is at once God the Creator, God the Father, and God the Mother, offering a direct link with the highest. And relative to its symbolism as bearer of the Supreme Throne, the card of *The Chariot* is unique in that it shows *movement*. This movement is a reference to the "first movement" of *The Lover*.

The Chariot is the as yet unrecognized Self's continual point of contact with Pure Spirit. The card suggests a correction to the laws of the Lesser Creator within which life takes place. And although the existence of *The Chariot* may be hidden by the Demiurge, the Son is always in contact with the Father—whether he accepts that fact or not. No matter what forces may act upon Original Man, and no matter to what extent he may appear subject to the whim of the Lesser Creator, the Pure Spirit of *The Chariot* gives him a direct channel to the Most Divine in any condition of waking or of sleeping consciousness.

The Chariot is without limitations. It is without boundaries. It is without regulations. *The Chariot* is not subject to the time/space continuum of *The Hierophant*. This Chariot, which carries the Crown across the Abyss, knows no dimensions. It knows no laws. Its only motive power is the thought of the Crown.

In the Jungian Tarot design, the Chariot is shown passing through all four elements, arranged in a scheme which is more artistically practical than symbolically accurate.[3] Technically, each wheel is understood to be a wheel within a wheel, and capable of moving in all directions at once. The inner wheel of the mandala is divided into twelve sections, each of which is colored according to late nineteenth-century attributions for paths on the Tree of Life related to the twelve signs of the Zodiac.[4]

Symbolically, the chariot (of four parts in one) is that which turns the Wheel of Fortune, the circle of Original Man's experiences (shown as the zodiac) below that *Abyss* postulated as a separation between the highest realms and manifestation.

Hebrew Mysticism: Merkabah

The earliest form of Jewish mysticism is Throne Mysticism[5] based on the vision of Ezekiel. Rather than contemplation of the true nature of God, this concerns a perception of His appearance on the Throne. This Throne World is almost identical to the realm of the upper gods called the *Pleroma* by the Hermetics and by the Early Christian Gnostics.[6] Merkabah (Chariot) literature, much of which stresses magic, is very similar to a number of Greek magic papyri of the second or third centuries B.C.E. and to Gnostic literature such as the *Pistis Sophia*[7]

The first biblical reference to a chariot is to the fiery chariot of the ninth century B.C.E. Prophet Elijah, which appeared drawn by fiery horses and which carried the prophet up to Heaven in a whirlwind.[8] Here one may recall that in the Hermetic Kabbalistic system the Godhead, Kether, is called "The Root of the Powers of Air." In fact, wind and fire seem to be archetypal tools of the Supreme Creator.

The most important chariot is that described in the vision of Ezekiel (early sixth century B.C.E.). About 400 years later the text began to be interpreted in terms that were to emerge as Merkabah mysticism. A primary example is the pseudo-epigraphic *Book of Enoch*[9] (150 B.C.E-100 B.C.E.), which has all the elements of Merkabah thought. That book was of special importance to the Essenes, a Jewish monastic sect colonizing the Dead Sea area in about 100 C.E., which may have counted Jesus Christ among its members.[10] The chronology here is simple: the Essenes were succeeded by the Merkabah mystics who in turn were succeeded by the medieval Kabbalists.[11]

In the text of Ezekiel (1:4-28) the prophet saw a storm coming from the North (traditionally called "the place of greatest darkness," and the compass direction related to elemental Earth.) Out of a dark cloud came a fire containing four living creatures. Each had four faces—that of a man, a lion, an ox, and an eagle[12]—and each had four wings. Their legs were straight with hooves like those of a calf. And each creature had two sets of wings, one covering its body, the other touching its neighbors. They looked like "fire from burning torches." Beside each of the four was a wheel, the rim of which was covered with eyes (see *The Wheel of Fortune)*. And as the creatures moved, the wheels moved with them. Above their heads was "a vault glittering like a sheet of ice" above which was a throne bearing a human figure.

The Chariot carries the Throne which is the united spirit of Father and Mother—as is eloquently expressed in Kabbalistic symbolism. Among the symbols attached to Chokmah (the Great Father) are the order of angels called *auphanim,* meaning *Wheels*.[13] And on the other hand Binah (the Great Mother) is represented by the order of angels called *Aralim,* or *Thrones*.[14] So the Chariot, i.e., Wheels carrying the Throne, refers to the original Father and original Mother. The wheels (activating principle) of the Father carry the Throne (formative principle) of the Mother into the perceived conditions of manifestation of the Son, whose order of angels is the Malachim, or *Kings*.

In commenting on *Ezekiel,* Jung emphasizes the wheel, rather than the Chariot (which is certainly legitimate, and in fact it was only later interpreters who saw a chariot in the wheels of Ezekiel's vision). The wheel of *The Chariot* is also that of *The Wheel of Fortune* and of the mandala, the archetype of the Wheel as Self. In the Jungian Tarot, the relationship of these two tarot keys is indicated by their mandalas, both using the twelve color rays of the zodiac to symbolize the totality of human experience.

Jungian scholars tend to agree that Ezekiel's vision describes a mystical totality. The reduction of the four elements into one is the "squaring of the circle," graphically shown here as the circle within the square. Jung said that "the squaring of the circle is one of the many archetypal motifs which form the basic patterns of our dreams and fantasies...it could be called the *Archetype of Wholeness*. Because of this significance, the 'quaternity of the One' is the schema for all images of God as depicted in the vision of Ezekiel."[15] And in Jungian terms, Circle=Self=Original Man= Mandala. Jung explains Ezekiel's vision as "arranged in such a way that a horizontal section through it would produce a mandala divided into four parts."[16]

All of this is very complicated, but literature provides clues about what visionaries have meant to express with their convoluted symbolism. Jung quotes Dorn, for example, who says that "The Wheel of Creation takes its rise from the Prima Materia, whence it passes to the simple elements."

To reiterate: Circle means Self, and Self, as Original Man, a quaternity of four elements, emerges from the collective First Matter of *The Magician*. These four simple elements are the four animals of Ezekiel's vision; they are the four quarters and the four seasons. The wheels of the Chariot are turned by the alternation of these four.

Initiatory Fire—The Serpent—Sun

The relationship of fire to Chariot is sufficiently common as to be called archetypal. In fact the spiritual fire which surrounds the Throne is initiatory—it pulls upward. In the first chapter of Ezekiel, *chashmal,* usually translated as fire (but more accurately as "shining"), is a divine substance which reveals God's Throne and His countenance in splendor. In modern Hebrew the word "chashmal" has come to mean *electricity.*[17] There was, in fact, an ancient association of the power of God with lightning.' And, probably based on Elijah, the *Book of Enoch* describes flashes of lightning and winds elevating the prophet to Heaven, where he discovers a throne surrounded by fire.[18] The fire which confronts Elijah and Ezekiel may be interpreted to be the "sacred fire" which has been variously called "Kundalini" and "Serpent Power." This is the pure sexual energy which is manipulated through yoga exercises. Its encounter underscores an aphorism of the mysteries that "God is sex."

The serpent, pictured in the lap of the charioteer in the *Jungian Tarot,* represents the fiery creative energy which is carried from one (so-called) level of consciousness to another. It is also a symbol of solar energy and thus of Christ, Apollo, and of other gods central to the Microcosm.

Chariot as "Vessel"

Jung (who called Alchemy "the forerunner of our modern psychology of the unconscious"[20]) cites a provocative passage from an early alchemical text which he calls a "recipe," and which begins: "Take the serpent [meaning the *prima materia* and the *Nous*] and place it in the Chariot with four wheels, and let it be turned about on the earth until it is immersed in the depths of the sea, and nothing more is visible than the blackest dead sea." The text continues to describe an essentially alchemical process in which the Chariot is clearly the vessel in which the transformation takes place. The vehicle (Chariot) is immersed in the sea of the unconscious, where it is heated and incubated, which Jung explains as meaning "a state of introversion in which the unconscious content is brooded over and digested." The black, dead, sea means that "consciousness has not completed the process of integration." But "through the incubation, the snake-like content is vaporized, literally 'sublimated,' which amounts to saying that it is recognized and made an object of conscious discrimination."

Eventually the Chariot reaches dry land, which as Jung says, suggests that "the content has become visible and remains conscious." Then, he continues, "the four natures or elements [four wheels of the Chariot] are gathered together and are contained in the spherical vessel, i.e., the four aspects of functions are integrated with consciousness."[21]

A more practical and basic discussion of the Chariot is offered by Aryeh Kaplan, who writes that Talmudic tradition "teaches that the vision of Ezekiel contains at least an allusion to the mystical techniques of the prophets." He states that "The word *Merkava* comes from the root *Rakhav,* 'to ride,' and hence refers to a 'riding vehicle.' In general, then, it refers to the complete system and mechanism through which God 'leaves his place' and reveals himself to those who are worthy." Kaplan goes on to explain that "What the prophet must do is blank out all of these sensations of storm, cloud and fire, which are aspects of the *Klipah*[22] and spiritual darkness, and concentrate on the light that shines out from this darkness...When the prophet reaches this level his ego is totally nullified and all sensation is hushed. He then reaches the level of the *Chashmal,* which is identical with the 'small still voice' of Elijah."[23]

The Indwelling Presence

The Chariot is the indwelling Divine Presence. It is, in some respects, what has been called the *Shekinah* by Jewish mysticism, although this term has a rather Byzantine history. It originally expressed the presence of God in the world, but was later used to mean something separate from God. One spoke of God and of his Shekinah standing before him. Later, the term Shekinah was used to describe the relationship between God and the community of Israel (which may be interpreted to mean the collective unconscious). This idea was transmuted into the Gnostic concept of Shekinah as Daughter,[24] and then to the Kabbalistic principle of earth as the "Bride" of Microprosopus. In all, the earliest and most simple definition is the most useful, and is most descriptive of the experience of *The Chariot*.

Whatever it may be called, there is nothing symbolic about this divine presence. Once its existence has been recognized and accepted, its reality is increasingly felt, and one enters into a dialogue with this "other,"[25] which assumes the proportions of a formidable adversary. And to call this adversary, this ever-present beckoning spirit which moves with the speed of thought, *The Chariot*, is actually quite appropriate.

Dangers of the Holy Spirit

"We ought to abandon ourselves to the Divine Will as much as we can," said Carl Jung, "but we admit that to do so is difficult and dangerous. So dangerous indeed, that I would not dare to advise one of my clients to 'take' the Holy Spirit or to abandon himself to him until I had first made him realize the risks of such an enterprise"[26]

In Greek legend, Helios drove the Chariot of the Sun from East to West each day. The story of his son, Phaeton, is the best-known of the solar myths. Phaeton asked to drive the Sun Chariot for one day, but could not handle the powerful horses, which bolted and threatened to set the world on fire. Finally Zeus killed Phaeton with a thunderbolt.[27] This myth certainly underscores the danger of direct contact with the fiery powers of the sky which are carried by the Chariot.[28] It also suggests that only the Supreme Deity can bring the Chariot under control once its power has been unleashed through abuse.

After one has allowed for perception of this so-called "Holy Spirit," there is no return. Life becomes a subtle dialogue between oneself and an Other. Sleep changes and is infused with constant "dreaming" about learning—which becomes a life parallel, in its reality, to the waking experience. And in sleep, as in waking, there is adversarial dealing with this Other. One may be faced with blank whiteness, a vision of an absolute nothing where seconds before there was something known. Interaction and confrontation with the Other, which is *The Chariot*, may be amusing, surprising, and cajoling—or it may be merciless and relentless. It is, overall, deeply disturbing to the security of the personality. Nevertheless, painful work eventually leads to a peaceful and balanced overcoming of fear and of the subject-object perspective, and to the true recognition of the nature of Self as is represented by *The Lover*.

Notes: *The Chariot*

1. See especially, *The Chariot* card from the *Visconti-Sforza* deck.

2. The *Triumph* was originally an elaborate parade-ceremony called by the *Imperator* to give thanks and to ask the protection of Jupiter during battle. The Triumphal procession was a formal event, in which the order of participants, from the Emperor through the members of the Senate, to the prisoners to be executed, was established. During the Empire, only the Emperor could celebrate a Triumph. So the reinstitution of these Triumphs on a spectacular scale by the merchant-princes who had essentially bought their principalities, was an assertion of legitimacy; it was a visible show of wealth and power linking them to the grandeur of Rome. Pierre Grimal, *The Civilization of Rome,* New York 1963, 177-179. These merchant-princes, including the Borgia, the Sforza, and the Medici, controlled both church and state absolutely, and without scruples. The story of the excesses of the popes placed in office by these families is truly unbelievable by today's standards. See E.R. Chamberlin, *The Bad Popes,* New York, 1986. The section on Leo X, 209-249 describes the great cost and political importance of outward shows of princely power such as the *Triomphi.*

3. It would appear odd if painted in the generally accepted hierarchical ladder of fire, water, air, and then earth—with a body of water between flames and clouds. Another way in which the design defers to practicality rather than symbolism is the simplicity of the wheels.

4. Late nineteenth century English and French occultists delighted in creating long and complicated charts demonstrating correspondences between systems. Some of these schemes are quite interesting, particularly those collected in 777, a book privately published in 1909 by Aleister Crowley, and presumably based on work by MacGregor Mathers, a founder of the Hermetic Order of the Golden Dawn. The attributions of colors, plants, animals, etc., to the Kabbalistic *Tree of Life* in this work should not, however, be assumed to have been handed down through some mysterious line of adepts. Although (particularly in the attribution of God names and angelic names to the Paths) there is a basis in Hebrew tradition, much of the material of the charts is original. The best book describing the activities of this remarkable Victorian order is *The Magicians of the Golden Dawn,* by Ellic Howe, London 1972.

5. Scholem describes the origins of Merkabah mysticism as follows:

"Merkabah mysticism, or *ma'aseh merkavah,* was the name given in Mishnah Hagigah, 2:1 to the first chapter of Ezekiel. The term was used by the rabbis to designate the complex of speculations, homilies, and visions connected with the Throne of Glory and the chariot (merkavah) which bears it and all that is embodied in this divine world. The term, which does not appear in Ezekiel, is derived from 1 Chronicles 28:18 and is first found with the meaning of Merkabah mysticism at the end of Ecclesiastes 49:8." Gershom Scholem, *Kabbalah,* New York, 1987.

6. Gershom Scholem, *Major Trends in Jewish Mysticism,* New York, 1977, 32.

7. Scholem, *Kabbalah,* 15-16.

8. II *Kings,* 2:11.

9. The *pseudoepigrapha* (meaning things falsely ascribed) are Christian and Hebrew texts which appear to be authentic early texts, but which are actually non-canonical writings for which false authorship and date have been claimed. However, such "deception" may have been social necessity. By the third century B.C.E. in the Hebrew world, it was accepted that the Pentateuch of Moses was the final revealed word and that any person claiming new and different revelations from the ancient mystics should be put to death as a false prophet. So there developed a whole class of literature where writers ascribed their own personal experience to figures of the past, such as Enoch, Jeremiah, Baruch, or Isaiah. See Edmund Wilson, *The Scrolls from the Dead Sea,* New York 1955, 63.

The *Book of Enoch,* as it exists today, is a collection of highly edited apocalyptic texts written during the last two centuries before Christ. The texts were originally written either in Hebrew or in Aramaic, but were later translated into Greek and then into Ethiopic and Latin. For a very clear discussion of this topic, see "Pseudoepigrapha," *Dictionary of the Bible,* James, Hastings, ed., New York, 1963.

10. The Essenes are best known through the discovery of the *Dead Sea Scrolls,* although they are mentioned by three first-century writers, Pliny, Philo, and Josephus (who was a member of the sect). The significance of the Dead Sea scrolls, which began to be unearthed in the late 1940s, is that they provided a previously unknown link between Hebrew and Christian literature. These works, and those of Gnostic Christianity discovered in Nag Hamadi, Egypt, during the same period, have revolutionized biblical studies. Among the best books on the subject is that of Edmund Wilson (cited above). Originally written for the *New*

Yorker Magazine, his *The Scrolls From the Dead Sea*—based upon experience at the actual sites, and upon interaction with the scholars who originally dealt with these scrolls—is a first-hand description of the excitement and importance of this archaeological discovery as it was happening.

11. Scholem, *Kabbalah,* 10-11. Discussing later developments, Scholem explains that: "In the Kabbalah, the contemplation of the ten *Sefirot,* which reveal the action of the Divine and comprise the world of emanation, was superimposed upon the Merkabah world. The contemplation of divine matters does not end, according to the Kabbalah, where the vision of Merkabah mysteries ended, but is capable of ascending to greater heights, which are no longer the objects of images and visions." *Kabbalah,* 370.

12. In art, these four related images are first seen in Assyrian works. In the fourth and fifth centuries C.E., Man (or Angel), Lion, Ox, and Eagle, assume great significance in Christian iconography as symbols of the four Evangelists, Matthew, Mark, Luke, and John.

13. The "mundane chakra" related to Chokmah is The Zodiac.

14. On the Kabbalistic Tree of Life, the path of *The Chariot* connects Mother and Son, Binah and Tiphareth.

15. Jung, *The Archetypes and the Collective Unconscious,* New York, 1977, **716.**

16. Jung, *Aion,* Princeton, 1978, **379.**

17. Kaplan points out that the word *Chashmal* is composed of *Chash,* meaning silence and *Mal* meaning speech. It means, he says, the silence through which the prophet can hear the word of God. *Meditation and the Bible,* New York, 1978, 41.

18. Robert Graves, *Hebrew Myths,* New York 1983, 38.

19. *The Book of Enoch The Prophet,* trans. Richard Laurence, San Diego, 1977. Photo reproduction of the London, 1883, edition, 17-18.

20. Carl Jung, *Alchemical Studies,* Princeton, 1976, **237.**

21. Carl Jung, *Mysterium Coniunctionis,* Princeton, 1976, **260-270.**

22. This word was spelled "Qlippoth" by nineteenth-century writers.

23. Kaplan, *Meditation and the Bible,* 39-42.

24. Gershom Scholem, *Kabbalah,* 31-32.

25. It was earlier noted that all subject-object relationships relate to

The Hierophant . The experience of this "other" is the prime example as this dialogue is the means for altering the perspective of subject-object.

26. Carl Jung, *The Symbolic Life,* Princeton, 1980, **1540.**

27. Robert Graves, *The Greek Myths,* New York, 1957, 156-157. Although this story has been interpreted in simple moral terms, it is actually a rather complex myth relating to the annual sacrifice of a royal prince. "The sacred king pretended to die at sunset; the boy *interrex* was at once invested with his titles, dignities and sacred implements, married to the queen, and killed twenty-four hours later." (157, note 2).

28. In Hermetic Kabbalah the Hebrew letter Cheth, meaning fence, is assigned to *The Chariot.*

9 / STRENGTH

Archetype of Original Woman

The complex history of this card underscores the ways in which tarot has evolved. In the earliest (uncaptioned) tarot decks,[1] such as the *Visconti Sforza Tarot,* the image of *Strength* was that of a man battling a lion with a club. The theme is well known in ancient art, and represents the first labor of Hercules, the slaying of the Nemean Lion. The story tells that Hercules kept the skin of the lion which, when worn as a garment, made him invincible.[2] This hero myth, a source of particular inspiration to Greek vase painters and to late Roman sculptors, began to be transformed in the art of the late Middle Ages.[3]

During the tarot's developmental period Hercules was replaced, and the lion was shown being "tamed" by the Virtue of Strength personified as a female (the ideal of innocence conquering a raging animal quite similar to that of the mythical virgin who captures a unicorn in her lap). But the theme of woman and lion did not immediately become the accepted standard. There are many decks, from the fifteenth and sixteenth century, where the Virtue stands beside a column—simplistically meaning the "Pillar of Strength."[4]

Virtues and Vices

The idea of Virtues and Vices, found as far back as Plato, and most eloquently expressed in Virgil's *Aeneid*, was of great importance to the art of the Middle Ages. The primary source of inspiration was an allegorical work by a poet of the fourth century C.E., Aurelius Clemens Prudentius, called *Psychomachia,* or "The Battle of the Soul," which, following classical tradition, personified the Virtues and Vices as females.[5] Based upon the *Psychomachia,* medieval church sculpture showed Virtues and Vices paired and in battle against one another. Strength wielded a powerful sword while its opposite, Cowardice, was shown throwing a sword down.

In the thirteenth century, the *Psychomachia* was abandoned and Virtues and Vices began to appear in an entirely new way. This century, which was intellectual precursor to the tarot, was one of imagination and of creative reassessment of earlier iconography. As Katzenellenbogen asserted: "Up to the thirteenth century attributes were only used as stereotyped formulae...and once the spell of the rigid and narrow tradition was broken, nothing stood in the way of a generous elaboration of the motives."[6] The Virtues were now shown as placidly seated women, while Vices, were represented in small scenes below each Virtue.[7] Twelve or more Virtues appear in some works, but seven became standard.

Of the seven, three were called *theological.* These included Honor, Hope, and Charity. The *cardinal* virtues were Strength, Justice, Prudence, and Temperance.[8]

This clear, fundamentally classical, system of four cardinal virtues was an essential theme of medieval art. "Socrates," Katzenellenbogen explained, "had defined them as forces of the soul, which work to perfect the human being—Cicero had handed them on to Christian thinkers, and Ambrose had stamped them as gifts of divine grace."[9] And although only three Virtues —Strength, Justice, and Temperance—remain in the standard deck,[10] it is absolutely inconceivable that the medieval mentality which originated the tarot would have omitted Prudence.

To digress briefly from the Virtue of Strength: one must inevitably search for the "lost" virtue of Prudence among the earliest known cards of the tarot—establishing two essentials of identification: The card must show a woman, and it must show at least one of the three traditional attributes of Prudence, a dove, a snake, a book (or scroll), or some variation on those themes.

It appears almost certain that *The Popess* (later called *High Priestess*) is based on a lost prototype card of Prudence in which a female figure held a book in one hand and probably a snake in the other (which may have been turned into a staff). *The Popess* does not fit into the medievalist's logical story of court and countryside which includes king, queen, bishop—or in tarot, *Emperor, Empress,* and *Hierophant*—with a court juggler (*Magician*) and a collection of symbolic figures such as Virtues and Foolish Man. *The High Priestess* is inconsistent with the other members of the royal court. She is explicable only as an exception, such as Pope Joan, or as a reference to Astarte as Waite suggested.

The substitution of a bizarre and incongruous *Popess* for the classically requisite fourth Virtue of Prudence must have been done with good reason. Gertrude Moakley suggests that this card entered the tarot vocabulary to aggrandize a member of the Visconti family, a sister Manfreda who is said to have actually been elected Pope by a minor sect of the Church.[11]

In any event, *The Popess,* and then *The High Priestess* assumed a key attribute of Prudence—the *book*—which has often been incorrectly identified as that of the Virgin Mary in Paradise. Rather, it is that of the *scientia scripturarum* (knowledge of writing), which was understood by medieval theologians to be a symbol of discernment between good and evil.

Original Woman

The principle has been established that *The Magician* is both male and female, and that the separated-out female aspect of this energy is *The High Priestess*. This is the principle of the *collective*.

The individual in incarnation is represented by the androgynous *Lover*, whose female aspect is *Strength*. She is the first female below the Abyss, that is, in manifestation. She is Original Woman. She is the individual Eve whereas *The High Priestess* is the collective Eve yet to be expressed in the collective unconscious as *The Empress*.

Within the microcosmic kingdom of the Demiurge she is the First Mother, and thus also the First Daughter. She is the consort of Original Man and is the vehicle of reproduction.

The totality of the Microcosm is within her. She is the mother of manifest creation.

In the *Jungian Tarot* the relationship of *Strength* to *The Lover* is stressed by the small figure with arms outstretched in the upper right hand side of the card. As in *The High Priestess*, candles float on the waters of consciousness. They form a triangle of light here which is the female aspect of the six-pointed star. The dark cave from which the waters flow in and out represents the channel between the conscious and the unconscious mind.

As is traditional, the woman holds her hand upon the head of a lion. Her function, as the Virgin Daughter, is the "taming" (i.e., enclosing/forming) of the sexual energy which is outgoing from *The Lover*. Like all female figures in the tarot, she is an organizing principle. Moreover, in Jungian terms, this card describes the profound interaction of the male and female sides of Mercurius (First Matter) as they express themselves in manifestation.

The Bright and Dark Daughter

Strength is the woman of the *Apocalypse* described by Saint John as "robed with the Sun, beneath her feet the Moon, and on her head a crown of twelve Stars." The text continues, saying that "she was pregnant," and that "she gave birth to a male child who is destined to rule all nations."[12] This is *Strength* as the archetype of the Virgin Mother, the aspect which is shown in most tarot decks. She is a figure of inherent contradictions. On the one hand she is virtue conquering primitive force, but on the other she is the archetype of helpless Maiden, exposed to great dangers, such as being devoured by reptiles, or being subject to bloody, cruel, and obscene orgies, and being forced to descend into Hades. It is the Terrible Mother who brings the Daughter to such trials.[13]

Despite a powerful sexual content here, the Maiden aspect of *Strength* (as opposed to its Whore aspect) is "ever virgin." She is like the ancient Vestal Virgins who protected the sacred fire. Only in her phase of virtue and innocence can she bring under control what is represented by the red lion.[14] The richness of her activity is explained by the myth of Demeter and Kore, which illustrates the Jungian principle that "every mother contains her daughter in herself, and every daughter her mother, and that every woman extends backwards into her mother and forwards into her daughter. The conscious experience of these ties produces the feeling that her life is spread out over generations—the first step toward the immediate experience and conviction of being outside of time, which brings with it a feeling of immortality."[15]

The corn goddess, Demeter, was a gentle and loving temperament who bore Kore and Iacchus out of wedlock to her brother Zeus. Her natural gaiety was destroyed when Hades fell in love with the young Kore, and asked Zeus for her hand in marriage. Zeus, did not want to offend his oldest brother, but knew how Demeter would feel if he agreed. So he permitted Hades to rape and to abduct the girl while she was picking flowers in a field. It was unclear where Kore was abducted, but Demeter's priests told her that it was at Eleusis.

Upon learning the truth of her daughter's kidnapping, Demeter angrily refused to return to Olympus, a stand which embarrassed Zeus, and caused him to send Hermes to Hades with the message that Kore must be restored. A compromise was eventually reached, and it was determined that Kore should spend three months of each year with Hades as the Queen of Tartarus, where she would be known as Persephone. The remaining nine months she was to spend with her mother, Demeter. Hecate was to keep watch over Kore, and to insure that this arrangement was maintained.[16]

The disappearance and return of Kore was occasion for great festivals in Greece. The *Thesmorphoria,* celebrated in Attica in the month of October, marked the departure of Kore for the underworld.[17] The return of Kore was celebrated in the *Lesser Eleusian Mysteries* in February. The emphasis was agricultural, meaning the old and the new crops. As one scholar stated (and despite eighteenth and nineteenth-century romantic notions about these famous Greek mysteries) at Eleusis "there were no doctrines, but only some simple fundamental ideas about life and death as symbolized in the springing up of the new crops from the old."[18]

The *Greater Eleusian Mysteries* took place every five years, and were in honor of Demeter.[19] As Graves described these rituals: "Demeter's ecstatic initiates symbolically consummated her love affair with Iasius, or Tripolemus, or Zeus, in an inner recess of the shrine."[20] So the Mother who is also Daughter is understood to have a profoundly sexual nature. She brings forth the Daughter who lives both in the above and in the below, in the bright sunlight and the underworld. This Daughter is both innocent Maiden and profligate whore.

The Whore is the dark side of the female aspect of Mercurius. She is the dark side of Original Woman in her role as Eve. The Whore relates to Lilith who, according to the Talmud was the first wife of Adam who became the mother of the Demons.[21] She is also the serpent who is at once the cause of the fall and the means of redemption. In some stories Lilith is described as taking the form of a beautiful woman to beguile and destroy young children. In that role she is a deceiver whose activities parallel those of Mercurius as Trickster.[22]

The Lion

The Jungian Tarot card of *Strength* reiterates the importance of the divine pair, or androgyne. As Jung expresses it: "The animals (dragon, lion, snake. etc.) stand for evil passions that finally take the form of incest. They are destroyed by their own ravenous nature, just as are Sol and Luna, whose supreme desire culminates apparently in incest."[23] And he explains that "In Alchemy the lion...is a synonym for Mercurius, or to be more accurate, for a stage in his transformation."[24]

The dark aspects of the Daughter are symbolically represented by the serpent (recalling that Hecate is also a snake goddess), and by the lion—meaning the erotic aspect of Mercurius. The lion also means the male partner in Alchemy. *Strength* describes two important relationships—that of Mother to Daughter as we have seen, and that of male to female. In alchemical manuscripts a pair of lions is often used to represent Spirit and Soul (*Anima* and *Animus*) united in the body.

That the ultimate unity of Daughter and Son results from spiritual incest is suggested by the Eleventh (pictorial) Key of Valentinus. There twin females, both of which are Sun and Moon (and which together represent the quaternity), ride lions. One lion is devouring the other—symbolizing a principle also shown by the serpent with its tail in its mouth.

The lion's red color has become traditional in tarot because of the sixteenth-century alchemical reference to the "Red Lion," in the process of turning lead into gold.[25] But of course, as one modern alchemist points out, terms such as "Red Lion or Peacock'sTail," have become "impossible childish nonsense" because they have been supplanted by the technical language and symbols of the science of chemistry.[26]

In Western iconography red is also is the color of sin; scarlet is the color of the Great Whore of Babylon and of her beast. But as Jung asserts, it is also the color of the rose of Mary, "the chaste bride and whore who symbolizes the prima materia which 'nature left imperfected.' "[27] 'The bride is," he says, "not only lovely and innocent, but witch-like and terrible."[28]

It may be very difficult for some, no matter how open to new ideas they may be, to think of the Virgin Mary as having an orgiastic side. As Jung taught: "We think we have only to declare an accepted article of faith incorrect and invalid, and we shall be psychologically rid of all the traditional effects of Christianity or Judaism....We entirely forget that the religion of the last two thousand years is a psychological attitude, a definite form and manner of adaptation to the world without and within, that lays down a definite cultural pattern and creates an atmosphere wholly uninfluenced by any intellectual denials...because of this the unconscious was able to keep paganism alive "[29]

The Steps Downward

One of the most interesting aspects of Jung's philosophy is his specialized, and frequently obscure, use of language. The word *supraordinate* is a good example. It is taken from the Latin words *supra,* meaning *above,* and *ordinare,* meaning *to arrange.* So the word means something more than the given order, something which functions in more than one way, something which is more than the apparent sum of its parts. In Jung's dictionary it is the total man, the "Self" which includes the conscious and unconscious components, as opposed to the Ego which relates only to the conscious mind.[30]

Jung describes the Mother as supraordinate (and thus as

daemonic),[31] which qualities are also ascribed to her counter-part, the Maiden. This leads to an important principle: Insofar as the tarot figures may be considered to be archetypes, they function differently—they are expressed differently—as they appear in the individual personality. Jung explains that the Maiden belongs "when observed in a man, to the Anima type; and when observed in a woman to the type of supraordinate personality. It is an essential characteristic of psychic figures hat they are duplex...they are bipolar and oscillate between their positive and negative meanings."[32] This is the symbolism in-herent in the steps behind the figure, leading to the underworld.

The necessity and inevitability of each person's descent into darkness is among the key principles of *Strength* shown both by the descending stairs and by the dark watery cavern. It would be difficult to improve on Jung's succinct explanation of this process: "The conscious mind, advancing into the unknown regions of the psyche, is overpowered by the archaic forces of the unconscious: a repetition of the cosmic embrace of Nous and Physis. The purpose of the descent as universally exempli-fied in the myth of the Hero is to show that only in the region of danger (watery abyss, forest, island, castle, etc.) can one find the 'treasure hard to attain.' "[33]

Notes: *Strength*

1. See Stuart Kaplan, *The Encyclopedia of Tarot*, v. I, New York 1978 and v. II, Stamford 1986, Passim.

2. *Larousse Encyclopedia of Mythology*, New York 1968, 170.

3. A striking example of renewed interest in the Hercules theme, from a period just prior to the invention of the Tarot is found on the pulpit in the Pisa Baptistery carved in 1260 by Nicola Pisano. The nude figure of Hercules with a lion is clearly identified as the virtue of Strength, and is linked with three other virtues —Temperance, Prudence, and Faith. John Pope-Hennessy, *Italian Gothic Sculpture*, London 1955, Plate 5, Notes, 176.

4. Decks which may be cited include the *Gringonneur Tarot*, Kaplan v.I, 111-116, and the Rosenwald *Tarot*, 130-131.

5. "Prudentius," *Oxford Classical Dictionary*, Oxford, 1978, 893.

6. Adolph Katzenellenbogen, *Allegories of the Virtues and Vices in Medieval Art*, Liechtenstein, 1977, 60.

7. Emile Mâle, *Religious Art from the Twelfth to the Eighteenth Century*, New York 1961, 71.

8. Louis Réau, L'*Art Chrétien*, v. I, 175. Réau traces three phases of the combat of the Virtues and Vices: 1) the epoch of the *Psychomachia*, 2) the Virtues unarmed and seated above the vices and 3) the seven theological and cardinal virtues opposing the seven deadly sins. A further development on this theme is that of the *Triumph of the Virtues* found especially in Italian funerary monuments. Panofsky relates the secularization of the virtues to the secularization of biographical eulogy. See Erwin Panofsky, *Tomb Sculpture*, New York 1964, 75. At Paris and at Amiens, twelve virtues are represented.

9. Katzenellenbogen, *Allegories*, 30.

10. In early art the Virtues almost always have the nimbus (halo). See: Alphonse Napoleon Didron, *Christian Iconography*, New York 1965 (reprint of the 1851 translation from the French), 83. On the basis of this scalloped nimbus identifying Virtues in some decks such as the *Rosenwald Tarot*, one may conclude that only three of the Virtues were generally represented by this tine.

11. See: Gertrude Moakley, *The Tarot Cards Painted by Bonafacio Bembo for the Visconti-Sforza Family*, New York, 1966. The serpent and the dove have been attributed to the Virtue following Matthew 10:16:

"Behold, I send you forth as sheep in the midst of wolves: so be wise as serpents and innocent as doves." Katzenellenbogen provides the most comprehensive overview of this study in his *Virtues and Vices.*

12. *Apocalypse,* 12.

13. Carl Jung, *The Archetypes and the Collective Unconscious,* Princeton, 1977, **311-312.**

14. The Vestal Virgins guarded the Roman people by keeping the fire of the city ever burning. They were selected from girls between the ages of six and ten, and were consecrated for a period of thirty years. Their power depended entirely upon their virtue, and whoever lost this was buried alive in an underground tomb, and the male partner was immediately executed. See: Eliade *History of Religious Ideas, vii,* 121.

15. Jung, *Archetypes,* **116.**

16. Robert Graves, *The Greek Myths,* New York, 1957, 89-93. "Kore, Persephone, and Hecate were, clearly, the Goddess in Triad as Maiden, Nymph, and Crone, at a time when only women practiced the mysteries of agriculture. Core stands for the green corn, Persephone for the ripe ear, and Hecate for the harvested corn...." It has been argued that Kore, rather than being wife of the death god, Hades, was originally linked to Pluton, god of wealth—especially the wealth of corn. *Oxford Classical Dictionary,* 324. Relative to the Eleusian mysteries it may be noted that *Demeter Thesmophosos* was the "bringer of treasures."

17. Herodotus claims that all of these festivals came originally from Egypt. He equates Demeter, mother of Kore, with the Egyptian Isis. *The Histories of Herodotus,* London 1964, v. 1.143. Herodotus (c.484 B.C.E. 424 B.C.E) was a Greek historian who traveled widely and who was especially known for his description of the Persian Wars. Cicero called him "the Father of History" because of his ability to present facts in epic form.

18. Eliade, *History of Religious Ideas,* Chicago, 1978, v.I, 460.

19. *Larousse Encyclopedia of Mythology,* New York, 1968, 155.

20. Graves, *Greek Myths,* 94, note 7. Robert Graves claims that in a bizarre ritual a phallic object was worked up and down a woman's boot. Goldberg described this ritual somewhat differently. He states that the marriage of Zeus and Demeter was represented by a priestess of Demeter and a hierophant. "the torches were extinguished and the pair descended into a murky place, while the throng of worshippers awaited in anxious suspense the result of the mystic union, upon which they believed their

salvation depended. After a time the hierophant reappeared and, in the blaze of the night, silently exhibited an ear of corn—the fruit of the divine marriage. However, their intercourse was only dramatic and symbolical, since the hierophant incapacitated himself by the application of hemlock." B.Z. Goldberg, *The Sacred Fire; The Story of Sex in Religion,* New York 1958, 54.

21. Hastings, *Dictionary of the Bible,* New York, 1963, 586.

22. Hastings mentions the rabbinical tradition of Lilith as a beautiful nocturnal specter. *Dictionary of the Bible,* 586.

23. Carl Jung, *Mysterium Coniunctionis,* Princeton, 1976, **188.**

24. Jung, *Mysterium,* **404.**

25. Solomon Trismosin, *Splendor Solis,* with explanatory notes by J.K., Kegan Paul, Trench, Trubner & Co, Ltd., London, undated, 90-93.

26. Frater Albertus, *The Alchemist's Handbook,* New York, 1978, 11.

27. Jung, *Mysterium,* **421.**

28. Ibid., **24**

29. Carl Jung, *Psychological Types,* Princeton, 1977, **313.**

10 / THE HERMIT

Archetype of the Wise Old Man

As is the case with most other cards, the original *Hermit* expressed very different principles than does the card today. In the *Visconti-Sforza* deck *The Hermit* carries an hourglass as an apparent *memento mori* (reminder of death) of which the Middle Ages was so fond.

It may be interpreted as a warning directed to foolish man, that he, "everyman," will come to judgment sooner than he may expect. In other early decks, *The Hermit* is shown as an old man with a staff which, like the hourglass of time, is an attribute of *Saturn*.

The original hourglass of *The Hermit,* transformed into a lamp, appeared in the seventeenth century and became a standard in the eighteenth century when Court de Gebelin's fanciful and romantic ideas began to gain in popularity.[1] Thus *The Hermit* as Father Time became the Wise Old Man as *Light Bearer*

The Wise Old Man

Of all archetypal images, the Wise Old Man is among the most agreed-upon. This image appeared in tarot as early as the sixteenth century. But modern philosophical interpretations of the Hermit as an old man with long white hair and beard, wearing flowing robes owes a great deal to the Theosophists, whose influence tended to graft the features of some ideal Hindu guru onto earlier figures such as Moses and Hermes Trismegistus. Jung explains that the archetype appears with great plasticity in meditation ("active imagination"). It can be magician, priest, grandfather, dwarf, or even animal, and it frequently appears as guru or Master.[2]

Popular Western ideas about a race of Masters trace back to Helena Petrovna Blavatsky, who founded the Theosophical Society in 1875. She wrote about Masters called *Mahatmas,* to signify their awakening to the *Mahat,* a condition commensurate with what has been called "First Matter."[3] Blavatsky described these Masters, as "heirs to the early heavenly wisdom of the first forefathers, they...keep the keys which unlock the most guarded of nature's secrets, and impart them only gradually and with the greatest caution."[4]

According to Theosophical doctrine, the Masters live in various countries around the world and have a mysterious network of communication to which Blavatsky claimed to have been privy as their supposed messenger and as the student of one of the greatest among them.

Contemporary society today is sufficiently removed from the romantic theatricality of the late nineteenth-century occult movement to put that movement into rational perspective. Interest in spiritual phenomenon and in the occult was to some extent a response to industrialization and to fears of a Kaflka-like machine dominated future which many feared would actually destroy humanity's individuality and originality.

With its involvement in India, England came face to face with a culture rooted in the belief that an unseen reality was of far greater import than what could be seen and touched. And, divorced from any value judgment about the movement's spiritual legitimacy, Theosophy was a Western response of wonder and amazement to the philosophy of the East. One need only skim the London newspapers of the day to appreciate the fascination of the man in the street with the unusual and the bizarre. With such an overview one can appreciate the occult movements which emerged. This period of "willing suspension of disbelief" helped to shape the tarot as it is known today and added immeasurably to the mystique of the archetypal image of the Wise Old Man in the West.

Attributes of the Wise Old Man

This is an especially profound and magical archetype. It touches upon everyone's deep-rooted and self-protective fantasy that a guide of great wisdom will appear to lead one out of the wilderness—a very different matter than a Christ or Krishna figure who may be called upon in time of stress and danger. The Wise Old Man is a more primitive and ill-defined presence (Jung referred to his "plasticity") who, like all archetypes, is encountered at the edge of a shadowland between the conscious and the unconscious.

The Wise Old Man affirms two important points: first, that knowledge of the true meaning of life is actually possible, and second that one is not alone in the pursuit of this knowledge. The desire for a teacher and the very belief that teachers *per se* exist in an unseen world is a natural result of self-enquiry. The archetype fulfills a cultural need, such as that expressed in the aphorism "When the student is ready, the master appears." The question of whether this master is a real person on earth, or a figure who exists in a "spirit world," or even whether he may be an artificial construct is of no importance.

Jung calls the Wise Old Man "the superior master and teacher, the archetype of the Spirit, who symbolizes the pre-existent meaning hidden in the chaos of life. He is the father of the soul, and yet the soul, in some miraculous manner, is also his Virgin Mother, for which reason he was called by the alchemists "the first Son of the Mother."[5]

It is the Wise Old Man who intervenes when the Hero is in a desperate situation from which he cannot extricate himself alone. He provides something missing, of which Jung says that: "the knowledge needed to compensate the deficiency comes in the form of a personified thought, i.e., in the shape of a sagacious and helpful old man."[6] This is necessary because "the conscious will by itself is hardly ever capable of uniting the personality to the point where it assumes this extraordinary power to succeed."[7]

The Hermit represents a prophet who, living in two worlds, teaches about the unseen and about the nature of life and death, affirming a principle of Plato that "true philosophers make dying their profession."[8] Plato is, in fact, as propagandist of Pythagorean doctrine, the key Western source for the idea of *me-*

tempsychosis, or "transmigration of the soul," and of the principle of the immortality of the soul unacceptable to Buddhism.

The Western tradition of an individual immortal soul began in about the sixth century B.C.E. With the collapse of Homeric religious values, the Greeks began to speculate on the relationship of the individual to the divine, the relationship of the one to the many. As in India after the *Upanishads,* the individual soul came to be accepted as indestructible but condemned to transmigration until it was ultimately released from its bondage.[9]

Immediately before his death, Socrates asked: "Do the souls of the departed exist in another world or not?" He concluded "that they do exist there, after leaving here, and that they return again to this world and come into being from the dead."[10] Socrates explains that, "The soul, since it is immortal and has been born many times, and has seen all things both here and in the other world, has learned everything that is," and he concludes that "seeking and learning are nothing but *recollection."*[11]

The relationship of *The Hermit* to the Self which is beginning the process of recollection is complicated, but manageable: the grandfather Hermit helps the young Son (*The Sun*) to recognize that he is, himself, the Logos (i.e., the expressed "word" or "action'') and that his task—as the emerging Hero, is to kill his own Mother, meaning the destruction of the collective unconscious itself.[12] The Wise Old Man first helps the Hero to accept his own mortality, and then to recognize (and thus annihilate) the very source of the myth of Self.

But this labor is Herculean. The soul exists on the earth in great darkness; it does not understand the "signs" of the gods. So the Hermit, as prophet, becomes an interpreter of divine omens for the emerging Self-Consciousness. He is an oracle pointing toward the value of some earthly paths and warning about the danger of others.

The Hero must always be on guard. There is a dark side to the Wise Old Man. He may be an evil sorcerer; he may be a deceiver; he may be the instigator of great harm. Or he may simply be a fake. History abounds with people claiming to possess secret knowledge making them better than others, but who are basically charlatans. Even in ancient Greece, Plato decried those who preyed on others with false claims of great powers.[13]

Lao Tzu and the Buddha

One may reasonably assert that, although rooted in the Christian West, Jungian psychology has more in common with Eastern thought, particularly Taoism and Buddhism. The opposites of *yin* and *yang* are together the *Tao,* an indescribable quality from which all things are produced and which contains all possibilities. The Tao, like the Mahat, is similar to the First Matter of *The Magician* To the Taoist, as to the Jungian, life represents the alternation of opposites. To resolve these opposites is to achieve the Tao, or to attain what Jung called a condition of individuation.

In the *Tao Te Ching,* Lao Tzu describes a sage who has qualities of the Hermit. He is a man of supreme knowledge who moves in and out of the *Tao.* The advanced age of the Wise Man is due to the fact that direct encounter of the *Tao* confers longevity.[14] The goal of certain adepts is to attain physical immortality and indeed, Taoists believe there to be a whole class of adepts who, as Blavatsky described, live for centuries in a sort of earthly paradise.[15] Interestingly enough, the Chinese ideogram for the Immortal *(hsien)* represents a hermit-like man and a mountain. Indeed, there is considerable cross-cultural agreement about the relationship of the Wise Old Man archetype to the mountain, such as that on which Moses receives the tablets of the ten commandments.

In the East the one who most characterizes the Wise Old Man is the Buddha, who (unlike the Christ) was married, had two children, and had experienced all aspects of life before he entered into *nirvana.* As Eliade observed: "Buddhism is the only religion whose founder declares himself to be neither the prophet of a god nor his emissary....But he proclaims himself 'awakened' *(buddha)* and hence guide and spiritual master. The goal of his preaching is the deliverance of mankind."[16]

The Buddha, like the Hermit, is a wandering ascetic. He is also a magician. For on the road to nirvana one achieves miraculous powers which (although they should never be flaunted before the common man) demonstrate that the sage has suspended the laws of nature.[17]

Moses and the Logos

In the West, it is Moses who best represents the Wise Old Man as Spirit. It is he who leads his people across the Egyptian desert and out of bondage. He is a prophet and the giver of law. And, like the Buddha, he has magical powers. He turns his staff into a serpent (presumably a phallic reference to the ability of the thaumaturge to transmute sexual energy), and he parts the Red Sea, which one might explain as creating a protected road for the seeker into the waters of the collective unconscious.

Moses is an archetype of intermediary. God speaks directly to him, and he then gives the message to his people. It was the Gnostic Simon Magus who connected Moses to Logos. Simon "The Magician" mentioned briefly in the *Acts of the Apostles,*[18] was an object of vituperation to Hippolytus who accused him of being "an adept in sorceries," who "partly also by the assistance of demons perpetrating his villainy, attempted to deify himself."[19] But Simon's interpretation of Moses is really quite profound.

According to the text of *Exodus,* after the crossing of the Red Sea, the Israelites found water which they could not drink. But the Lord showed Moses a log which, when thrown into the water, caused it to become clean and pure.[20] Simon Magus explains *Exodus* as an allegory of the soul being led out of darkness. He says that crossing the Red Sea led to a knowledge of the meaning and toils of life, and that Moses—as Logos—makes what was "bitter water" into "sweet water."[21] Moses is considered to be more than a prophet of God. He is endowed by Simon with a divinity of his own. As Logos he is in the same essential intermediary position to God the Father as is Christ.

Hermes Trismegistus

The quintessential archetypal image of the Wise Old Magician is that of Hermes Trismegistus. His character was originally based on the Egyptian Thoth, the scribe of the gods who, identified by the Greeks with Hermes, was sometimes called "Thrice Greatest." A considerable amount of literature in Greek, texts on astrology and the occult, appeared under this name. And although Renaissance scholars believed these works to be of great antiquity, they were actually produced in the second and third centuries C.E.[22]

Regardless of the actual origin of the *Corpus Hermeticum,* it was of inestimable influence on Renaissance philosophers, who thought that these books contained the secrets of the ancient Egyptians, and that they held the key to all knowledge and power. So the mystical figure of Hermes Trismegistus began to appear increasingly in works of art, borrowing no small amount from earlier representations of Moses and adding considerably to the archetypal image of a Wise Old Man in flowing robes and long white beard.

Merlin

A key figure in Arthurian legend, Merlin may be singled out as the best personification of the Magician aspect of the Wise Old Man archetype because his qualities are the most human. He lacks the implied perfection of Moses and Hermes Trismegistus (he is not a great religious leader), being rather eccentric in his behavior. Moreover, his relationship to Arthur from youth through kingship, may be explained as one of nurturing the emerging Self-Consciousness.

Sir Thomas Malory's *Le Morte d'Arthur* (in English based on French texts) was first published in 1485. It is a compilation of folk stories about an early king whom historians speculate may have been a king of the *Brythons* (the *Comes Britannae)* at the time of Roman rule.[23] The quest of the Knights of the Round Table for the *Holy Grail* has itself become an archetype in the West. And, although allegory may not have been the intention of the storytellers, Arthurian legend lends itself to some very tight-knit Jungian interpretation.

Merlin plots the birth of Arthur from a liaison with King Uther and Igraine, another man's wife. He says to Uther: "Sir, this is my desire: the first night that ye shall lie by Igraine ye shall get a child on her, and when that is born, that it shall be delivered to me for to nourish there as I will have it."[24] So the Old Magician causes the birth of a soul which he claims as his own, to teach as he pleases! This is to say, symbolically, that he has brought an aspect of himself into new being.

And a principle which Jung has often addressed, that of the relationship between Old Man and Young Boy, is found at the very first meeting between Merlin and Arthur. Merlin appears to Arthur as a fourteen-year old boy and then changes into an old man and says ominously: "God is displeased with you, for ye have lain by your sister, and on her ye have gotten a child that shall destroy you and all the Knights of your realm."[25]

Merlin, as the Higher Consciousness, conspires to express a personality which is his own (the perception of separate existence) into the world. Then, on his first meeting with his separate Ego, he describes to it an act of *incest* that will result in its destruction, and in the destruction of the very world (Camelot) in which that Ego perceives itself to exist. This is the alchemical union of Brother Sun and Sister Moon (clash of conscious and unconscious) that causes a destruction (blackness) from which gold is ultimately produced. In Arthurian terms this means the discovery of the Holy Grail.

Notes: *The Hermit*

1. Remarkably, there are many today who, following Court de Gebelin's bizarre and distorted history of tarot in his *Monde Primitif,* insist that the cards are of Egyptian origin, and who, despite clear historical evidence to the contrary, claim that the cards were originally intended to encapsulate high spiritual principal.

2. Carl Jung, *The Archetypes and the Collective Unconscious,* Princeton, 1977, **398**. According to Jung, the Wise Old Man appears in many different forms, including that of dwarf, hobgoblin, and a variety of animals. Jung states that the animal form implies no devaluation for "in certain respects the animal is superior to man. It has not yet blundered into consciousness nor pitted a self-willed ego against a power from which it lives; on the contrary, it fulfills the will that actuates it in a well-nigh perfect manner." *Archetypes,* **420.**

3. H.P. Blavatsky, *The Secret Doctrine,* Pasadena, 1952, v.I, 162; v.II, 173.

4. Charles J. Ryan, *H.P. Blavatsky* and *the Theosophical Movement,* San Diego, 1975, 66, 92-92. This book is a Theosophical Society publication and thus, by definition, depicts Blavatsky in the most favorable light. A somewhat more objective account of the lady and her organization will be found in *The Lady* with *the Magic Eyes,* by John Symonds, New York, 1960.

5. Jung *, Archetypes,* **74.**

6. Ibid., **401.**

7. Ibid., **404.**

8. Plato, *Phaedo* 67.e.

9. Mircea Eliade, *History of Religious Ideas,* Chicago, 1984, v.II, 184.

10. Plato, *Phaedo,* 70.c-d.

11. Plato, *Meno,* 81.c-d.

12. The literature of Western mysticism contains many veiled references to the idea that at the most advanced level, the male teacher turns the student over to a female teacher. In Jungian terms this may be interpreted to mean that the teacher points the student toward the Anima/Animus, or it may be explained as direct reference to conscious involvement with the collective unconscious.

13. Plato, *Republic,* 364b-365a.

14. *The Texts of Taoism,* Translated by James Legge, New York, 1962 (Republication of 1891 Oxford University text), 54, 103.

15. Eliade, *History of Religious Ideas,* v.II 33-34.

16. Ibid., v.II, 72.

17. *A Buddhist Bible,* (collected Buddhist texts) ed. Dwight Goddard, Boston 1970, 50. A Pali scripture describes four different magical powers: The Heavenly Ear, an ability to hear both earthly and heavenly sounds; Remembrance of past lives; Insights into the hearts of others; The Heavenly Eye, the vision of truth; and self-knowledge which delivers the mind.

18. *Acts,* 8:9-24.

19. Hippolytus, *Refutation of All Heresies,* Grand Rapids, 1986, 78.

20. *Exodus,* 15:21-25.

21. Hippolytus, 78.

22. Frances A. Yates, *Giordano Bruno* and *the Hermetic Tradition,* Chicago, 1964, 2.

23. Sir Thomas Malory, *Le Morte D'Arthur,* London 1956, v.I, ix.

24. Ibid., v.I, 7.

25. Ibid., v.I, 37.

11 / THE WHEEL OF FORTUNE

Archetype of the Mother as Fortuna

This card's history points to a mind-set of the original tarot artists. As Emile Mâle said, the Middle Ages "took everything in a literal sense and loved to clothe the most abstract thought in concrete form."[1] And to this insight one may add Katzenellenbogen's observation that "the systematically-thinking medieval writer attributes moral significance to every detail of his work."[2] So as a product of late medieval thought, the tarot cards may be taken as very literal stories and as simple behavioral models. In fact the tarot represents the most popular and common themes of late medieval art. Nowhere is this inclination more evident than in *The Wheel of Fortune*, a card which illustrates life's "ups and downs."

The Wheel of Fortune, and the circular pattern in general, appear often in medieval art. The most prominent of these wheels are the magnificent rose windows in French Gothic cathedrals. On the South porch of Amiens, for example, Fortune is shown as a half-round wheel to which seventeen figures are attached. Eight of these are carried up while another eight, dressed in rags to show their bad luck, are carried downward. At the very top sits a man wearing a crown and carrying a scepter.[3]

In classical times, Lady Fortune was carried about on a winged wheel. But the Middle Ages incorporated this figure into the wheel itself. This new theme, apparently an innovation of thirteenth-century Italian manuscript painting, appeared in the program of the *Visconti-Sforza Tarot*. Such developments on the iconography of the wheel largely resulted from renewed attention to the work of Boethius, (480-554 C.E.), a philosopher and statesman who has often been called "the father of the Middle Ages."[4]

Under the rule of the Ostrogoth King, Theodoric,[5] Boethius was accused of plotting with the Byzantine Emperor, Justinian, for the king's removal. And in a move which he lived to regret, Theodoric put the philosopher into prison and sentenced him to death. While awaiting execution, Boethius wrote *The Consolation of Philosophy,* a lengthy "dialogue" concerning the true nature of fortune. The book tells how, in a state of despair, there appears to him a beautiful woman who is the embodiment of Philosophy, and who expresses deep concern for him, and who—before death —helps him to find the meaning of life.[6] The first thing she does is to chase away the "Muses of Poetry" which were, as he says "standing by my bed, helping me to find words for my grief." To them, Lady Philosophy says: "Who let these theatrical tarts in with this sick man? Not only have they no cures for his pain, but with their sweet poison they make it worse."[7]

The arts, and all else, she instructs, must be put into a proper perspective. And Lady Fortune herself is indeed fickle. "I know, says Philosophy, the many kinds of tricks of that monster, Fortune, and especially her charming and friendly manner with those she is trying to cheat, when she crushes with unbearable grief those whom she leaves when they least expect it....you have never had anything worth having at her hands, nor have you lost anything." And she insists that once "you have given yourself over to Fortune's rules, you must accommodate yourself to your mistress's ways." And she offers a remarkable challenge: "Will you really try to stop the whirl of her turning wheel? Why, you are the biggest fool alive—if it once stop, it ceases to be the Wheel of Fortune."[9]

Philosophy insists that Fortune is utterly ruthless:
So with imperious hand she turns the wheel of change
This way and that like the ebb and flow of the tide,
And pitiless tramples down those once dread kings,
Raising the lowly face of the conquered—
Only to mock him in his turn;
Careless she neither hears nor heeds the cries
Of miserable men: she laughs
At the groans that she herself has mercilessly caused.
So she sports, so she proves her power,
Showing a mighty marvel to her subjects, when
The self-same hour.
Sees a man first successful, then cast down.[10]

It was in this spirit that artists from the twelfth through the fifteenth centuries depicted a wheel on which man rises and falls in sudden changes of fortune. But the circle meant more than the Wheel of Fate. As a perfect form, it was also related to Divine Light. Under the influence of Neo-Platonists such as Pseudo-Dionysius (the Areopagite), and by the structural accomplishment of flying buttresses, the walls of Gothic churches were almost eliminated, as "Divine Light" flooded the churches. The primary vehicle of this light was the rose window, which may legitimately be called a *mandala*, a form among the most powerful of all archetypal images.

Boethius would certainly have agreed with Jung's references to the idea of God as a circle, or to "the circular motion of the mind." Whereas his spiritual mentor, Plato, spoke of the "circles in the world soul," and the Stoics, who so attracted him, described the heavens a "round and revolving God,"[11] Boethius speaks of a divine substance which "turns the moving circle of the universe while it keeps itself unmoved."[12]

The Archetype of the Mandala

If the principle of archetype is more than merely a seductively clever philosophical postulate, and if there is actually such a thing as an "archetypal symbol," a cross-cultural look at ideas about the circle should reveal a great deal about the nature of the most "pure" archetypes. Does the image of a circle evoke something similar in everyone, regardless of their cultural orientation? The answer seems generally to be yes. Indeed Jung said that he felt it "probable that we are dealing with an *a priori* 'type,' an archetype which is inherent in the collective unconscious and thus individual birth and death."[13]

The mandala is the most important visual sign of Jungian psychology in that it represents the totality of Self, both conscious and unconscious.[14] It is enclosing and protecting, like the Greek *temenos* (temple compound). Jung taught that "insofar as the mandala encompasses, protects, and defends the psychic personality against outside influences and seeks to unite the inner opposites, it is at the same time a distinct individuation symbol and was known as such even to medieval Alchemy."[15] The figure of Fortuna on the Jungian Tarot card is that of the Mother who determines the experience of the Son, but who may be also be protective. Jung stressed that the mandala can be a form of Mother archetype.[16]

The practical value of the mandala is to focus what would otherwise be diffused and chaotic. Jung stated that all of the unconscious mythological materials (such as those encountered in the tarot) form a multiplicity that "culminates in a concentric or radial order which constitutes the true center or essence of the collective unconscious."[17]

A similar point is made by Plato, who says that "the universe is in the form of a sphere,"and that "the center of the world cannot be rightly called above or below, but is the center and nothing else."[18] The soul of man reflects that of the universe, and is also considered to be spherical. The philosophies of Jung and of Plato are in complete agreement about the special nature of the central point of this sphere. Jung took the Sanskrit word for circle, *mandala,* to describe this form because of what he called a "remarkable agreement between the insights of yoga and the results of psychological research."[19]

The basic motif of the mandala, Jung explains, "is a premonition of a center of personality, a kind of central point within the psyche to which everything is related, by which everything is arranged, and which is itself a source of energy. This center is not felt or thought of as the ego but, if one may so express it, as the *Self*. Although the center is represented by an innermost point, it is surrounded by a periphery containing everything that belongs to the Self—the paired opposites that make up the total personality. This totality comprises consciousness first of all, then the personal unconscious, and finally an identifiably large segment of the collective unconscious whose archetypes are common to all mankind."[20]

In his *Archetypes and the Collective Unconscious,* Jung lists nine formal elements of the mandala. On this scheme a mandala may:

1) be circular, spherical, or egg-shaped,
2) be elaborated into a wheel or into a flower
     such as a rose, or a lotus,
3) at the center have a sun, a star or a cross—
     usually with four, eight, or twelve rays,
4) have rotating figures (such as the swastika),
5) have a snake coiled around a center,
6) show the squaring of the circle
     (a circle in a square, or a square in a circle),
7) show an enclosed castle, city, or courtyard,
8) show an eye (pupil and iris),
9) when it is a "disturbed totality picture"
     deviate from the four and show
     three or five pointed figures.[21]

But Jung adds that: "The true mandala is always an inner image which is gradually built up through (active) imagination, at such times when psychic equilibrium is disturbed or when a thought cannot be found and must be sought for, because it is not contained in holy doctrine." And he points out that this is a most advanced exercise. It is "a mental image that can be built up only by a fully-instructed lama through the power of imagination."[22]

Squaring the Circle

The square (quaternity) is matter, the physical condition. It is thus the conscious self and the perception of a separate personality, which involves dualities and their internal opposite poles—light and dark, male and female. The circle is perfection, God, "a circle whose center is everywhere and the circumference nowhere."[23]

The circle in the square is God within man; the square in the circle is man within God. The squaring of the circle may mean perception of the mechanisms by which dimensions appear within the Creative Emptiness; it is the framework of "sane" consciousness by which the unconscious is excluded. In early magical treatises, such as that of Agrippa, a circle was consecrated using the same Prayer of Solomon used in the dedication of a temple.[24] Later magicians, including Barrett, offered more complicated and baroque formulae for consecration of the circle, with the names of deities and angels assigned to the day and hour of the operations.[25]

The circle was protection against those evil forces which the magus might evoke, whether by design or by accident. Jung puts this into psychological terms, suggesting that the evil spirits are within and that the creation of a magic circle through the *circumambulatio,* has the effect of preventing the unconscious from "breaking out," which is the equivalent of psychosis.[26]

Jung stresses the archetypal relationship of the square to the circle. He says that "the squaring of the circle was a problem that greatly exercised medieval minds. It is a symbol of the opus *alchymicum,* since it breaks down the original chaotic unity into four elements and then combines them again in a higher unity. Unity is represented by a circle and the four elements by a square."[27] The squared figure at the center of the mandala is considered to be the *lapis,* the *philosopher's stone.* And, in fact, pursuant to the Wheel of Fortune, it was believed in the Middle Ages that within the wheel, Lady Fortuna determined the four specific phases of human destiny.[28]

The *Fourth Book of Occult Philosophy,* attributed to Agrippa, offers a profound accounting of the symbolic square. It concludes that "the name of the Supreme and highest intelligence, which many suppose to be the soul of the world, is collected out of the four cardinal points of the figure of the world...and by the opposite and contrary way, is known the name of the great *Daemon* or evil spirit."[29] This is an interesting theological statement. It says, first of all, that the highest intelligence is based upon a quaternity. And second, it says that when these four points are brought together the intelligence is good, but that when these four points are separated, the intelligence is evil. Good and evil are different activities of the same thing. And presumably this intelligence of four points (traditionally symbolizing earth, or incarnation) happens within the perfect circle of God. By implication the four points, or square, of "good intelligence" is, as Jung suggested, like an enclosed house or temple.[30]

As has been considered, Jung called the circle the *temenos,* or area where the temple sits, and to call the square the *temple* implies that it is most logically represented within the circle.

The Mother Who Determines Experience

In the *Jungian Tarot* card, *The Wheel of Fortune*, the Mother stands behind the wheel, directing its rotation. The "Son" (*The*

Lover) is at the center with arms and legs extended like Leonardo da Vinci's design representing man as "the measure of all things." The colors behind the figure are of those of the twelve zodiacal paths on the Kabbalistic Tree of Life, calling into play an old aphorism of astrology that a person lives successively in each of these signs. The eyes around the wheel relate it to the wheels of Ezekiel's chariot. The four candles suggest the relationship of the circular figure to the four points, the square of physical dimensions.

To the medieval artist, a simple soul unconcerned by the fact that irrational "fatalism" is essentially antithetical to Christianity, this card meant chance or luck.[31] Artists invoked Fortuna with little concern for philosophical contradiction. A philosophically homogeneous society felt no ideological threats and managed to bend everything into a Christian context.[32] Of course, earlier, the Christian principle of salvation had supplanted that of the Roman goddess Fortuna, and of the Greek *Tyche* who, although closely related, were not exactly the same deities. Evidence suggests that Fortuna was not originally a goddess of chance or luck, but that she was a bringer of fertility and increase which, as an aspect of the Earth Mother, makes her a fine candidate for inclusion into a Jungian pantheon.

The Greek goddess Tyche was pure chance or fortune, a basically indifferent force. She brought good or bad things unpredictably, with no judgment about consequences. And it was in this spirit of antique fatalism that the originators of tarot created *The Wheel of Fortune*. The card reflected the very popular theme of fickle and blind fortune, which raises people to positions of wealth and power, and then dashes them back down to earth.

Wheel of the Zodiac

The wheel of the Zodiac which, as Ptolemy said "in its nature as a circle can have no beginning nor end,"[33] is to the astrologer the wheel of life and of experience. Insofar as life changes are involved, the wheel is also a measure of *time.* Behind the Mother as Fortuna stands the Old Man, Saturn-Kronos.[34] In fact, in Hermetic Kabbalah, the relationship of the mother *Binah* to Saturn/Kronos and, thus to manifestation and the inevitability of death, is very direct.[35] The Mother encloses the creative principle of the Father to produce a Son who is subject to the rules of matter, and to the sequence of time and *deterioration* of the perceived reality. Nevertheless, the Mother tries, by imposing experience, to convey to her Son the means for escaping the wheel of this earthly condition.

Jung called attention to the dark side of all of this. "The horoscope," he said, "is itself a mandala (a clock) with a dark center, and a leftward *circumambulatio* with 'houses' and planetary phases."[36] Circumambulation to the left (*sinister*) is movement into the unconscious, whereas a clockwise movement is toward consciousness. Jung said that "presumably the leftward circumambulation indicates that the squaring of the circle is a stage on the way to the unconscious,"[37] by which he is suggesting that life experience as represented by the Zodiac-clock-mandala, is ultimately working toward assimilation into the unconscious.

1. Emile Mâle, *The Gothic Image,* New York 1958, 97

2. Adolph Katzenellenbogen, *Allegories of the Virtues and Vices in Medieval Art,* Liechtenstein, 1977, 71.

3. Didron argues unconvincingly that these figures are an allegory of the ages of man. The half-rose window is clearly a wheel of fortune.

4. Apparently educated in Athens, he was among the last of the philosophers to be taught in the, by then, unfashionable Greek language. He thus forms a bridge between the ancient world and that of medieval Christianity. His *Consolation of Philosophy,* nominally a Christian book leaning upon Neo-Platonic and Stoic ideas, was influential to the early scholastic period (1000-1150) during which many of the ideas and images later incorporated into Tarot appeared. See also: David Knowles, "Boethius," *The Encyclopedia of Philosophy,* New York, 1972, v.I, 328-330.

5. Theodoric "The Great," elected King of the Ostrogoths in 471, (c.454-526 C.E.) led an attack into Italy and took over several important cities, including Ravenna. His rule was relatively benevolent, but was so strong that he could avoid any real control from the Byzantine Emperor. The end of his career was marked by disagreement with his Roman subjects, and by a quarrel with the Pope. His hasty execution of Boethius was extremely unpopular.

6. Mâle, 96. The interaction between Boethius and the Lady who personifies philosophy appears to be an almost perfect example of Jung's postulate that a man deals with his own *Anima.*

7. Anicius Manlius Severinus Boethius, *The Consolation of Philosophy* Cambridge, 1973, Loeb Classical Library, 133-135.

8. Ibid., 175.

9. Ibid., 179.

10. Ibid., 179-181.

11. Carl Jung, *The Archetypes and the Collective Unconscious,* Princeton, 1977, **573**, also Cornford *Timaeus,* 72ff.

12. Boethius, 307.

13. Carl Jung, *Psychology and Alchemy,* Princeton, 1977, **329.**

14. This interpretation is of the mandala as *circle,* insofar as the mandala is an archetypal wheel is used to describe an action or series of actions. For example, in one school of Buddhist thought, the initiated mind turns "the Wheel of Right Dharma," in contrast to those in the

world who are "turned upside down by the wheel of birth and death." Luk K'uan YG, *The Secrets of Chinese Meditation,* New York 1979, 154.

15. Jung, *Archetypes,* **318.**

16. Ibid., **156.**

17. Carl Jung, *Psychology and Religion: West and East,* Princeton, 1977, **945.**

18. Plato, *Timaeus,* 62, d.

19. Jung, *Psychology and Religion,* **945.**

20. Jung, *Archetypes,* **634.**

21. Ibid., **646.**

22. Jung, *Psychology and Alchemy,* **12.**

23. Jung, *Psychology and Religion,* **229.**

24. Cornelius Agrippa, *Fourth Book of Occult Philosophy,* London 1655 (First English translation), 33. The original was claimed to have been published in Latin in the early sixteenth century, however some scholars insist that this is a spurious work. Regardless of authorship the *Fourth Book* contains some brilliant insights. Agrippa's first three books are not in dispute.

Agrippa presented a tight and reasoned magical system which was to influence generations that followed him (Barrett's *Magus* is the best-known example). This father of Western magical systems worked entirely within the context of the Catholic Church. Dedicated to Charles V., the book appeared with an imprimatur stating that "This book has been lately examined land approved by certain prelates of the church, and doctors, thoroughly versed both in sacred and profane literature." *Philosophy of Natural Magic,* Princeton 1974, 2. This is the first of the three books. It was originally published in Antwerp in 1531. See also Charles G. Nauert, Jr. *Agrippa and the Crisis of Renaissance Thought,* Illinois, 1965.

25. Francis Barrett, *The Magus,* London, 1801, 105.

26. Jung, *Psychology and Alchemy,* **188.**

27. Ibid., **165.**

28.The life of Christ is also divided into four phases. Katzenellenbogen, *Allegories,* 70.

29. Agrippa, *Fourth Book,* 55.

30. Jung, *Psychology and Alchemy,* **166.**

31. Ante-Nicene Christianity happened in a climate of syncretism

when there was a far greater willingness to allow for a free flow of ideas. It was later periods which affirmed this ideological distinction.

32. Twelfth century writers extended the metaphor of Boethius, gave the wheel a key moral significance related to the monastic life, and eliminated any philosophical contradictions. In the *Wheel of True Religion* the goddess of blind fate is missing because the wheel turns entirely by itself. Katzenelenbogen, 70-72.

33. Ptolemy, *Tetrabiblios,* North Hollywood, 1976, XII.

34. Erwin Panofsky, *Studies in Iconology,* New York 1962, 69ff.

35. There are a number of legends in which death and the wheel are linked. In Bohemia, for example, on the fourth Sunday in Lent children fastened a straw man, representing death, to a wheel, set the figure ablaze and rolled it down a hill. This playful ritual meant the banishing of death (Winter) by the Spring.

36. Jung, *Psychology and Alchemy,* **327.**

37. Ibid., **166-167.**

12 / JUSTICE

Archetype of Punishment and Reward

This is another of those tarot cards which have been used to carry many (often divergent) messages. It has been described as a Virtue, as the essence of divine justice, as the often arbitrary injustice of the Demiurge, and as a system of psychological self-regulation.

To the late Middle Ages, the Virtue of Justice was a behavioral model for a perfect justice so clearly lacking in real society. The figure, with its scales, suggested a justice which was as old as time itself. And in fact, the origin of justice shown as a woman with scales is found in ancient Egypt. This theme, like many others, was transmitted from the Egyptians to the Greeks, to the Romans, and then into the vocabulary of the Western Middle Ages.

In Egypt the goddess *Maat* personified justice, moral law, order and truth. Her attribute, *the feather of Maat,* was weighed against the heart of the deceased, *Maat* being at once the goddess and the principle of justice; she often appeared as the balance itself.[1] Presumably the idea of a goddess whose name is synonymous with the principle of justice was borrowed by the Greeks as *Themis,* the second consort of Zeus.[2] The personification of justice, her name had the abstract meaning of both justice and righteousness. The principle called *Themis* is very ancient and, like the essential rightness of *maat,* precedes all known systems of laws.

The Themis was a divine agent which suggested to kings, and even to gods, what judicial awards were appropriate. The plural of the word, *Themistes,* came to mean the awards themselves. In this context Zeus is a lawmaker, a judge with his own store of Themistes emanating from above.[3] The same principle of divine judgment is present as "the wisdom of Solomon."

In *The Iliad,* Homer described the goddess of justice as so powerful that she was the assessor of Jupiter himself. And by the time of Plato, Themis had become one of a trinity of deities, (including Zeus and Apollo), by whom one swore to be telling the truth in a court of law.[4]

The tarot card of *Justice* also assumes the existence of some abstract ultimate justice, a "natural law" transcending all earthly systems. The sixth-century emperor Justinian, who codified Roman law, spoke of the laws of men as "civil law," but of natural law as the "law of nations" because all nations use it[5] It is this sort of law which the figure of Justice, later shown as blindfolded, administers—a natural law which is beyond all known authority. Of course, as history demonstrates, natural law is a concept itself subject to many interpretations. For example, democratic systems claim that "all men are created equal," monarchist governments claim the "divine right of kings," and modern constitutional monarchies straddle the fence claiming that, as Orwell suggested, all men are created equal, but that some men are created more equal than others.

In the tenth and eleventh centuries, almost no thought was given to laws. Feudal government was arbitrary and often cruel. Justice, as one scholar expressed it, became "an instrument of extortion, the essential object of which was to *exploit* the person under jurisdiction—that is to say, to overwhelm him with fines and confiscations."[6] But the twelfth and thirteenth centuries brought a rediscovery of Roman law through the works of Justinian, which had almost as stimulating an effect as the rediscovery of Aristotle. Judges and kings found in this system ideal solutions to every problem of human conduct.[7] Thus, by the time the game of tarot was created, justice had a very different meaning than it had earlier. The card pointed to an ideal justice which now seemed possible.

Although the origins of the tarot themes may never be proven exactly, there are two apparent reasons that Justice and the other cardinal Virtues appear in this secular device. First, there was the general revival of classical themes in the twelfth and thirteenth centuries. And second, virtuous behavior in daily life was stressed in the morality plays which personified the Virtues, and which were common at precisely the period in history (late 1300's) when the tarot cards first emerged.[8] The connection of tarot as descriptive of daily life with that of the medieval theater underscores an important art historical fact. There is limited information about the most common things, such as the secular theater, and scholars have been forced to place almost all of their emphasis on religious materials.

Thus one seeks a corrective in asking how an ordinary person of the fourteenth century would have viewed the card of *Justice*.

Medieval man probably saw a connection between this card and that of *Judgment*, which was certainly a "Last Judgment" in the early tarot. But *Justice* is a card of the earthly condition; it is the punishment and reward of this life, meted out to foolish man by civil or clerical authority.

Iconographically, a distinction can also be made between the scales of Lady Justice and those of the Last Judgment. The scales of justice are biblical. They are the scales so often referred to by the prophets, for example the passage in *Proverbs,* which says that "A just balance and scales are the Lord's."[9] But the scales of the last judgment, so ominously ubiquitous above the doors of medieval churches, have quite a difference source. The theme of the *psychostasis,* or weighing of souls, entered the western vocabulary through Coptic (Christian) Egypt. The role of the Egyptian god Anubis, weighing the heart of the deceased, was taken over by the Archangel Michael.[10]

The Virtue of Justice

The mode of portraying Justice, as well as that of the other Virtues, became established in the ninth century. They were shown standing, and in full-length: *Prudentia* carried a book, *Fortitudo* was armed, and *Justitia* held a balance as she had in the earliest times.[11]

Most of the development of the Virtues theme took place in manuscript painting, where the artists had a great deal more freedom to interpret themes than did the stone sculptors. And, particularly in the creative atmosphere of the twelfth-century classical revival, there was dramatic increase in the stock of attributes of the Virtues. In that time Justice was shown holding a set square, a plumb level, or a pair of scales and a measuring rod as a symbol of the accuracy of her decisions. That she can punish wrongdoing severely is shown by her sword.[12]

Pursuant to the exploration of such themes, it must be under-scored that those early tarot decks commissioned by royal courts are actually manuscript paintings. And although there may be some lost prototype which originated among the common people, the tarot as it is known today is clearly heir to the creative inventions of late medieval manuscript artists.

Punishment and Reward

Modern psychology and metaphysics have transported this card's meaning a great distance from the simplicity of medieval justice to an activity in a process of Self-revelation.[13] Late nineteenth-century Hermetic Kabbalists, who developed a very complicated system correlating the Kabbalistic Tree of Life, the Hebrew alphabet, and the tarot, put special emphasis on the card of *Justice.* As the card *of Lamed,* it bore a special relationship to *The Fool*, to which they assigned the letter *Aleph.* The implication was that *Justice* maintained the balance of opposites in the universe projected by *The Fool.*

Interestingly enough, Jungian psychology leads one to precisely this same observation. And, in fact, the punishment and reward of the Mother as Justice represents the very essence of Jung's ideas about what happens to the "inspired soul" seeking Self-knowledge. According to Jung it is, "just the 'inspired soul' that becomes god and demon, and as such suffers the divine punishment of being torn asunder like Zagreus."[14] He uses the term *enantiodromia* to mean "being torn asunder into pairs of opposites, which are the attributes of 'the god' and hence also of the godlike man, who owes his godlikeness to overcoming his gods."[15] Almost everyone is, in fact, "stuck" with the punishment of the dualities imposed by the unconscious. "The only person who escapes the grim law of enantiodromia is the man who knows how to separate himself from the unconscious, not by repressing it—for then it simply attacks him from the rear—but by putting it clearly before him as *that which he is not* "[16]

And Jung warns that the simple act of turning one's conscious attention to the unconscious may cause terrible problems: "Whenever the Father and Mother images have still to be overcome, whenever there is a little bit of life still to be conquered, then we had better make no mention of the collective unconscious."[17]

In these terms *Justice* is, beyond its obvious and simplistic meanings, a rather negative figure which serves to maintain some absolute balance of the perception of opposites. The Jungian point of view is that the perception of opposites (Father and Mother) is an affliction imposed by the Mother, the collective unconscious, which, having borne the Son into the material condition, imposes structure and order within that condition. To overcome the figure of Justice in this card is to symbolically destroy both the Mother and the Father, which means to eliminate the perception of opposites.

In brief, Justice may be called the constant affirmation of the "reality" (actually illusion) of opposite conditions and, most important, of the laws of cause and effect.

The Balance of Opposites

Another way to approach this inner cause-effect continuum is to consider the archetype of Justice to be an innate drive toward the maintenance of opposites within each individual the "good" of equal and opposite weights as opposed to the "evil" of unbounded energy. This is an automatic mechanism by which a person becomes uncomfortable with an extreme and strives for the opposite until a middle ground is reached. It is a mechanism which tells the body that it is too hot or too cold, or the mind that it is functioning inefficiently with an excess of either intellect or emotion. At a more complex level, Jung speaks of the "counterplay between inside and outside" which, he says, "represents, at bottom, the energetics of the life process, the polar tension that is necessary for self-regulation. However different to all intents and purposes these opposing forces may be, their fundamental meaning and desire is the life of the individual; they always fluctuate round this center of balance."[18]

Jung explains over and over again that analysis, meditation, or whatever may bring a person to look inside himself, causes a psychic disequilibrium and that this is a vital part of the process of Self-recollection. What happens, he explains, is that "the energy thus freed disappears from consciousness and falls into the unconscious."[19] And, he says, "I regard the loss of balance as purposive, since it replaces a defective consciousness by the automatic and instinctive activity of the unconscious, which is aiming all the time at the creation of a new balance."[20]

Jung's comments are rather clinical and dispassionate, but as a practical matter, this process can be overwhelming. In his book *Shamanism: Archaic Techniques of Ecstasy,* Mircea Eliade describes the "more or less pathological sickness, dreams, and ecstasies" which happen as one approaches the condition of shaman,[21] the tribal priest and magician who lives in two worlds and who is able to transcend the laws of nature.

Eliade examines the ways in which mental imbalance, even insanity, is followed by a rebalancing at a "higher" level: Among these experiences are often a feeling that the body is dismembered, followed by a feeling of renewal of the internal organs and viscera."[22] The underlying theme of these initiatory experiences is death and resurrection—psychic suffering and isolation being an inescapable part of this process.

This is another area of cross-cultural agreement which may signal a process that is archetypal. The alchemical state of *nigredo,* the descent of Christ into Hell (the Self descending into black-ness), and the encounter of the Shaman-candidate with madness all refer to the frightening encounter of the disorganized collective unconscious. It is a "reality" where the safe and secure rules of the waking consciousness do not apply.

"Divine" Punishment

Among the most profound of the philosophical questions asked by Jung—and a key to his thought processes—has to do with the reasons for the crucifixion of Christ. Why, he asks, did the God accept punishment? Did he really die to expiate the guilt of humanity? "If mankind is the guilty party," Jung observes, "logic surely demands that mankind should be punished. But if God takes the punishment on himself, he exculpates mankind, and we must then conjecture that it is not mankind that is guilty, but God (which would logically explain why he took the guilt on himself.)" [23]

Jung sees no answers to this question in Christianity, but finds some clues in the Old Testament and in Gnosticism: "Though Yahweh was a guardian of the law he was not just and...he suffered from fits of rage which he had every occasion to regret. And from certain Gnostic systems it is clear that the *auctor rerum* was a lower archon who falsely imagined that he had created a perfect world."[24]

So *Justice* does not necessarily administer a perfect natural law, but may function as an imperfect agent of the imperfect Demiurge. The implication is that, in reality, there is no justice, and that what has been called "the will of God," also does not exist. It is for this reason that the card of *Justice* in the *Jungian Tarot* is the only one of the deck that is represented indoors. It means that the Mother who punishes and rewards functions within a perspective that is highly restricted.

Notes: *Justice*

1. E. A. Wallis Budge, *The Gods of the Egyptians,* New York, 1969, v.II,418-419.

2. Hesiod, *Theogony,* Oxford, 1988, line 135. Hesiod describes Themis as the daughter of Earth and the mother of the *Horae* (Goddesses of the Seasons)— whom he names Right, Peace, and Good Government, and the *Morae* (Fates).

3. Henry Sumner Maine, *Ancient Law,* New York, 1989 (original 1861), 3-7.

4. Plato, *Laws,* 936e.

5. Maine, *Ancient Law*, 38.

6. P. Boisonnade, *Life and Work in Medieval Europe,* New York 1987 (original 1908), 151.

7. Roman law was incorporated into almost all European legal systems by the end of the thirteenth century. One of the most important ideas was a clear-cut distinction between civil and criminal cases. Interest in Roman law also brought new interest in the study of Canon law.

8. The Paternoster play of the late fourteenth century personified both Virtues and Vices. The use of allegorical figures is first found in a twelfth century German advent play, *Antichristus.* Like the early tarot, there are no remaining secular plays, although Latin records of the twelfth and thirteenth centuries show that there were theaters dedicated to secular drama. See: *Everyman and Medieval Miracle Plays,* edited by A.C. Cawley, New York 1959, vii-xvii.

9.*Proverbs,* 16:11.

10. Louis Réau, *L'Art Chrétien,* v.II, Nouveau Testament, 733. Didron cites the appearance of the theme in Greek vase painting, specifically one illustrating the second book of *The Iliad* where the gods debate the fate of Achilles and Hector. Alphonse Napoleon Didron, *Christian Iconography* v.ii,180-181. In the West, it is likely that this symbolism first appeared in Spain, which began to feel Coptic influence as early as the sixth century. Ernst Kitzinger, *Early Medieval Art,* London 1963, 75.The ancient Egyptians, like the Christians, believed that the souls of the dead (and perhaps also their bodies) were judged. The "weighing of actions" took place, represented by the human heart from which they thought all action and thought proceeded.

This was the *utcha metu,* the weighing of actions. But *metu* also meant word, and carried a philosophical principle similar to that of the Hebrew *dabhar* and the Greek *logos.* E. Wallis Budge, *The Gods of the Egyptians,* New York 1969 (original 1904), v. ii, 142-144. See also E.A. Wallace Budge, *Osiris,* New York 1961, 318-319. It is possible that the concept of "word-event" originated with the Egyptians. There appears to have been a definite division of judgment. In the name of Osiris, the God Thoth (Scribe of the Gods) examined the balances when words were in question. And although this is not absolutely clear, Anubis may have presided when the weighing involved action, so that the *utcha metu* was understood to represent the assessment of two qualities in the same way. If the term which meant both "word" and "action" had to do with a practical division of labor at the last judgment, there may originally have been less philosophical significance of the Greek and Hebrew words carrying these identical dual meanings, *logos* and *dahbar,* than has been generally assumed.

11. Adolph Katzenellenbogen, *Allegories of the Virtues and Vices in Medieval Art,* Liechtenstein, 1977, 31n1.

12. Ibid., 55.

13. There is an important conceptual difference between many aspects of the Western mystery tradition and Christianity. One such difference is a belief that "enlightenment" is either earned, or that it is part of a very natural process. Many schools of Christianity view inner understanding as "a gift."

14. Jung, *Two Essays on Analytical Psychology,* New York 1953, **113.**

15. Ibid., **113.**

16. Ibid., **112.**

17. Ibid., **113.**

18. Ibid., **311.**

19. Ibid., **253.**

20. Ibid., **253.**

21. Mircea Eliade, *Shamanism,* Princeton, 1972, 33.

22. Ibid., 34.

23. Carl Jung, *Psychology and Religion: West and East,* Princeton, 1977, **408.**

24. Ibid.,

13 / THE HANGED MAN

Archetype of Sacrifice

Because of the peculiar position of the figure, this card has provoked more curiosity and bizarre theories about its origin than any other in the deck. One eighteenth-century writer assumed that a mistake had been made and produced a deck in which *The Hanged Man* was standing right side up on one foot. It has been variously claimed that the card represents Judas, the god Odin, or a collection of other mythological figures related to trees.

The truth is that hanging by the heels, and being beaten (often to death) was a special punishment inflicted upon knights guilty of lying, of cowardice, or of desertion. This form of punishment was known in Italy as well as in Germany and in Scotland, where it was called "baffling."[1]

Whatever the origins of *The Hanged Man*, it is a card to which some very profound ideas have been attached. Nineteenth century English and French occultists were the first to suggest that at the card could represent a condition of Self-sacrifice leading to direct knowledge of life and death. As it was taught by one occult fraternity: *The Hanged Man* "is sacrifice—the submergence of the higher in the lower in order to sublimate the lower. It is the descent of the Spirit into matter, the incarnation of God in man, the submission to the bonds of matter that the material may be transcended and transmuted."[2] The card was also equated with a condition called *Samadhi,* a reversal of perspective where the waking consciousness is the object rather than the subject of experience. Eliade describes this state as "a real coincidence between *knowledge of the object* and *the object of knowledge* for the object, no longer presenting itself to consciousness in the relations that delimit and define it as a phenomenon is "as if empty of itself."[4]

Jung says precisely the same thing. He explains the relationship of the conscious and unconscious aspects of Self by describing the conscious mind as a smaller circle within a larger circle of the unconscious. The "Self" is an "unconscious substrate, whose actual exponent in consciousness is the ego. And Jung explains that "The ego stands to the Self as the moved to the mover, or as object to subject, because the determining factors which radiate out from the Self surround the ego on all sides and are therefore supraordinate to it. The Self, like the unconscious, is an *a priori* existent out of which the ego evolves."[4]

Thus it is, he says, "quite possible for the ego to be made into an object, that is to say, for a more compendious personality to emerge in the course of development and take the ego into its service. Since this growth of personality comes out of the unconscious, which is by definition unlimited, the extent of the personality now gradually realizing itself cannot in practice be limited either.[5] Jung's language is very formal, but he is expressing the principle which the Western mystery tradition has for centuries described as the operation of the "Higher Self."

Sacrifice: The Universal Key

There are some writers on tarot who state without hesitation that the principle of sacrifice, as represented by *The Hanged Man*, is the absolute key to everything about the human condition that has been classed as a "mystery." And perhaps Jung would have agreed, for it is in his discussion of sacrifice that he has most meticulously, and in precise psychological terms supplanting those of traditional mysticism, explained the process by which Self-realization takes place.

The Archetype of Sacrifice

The word "sacrifice is a common translation of the Hebrew *zebah,* an animal offering. *Zebah* literally means "slaughter," and hence the word for "altar," *mizbeah,* which is the place the ritual slaughter takes place.[6] The original of such sacrifices were probably of livestock, which were of far greater value than human life. Yet human sacrifice, of one type or another, was practiced all over the ancient Near East and as far away as China and Japan. It was common for the living to be buried with the dead in many early societies. And the practice of burying people alive beneath the foundations of new buildings (often children as in China) was common.[7]

Nor was such behavior a purely Eastern phenomenon. As Nigel Davies, author of *Human Sacrifice* writes: "All over pre-Christian

Europe every imaginable form of human sacrifice was to be found: infanticide, fertility rites, immolation of war prisoners, live buried under buildings, sacrifice of the god or of the ruler in his place."[8]

The history of religions is the history of sacrifice at many levels. Imbedded in every culture—from the pagan to the most complicated industrial society—is the idea that sacrifice, in one form or another, is essential to progress. The offering of human life, especially, was believed from the earliest times, to appease the gods, and to persuade them to bring good fortune. And often it was the gods themselves who were slain, and whose death marked the cycle of the crops. In all cultures, sacrifice expresses a relationship between life and death as well as between the individual and the collective consciousness (the gods).

Human Sacrifice: Life as "Divine Currency"

The history of the sacrifice of human life, horrible and brutal though it may be, is a history of the interpretation by different cultures of the very meaning and value of life. It will be seen that today's Western belief in the sanctity of human life is a product of early medieval Christian thought. However, the earliest Judaism and the earliest Christianity were far more in tune with the "relative" value of life found in primitive societies. There may be something of a paradox here. If one honestly believes that a comparative study of the earliest religious practices of mankind can reveal some unique truth to which primitive man was privy, a question must be asked: how does one then deal with the same societies' disregard for human life? Some may say that the answer is that the materialistic (death-fearing) West has grossly overvalued human life.

Ritual sacrifice of human life has often, throughout history, been believed essential to the relationship of living men with their "gods." The life-force of the victims was absorbed by their executioners, who by eating their hearts, by bathing in their blood,[9] or by wearing their skin, gained supernatural strength. And, far from being unwilling prey, the prisoners themselves often believed (as did thousands of Aztec victims), that they were going to a better world where they would become the god for whom they died.[10] Individual life meant little in the ancient world and, although the practice of human sacrifice was passionately decried by the prophets, when the Hebrews came out of Egypt and into the promised land they took on an unpleasant tradition of their Canaanite neighbors— the ritual sacrifice of children by burning.[11]

Beyond this question of violent sacrifice of human life is that of willing martyrdom. The free "gift" of one's life for some principle naturally raises the issue of *suicide*—which is exactly what many of the early martyrdoms were. And, in fact, suicide was acceptable to early Christian society—especially to the early fourth-century Donatist sect which encouraged self-sacrifice as a road to martyrdom and thus to eternal salvation.[12] But in the mid-sixth century C.E. under the influence of Augustine, funeral rites were refused to all suicides, who came to be known as the "martyrs of Satan."[13]

Previously suicide had been extolled in ancient Rome as well as in China and Japan. In India, suicide was considered to be a special privilege rewarding ascetics who had achieved perfection in this life. Since it was believed that suicides were never returned to earth, by taking his own life the holy man ended the cycle of birth and death to which every Hindu was condemned.[14]

Self-Sacrifice of The God

There are few topics which so interested Jung as did the nature of the sacrifice of Christ on the Cross which, he concluded, must have been because of the "sin" of God himself, rather than of man. But the most archetypal progression of self-sacrifice, death, and resurrection is not that of Christ, but of the Norse God Odin, often called the "Lord of the Gallows." His myth involves the "World Tree," or "Guardian Tree" called Yggdrasil, which, although suffering greatly, nourishes the animals that attach to it and feed on it. In caring for all living creatures, the Tree ensures eternal continuity. It is on this tree that Odin voluntarily hangs himself, in order to learn the wisdom of the dead.[15] After nine nights, Odin returns from death.

The archetype of the periodically self-sacrificed god demonstrates a renewal of the life-force. Thus, as an archetypal expression, the "event" of the sacrifice of Christ must be repeated regularly.[16] The significance of such myths, to Jung, is that they are archetypal descriptions of a natural course in the consciousness of each person.

The theme of a wilful sacrifice of one's life, and then a return from the dead as a "new" person (of which the Christ epic is a late version), is like the initiation described by Apuleius in *The Golden Ass*. "I approached the very gates of death," he wrote, "and set one foot on Proserpine's threshold, yet was permitted to return, rapt through all the elements. At midnight I saw the Sun shining as if it were noon; I entered the presence of the gods of the underworld and the gods of the upper-world, stood near and worshipped them."[17]

The Serpent

In the *Jungian Tarot* a profound emphasis has been placed on the serpent, which is wrapped around the body of the figure "hanged" in space. This is meant to express the importance of the serpent (kundalini-sex) energy aspect of libido in the process by which one "regresses," to use Jung's term, into the collective unconscious.

In tarot the serpent is ultimately that of *The Magician*; it is the *uroboros* which holds its tail in its mouth. And the principle that *The Magician* is both that which transmits and that which is transmitted, is one with which Jung clearly concurs. To him the snake "symbolizes the numen of the transformative act as well as the transformative substance itself." He says that "as the chthonic dweller in the cave she lives in the womb of mother earth, like the Kundalini serpent who lies coiled in the abdominal cavity at the base of the spine."

The serpent is, in fact, the quintessential instrument of sacrifice: "It is the knife that kills, but also the phallus as symbol of the regenerative power of the grain, which, buried in the earth like a corpse, is at the same time the inseminator of the earth."[18]

This idea that transformation and renewal happens through the serpent is an archetypal one found throughout history, and is perhaps best expressed by Kundalini Yoga. In the Early Christian West, the serpent energy was worshipped especially by two Gnostic groups to whom Jung often refers, the Naasenes and the Ophites.[19]

The Transformation

In addressing the principle of sacrifice Jung presents a bold and clear exposition of his philosophy. He asserts that in the beginning of this "sacrificial drama" energy is unconsciously transformed and the ego becomes increasingly aware of an upheaval of perception about the whole nature of self and of reality.[20] And there is a dawning appreciation that reality is not physical; it is psychological. For, as Jung says, "the world comes into being when man discovers it. But he only discovers it when he sacrifices his containment in the Primal Mother, the original state of consciousness"[21] The process is accomplished through the "libido," (which is not primarily a sexual energy—but is actually a psychic totality of individual energy) that may be consciously manipulated to attain contact with the deepest level of the collective unconscious.

The result of this purposeful contact between conscious and unconscious is something new and wonderful, for: "To the extent that the world and everything in it is a product of thought, the sacrifice of the libido that strives back to the past necessarily results in the creation of the world. For him who looks backwards the whole world, even the starry sky, becomes the Mother who bends over him and enfolds him on all sides, and from the renunciation of this image, and of the longing for it, arises the picture of the world as we know it today. This simple thought is what constitutes the nature of cosmic sacrifice."[22]

Jung cites Mithraic ritual as an especially powerful (metaphorical) description of the psychological process of "cosmic" sacrifice which is, he says, a sacrifice to the Terrible Mother. This means that the waking consciousness, the ego, gives itself up to the unconscious in an act that is the most terrible sacrifice of which a human being is capable. It is the sacrifice of the perception of individuality which "makes possible a union of opposites resulting in a release of energy." This is, according to Jung, a two-way process: "At the same time the act of sacrifice is a fertilization of the Mother: the chthonic serpent-demon drinks the blood, i.e., the soul of the Hero. In this way life becomes immortal, for, like the Sun, the Hero regenerates himself by his Self-sacrifice and reentry into the Mother"[23]

Among the most profound of Jung's writings are those in *Symbols of Transformation,* detailing the nature of the "regression of libido" back into the original undifferentiated state of mankind—which is the essence of the psychological sacrifice. He says that one regresses back into a deeper level of the "nutritive function" which precedes sexuality, and that within this framework of only primitively differentiated consciousness, the ego "clothes itself in the experiences of infancy."[24]

Jung proposes a complex sequence of regressions which may be repeated over and over again, a method inextricably related to the exercise of what he called "active imagination." As he explains it: "The regressing libido apparently desexualizes itself by retreating back step-by-step to the presexual stage of earliest infancy." And he says that "even there it does not make a halt, but in a manner of speaking continues right back into the intrauterine, prenatal condition and, leaving the sphere of personal psychology altogether, irrupts into the collective psyche where Jonah saw the 'mysteries' *('répresentations collectives')* in the whale's belly. The libido thus reaches a kind of inchoate condition in which, like Theseus and Peirithous on their journey to the underworld, it may easily stick fast. But it can also tear itself loose from the material embrace and return to the surface with new possibilities of life."[25]

Carl Jung has put into psychological terms what mystics have said for centuries. For example, in *The Voice of the Silence* Blavatsky writes: "before thou standest on the threshold of the Path; before thou crossest the foremost Gate, thou hast to merge the two into the One and sacrifice the personal to Self impersonal, and thus destroy the 'path' between the two."[26]

The experience of the collective unconscious and the immersion of the individual personality into the "Mother" is the first sacrifice. It produces the condition of *The Lover*, which has been grandly described as the "Higher Self," but which is actually a recognition of the conscious and unconscious totality of Self, a "union of opposites." What this means is not that the personality ceases to exist, but that there is an entirely new perception about the nature of this personality. As Jung expressed it, the perception of individual consciousness may now freely move "in and out" of the collective consciousness and its various man-generated "mysteries," scientific and religious.

1. Gertrude Moakley, *The Tarot Cards Painted by Bonifacio Bembo for the Visconti-Sforza Family,* New York, 1966, 95.

2. Israel Regardie, *The Golden Dawn,* Chicago, 1940, v.IV, 213.

3. Mircea Eliade, A *History of Religious Ideas,* Chicago, 1978, v.II, 67-68. Samadhi means union, totality, absorption in, complete spiritual concentration, conjunction. Eliade also makes clear that this condition is not "total deliverance." It is in essence a state wherein the Self ("Higher Self ") is recognized.

4. Carl Jung, *Psychology and Religion,* Princeton, 1977, **391.**

5. Ibid., **390.**

6. James Hastings, *Dictionary of the Bible,* New York, 1963, 869.

7. Nigel Davies, *Human Sacrifice,* New York, 1981, 37-38

8. Ibid., 43. Davies discusses a Christian martyr, St. Oran, whose legend tells that he volunteered to be buried alive under the church, at the founding of the monastery at Iona. Another story, one relating to the idea of spiritual experience which does not agree with accepted dogma, is especially interesting. Supposedly this saint was able to enter heaven, and then to return to earth. But because his experience forced him to refute orthodox teachings on the nature of heaven, he was buried alive.

9. One very gruesome example occurred in 437 C.E. when, believing that it would confer great strength, the Burgundians drank the blood of the vanquished Huns. Donald A. Mackenzie, *German Myths and Legends,* New York, 1985, 400.

10. Davies, 212.

11. Ibid., 18. Human sacrifice, especially that which was claimed to nourish the gods, was particularly repulsive to the early Church Fathers. In his *Against the Heathen,* Arnobius asked: "What man is there so ignorant of what a god is, certainly, as to think that they are maintained by any type of nourishment, and that it is the food given to them which causes them to live and endure throughout their endless immortality?" And, he asked "What pleasure is it to take delight in the slaughter of harmless creatures, to have the ears ringing often with their piteous bellowings, to see rivers of blood, the life fleeing away with the blood, and the secret parts having been laid open, not only the intestines to protrude with the excrements, but also the heart still bounding with the life left in it and the trembling, palpitating veins in the viscera?" Arnobius

concluded that the actual reason for such brutality was that it brought some people great sadistic pleasure. (Arnobius, *Against the Heathen,* The Ante-Nicene Fathers, v.VI, Michigan, 1987, 518ff.)

Others of the Early Christian Fathers, such as Origen, discussed sacrifice in the Christian context, especially in the sacrifice of Christ as the symbolic Lamb of God. Origen (whose own bizarre sacrifice was self-castration) stresses self-sacrifice of a life for the good of others. He relates that among the gentiles many people offered their lives as sacrifice for the "public good" in times of plague. His explanation for the utility of such sacrifice is that "he who has offered such a sacrifice overcomes the power which opposed him." (Origen, *Commentary on the Gospel of John,* The Ante-Nicene Fathers, v.X, 377-378). Yet he admits that he does not understand what influences the martyrs may have brought upon themselves through their voluntary deaths. "In some such ways we must suppose the death of the most holy martyrs to operate, many receive benefit from it by an influence we cannot describe." (Origen, 378.)

12. The Donatists were a puritanical North African sect which rivaled the Catholics. However, the rituals and beliefs of the two groups were almost identical, the most obvious difference being that the Donatists painted the inside of their churches stark white. Henry Chadwick, *The Early Church,* New York, 1986, 219.

13. In 533 C.E it was decreed that funeral rites would be withheld from persons who killed themselves while accused of a crime. Thirty years later these rites were refused to anyone who committed suicide. Davies, 130.

14. Ibid., 100.

15. Kevin Crossley-Holland, *The Norse Myths,* New York, 1980, 15-17.

16. Of course the liturgical calendar of the Catholic church does exactly this.

17. Apuleius, *The Transformations of Lucius Otherwise Known as The Golden Ass,* New York 1951, Robert Graves translation, 280.

18. Carl Jung, *Symbols of Transformation,* Princeton, 1976, **676.**

19. The title *Naaseni* comes from the serpent called *naas* (Hebrew *nachash).* Hippolytus related this group to ancient mysteries of the Assyrians, the Phrygians and the Egyptians. They believed in a Hermaphroditic Adam and in a very non-canonical Christ who is described

in *The Gospel of Thomas.* See Hippolytus, *Refutation of All Heresies,* The Ante-Nicene Fathers, v.V, 47.

The title *Ophite* comes from the Greek word for serpent. This sect argued that the serpent which gave Adam and Eve knowledge of Good and Evil was far greater than the inferior creator who produced Jesus Christ. They taught that the "Christ" descended into the man Jesus, then ascended into "the incorruptible Aeon" while the man Jesus was crucified. In their doctrine "as Jesus enriches himself with holy souls, to such an extent does his father suffer loss and is diminished being emptier of his own power by these souls." Irenaeus, *Against Heresies,* The Ante-Nicene Fathers, v. I, 357.

20. Jung, *Symbols of Transformation,* **669.**

21. Ibid., **652.**

22. Ibid., **646**. See p.613-682, "The Sacrifice."

14 / DEATH

Archetype of Transition

Death is the main theme of philosophy and of religion because the mysteries of death are the mysteries of life. Indeed, historians have always tended to categorize societies by the ways in which they view life and death.

Death is also a primary concern of Jung's investigation. And although his comments on that subject are somewhat overshadowed by his impressive postulates of a collective unconscious and of the archetypes which "inhabit" that realm, his conclusions about the nature and significance of death are among his most important contributions.

Jung believed that religions ideally serve the purpose of preparing one for death, although he expressed concern that some forms of religious activity are unduly extreme in their suggestion that the only real value in life is as the entrance way into death.

The Meaning of Death

Because the tarot emerged from a late medieval Christian world, it is important to consider that period's ideas about death and dying. Medieval theologians generally accepted Augustine's principle that death resulted from *"original sin"*—that mankind, the children of Adam, suffers mortality, pain, and death because Adam *chose* to sin. According to Augustine the descendants of Adam have lost the free will given to Adam; they have been deprived of the choice not to sin. This idea, a radical departure from previous Christian doctrine, was offensive to some of Augustine's Christian contemporaries. Many believed it to be a heresy undermining two key foundations of Christianity—the ultimate goodness of God, and the individual free will. There was a widespread belief that even if sin might exist at birth, it was completely wiped away by baptism.[1]

But the Augustinian point of view prevailed (largely because it presented the Church as the only salvation for original sin). Thus medieval artists adopted iconographic themes which related the sacrifice of Christ to the original sin of Adam. Christ was often shown crucified above a skull on a small mound of earth meant to be the burial place of Adam. Supposedly Adam was buried on Golgotha where Seth planted a twig from the Tree of Paradise on his father's grave. Over the millennia of human existence this symbolism developed into the cross of Christ, the "Tree of Death."

Jung also, crafting his own concept of original sin, relates death to Adam. He says that when the Son takes leave of the Mother—meaning being born—he leaves the animal unconscious. The psychologist argues that a deep-rooted and racial "incest prohibition" is what makes consciousness possible. In other words, internal strictures against free commerce between the conscious and the unconscious keeps man isolated. Thus Jung states that "through Adam's sin, which lay precisely in his becoming conscious, death came into the world."[2]

Beliefs about Death

Ideas about the *Death* card of the tarot have evolved significantly from the simplistic explanations of the medieval Christian artist. Today's philosophy of tarot has more in common with oriental religions than with Christianity. Indeed, as the "archetype of transition," *Death* is aptly described by a passage in the *Upanishads* which says that "The Tree of Samsara, or the relative universe, is characterized by a continuous series of births and deaths, without beginning or end. The only way to cut it down is through the knowledge and realization of Atman's identity with Brahman."[3] The *Katha Upanishad* teaches that the King of Death, who brings sickness and old age, has power only over those who are trapped in the cycle of earth. Those who achieve the merging of opposites are no longer subject to death but experience a cosmic life until the end of a cycle, when they are absorbed into the pure consciousness.

The requisite merging of opposites is, of course, what Western mysticism calls the *coniunctio,* the "mystic marriage" of opposites symbolized by Sun and Moon, male and female, conscious and unconscious. The means for the ultimate reunion of these opposites, and for escape from human suffering, is the underlying theme of the Eastern and Western mysteries.

The idea is very clearly expressed by Gnostic Christianity. In, for example, *The Gospel of Philip,* the Valentinian author attributes death to the separation of Eve from Adam (i.e., of Original Woman from Original Man). "If the woman had not separated from the man," he wrote, "she would not die with the man. His separation became the beginning of death. Because of this Christ came to repair the separation which was from the beginning and again unite the two."[4]

One particular influence on attitudes about death in Western mysticism was the Jewish Kabbalah, which began to attract the curiosity of intellectuals in the West after the expulsion of the Jews from Spain in 1492. This "later" Kabbalism, of whom Isaac Luria was the primary exponent, emphasized death and rebirth as an evolutionary process, the transcendency of which led to union with God.[5]

Kabbalistic thought addressed the migration of the soul before birth and after death, and is easily related to Death as the archetype of transition. The question of the "transmigration of souls," or "reincarnation," was of key concern. Reincarnation was generally taken for granted in the earliest written documents of the Kabbalah.[6]

The significance of the incorporation of Jewish Kabbalah into Western mysticism, from Pico della Mirandola to the present, is considerable.[7] In fact, the synthetic Western version of this philosophy called "Hermetic Kabbalah" has exerted more influence on modern tarot interpretation than any other system of metaphysics.

Death and Ancient Philosophy

It is often asserted that Western culture has been a pendulum swing between the ideas of Plato and those of Aristotle. Today's emphasis on the so-called "scientific" point of view, drawing conclusions from that which is observed, is the dubious triumph of Aristotle's materialistic rationalism. Accepting this, and recognizing also that the Western mystery tradition and the principles of Jungian psychology concur with Platonic thought, it is extremely interesting to compare the thoughts of Aristotle and Plato about death.

In his *Nichomachean Ethics* Aristotle says: "Now death is the most terrible of all things; for it is the end, and nothing is thought to be any longer either good or bad for the dead."[8] And in his *Rhetoric* he quotes Sappho as saying that "Death is an evil thing; the gods have so judged it or they would die."[9]

Plato, on the other hand, reports Socrates' complete lack of fear as he stood at the edge of death, and viewed death as a wonderful completion for those who have lived life appropriately.[10] "It seems natural to me," he said, "that a man who has really devoted his life to philosophy should be cheerful in the face of death, and confident in finding the greatest blessing in the next world when his life is finished." And he added that "ordinary people do not seem to realize that those who really apply themselves in the right way to philosophy are directly and of their own accord preparing themselves for dying and death."[11]

In this regard Jung says that "it is just as neurotic in old age not to focus on the goal of death as it is in youth to repress fantasies which have to do with the future."[12] "I am convinced," he states, "that it is hygienic—if one may use the word—to discover in death a goal toward which one can strive and that shrinking away from it is something unhealthy and abnormal which robs the second half of life of its purpose."[13]

And Jung states very clearly that he does not exactly believe in the immortality of the individual soul as it has been represented by Christianity. He calls death the "ending of individual existence" and says that "Life is an energy process. Like every energy process it is in principle irreversible and is therefore directed toward a goal. That goal is a state of rest. In the long run everything that happens is, as it were, no more than the initial disturbance of a perpetual state of rest which forever attempts to reestablish itself."[14]

It is in discussing the death of the Hero that Jung best defines the nature of personality and the relationship of that individual perspective to the collective unconscious. The Hero had to die because he "was really not much more than the personification of a regressive and infantile reverie, having neither the will nor the power to make good his aversion from this world by fishing up another from the primeval ocean of the unconscious, which would truly have been an heroic act."[15] The "Hero" is the personality, the individual consciousness, and "immortality is simply a psychic activity that transcends the limits of consciousnes..'beyond the grave,' or 'on the other side of death' means psychologically, 'beyond consciousness.' "[16]

Jung must have come to this conclusion very early, for in his autobiographical *Memories, Dreams, Reflections,* he describes a childhood recollection of what is apparently an earlier life.[17] And if, in fact, Jung is accepting a doctrine of reincarnation, he is once more in complete agreement with Plato.

Death in the Late Middle Ages

As with so many of the other tarot cards, the meaning attached to *Death* today is very unlike what was clearly intended by the inventors of the cards. The medieval artist would undoubtedly find an interpretation of *Death* as the "archetype of transition" very curious. There was nothing vague about death. It was the end of man when he was judged and sent to reward or punishment, a legacy passed down to him for the sin of Adam.[18]

In the Greek world, death had been represented by the winged

Thanatos,[19] who was known as a healer, as one who eases pain and suffering. He was a gentle figure described as "coming like the evening of a beautiful day."[20] This image was in radical contrast to representations of death in medieval Europe, where the black plague was rampant at the same period when the tarot presumably was being invented. Between 1348 and 1350 two thirds of the population of Italy, and two-thirds of the populations of France, England, and Germany perished. Eight hundred deaths a day were recorded in Paris alone. By the early 1400s twenty-four to twenty-six million people had lost their lives.[21]

The horror of death was inescapable, and its image was anything but gentle. It was as Daniel Defoe wrote of a later plague in London: "On one side there was scarce any passing by the streets, but that several dead bodies would be lying here and there upon the ground....at first the people would stop as they went along...yet afterwards no notice was taken of them."[22]

In the fourteenth century the artistic representation of death, shown a hundred years earlier as a beautiful event, took a turn toward the ugly. Rotting flesh crawling with larvae and ghostly specters drawn from popular Greek and Latin art became common. Artists began to associate death with the skeleton (found in Etruscan art) and with the Devil. Death, *mors,* was considered to be the Queen of Hell, the spouse of Satan.[23] At about the same time, the *Danse Macabre,* the Dance of Death was first presented in the form of a drama. Invented by a mendicant Dominican or Franciscan monk, it was a mimed illustration of a sermon on death and was performed inside the church.[24]

An image which became almost interchangeable with that of Death at this period is *Saturn,* a figure typically shown as an old man carrying a scythe (or occasionally as a cripple leaning on a stick). Saturn was a sinister figure who brought pain and hardship and who was also identified as Father Time. The hourglass carried by Saturn was first used in representations of Death toward the end of the fifteenth century.[25]

In the earliest extant tarot, the *Visconti Sforza, Death* is shown as a skeleton carrying the bow (perhaps that of the first horseman of the Apocalypse), whereas *The Hermit* carries the staff and hourglass which are attributes of Saturn/Kronos/Father Time. In the *Jungian Tarot*, as in other modern decks, *The Hermit's* hourglass has become a lamp. It is *Death* which now carries the hourglass and scythe of Saturn/Father Time.

The Jungian Death Card

As the "archetype of transition," *Death* is ideally represented with the attributes of Saturn/Kronos in the *Jungian Tarot*. The figure stands symbolically on a crumbling bridge from which there is no turning back once passage has begun. The stones of rational consciousness fall back into the unconscious from which they came.

Jung describes death as the return to the Mother, meaning the dissolution of the individual personality into that which gave it birth. This idea, although appearing to be a very complex philosophical metaphor, is found in the most primitive of societies and has to do with the discovery of agriculture. The planning and harvesting of crops, which was the primary responsibility of women, radically changed the conception of human existence. Birth, growth, and death were understood as a mystical cycle presided over by Mother Earth, who for centuries gave birth to herself.[26] And centuries before Jung theorized about Mother as the collective unconscious, the Vedic poet wrote that "Born of the Earth, man when he dies, returns to his mother."[27]

The black horse in this card is the Mother. Jung explains that "as an animal it represents the nonhuman psyche, the subhuman animal side, the unconscious. That is why horses in folklore sometimes see visions, hear voices, and speak. As a beast of burden it is closely related to the Mother archetype...'horse' is an equivalent of 'Mother' with a slight shift of meaning. The Mother stands for life at its origin, the horse for the merely animal life of the body."[28]

In this regard Jung calls special attention to the cosmic significance of the horse sacrifice according to the Upanishads, something "which signifies a renunciation of the world." The symbolism here is at once mystical and psychologically rational. "Since the horse is man's steed and works for him, and energy is even measured in terms of 'horse power,' the horse signifies a quantity of energy that stands at man's disposal. It therefore represents the libido which has passed into the world." Moreover, according to Jung, as "The Mother-libido must be sacrificed in order to create the world; here the world is destroyed by renewed sacrifice of the same libido which once belonged to the mother and then passed into the world....The sacrifice of the horse can only produce another phase of introversion similar to that which prevailed before the creation of the world."[29]

Notes: *Death*

1. Elaine Pagels, *Adam, Eve and the Serpent,* New York, 1988,131. Pagels argues that Augustine's principles of original sin were accepted for socio-political reasons: "Why did Catholic Christianity adopt Augustine's paradoxical—some would say preposterous—views? Some historians suggest that such beliefs validate the church's authority, for if the human condition is a disease, Catholic Christianity, acting as the Good Physician, offers the spiritual medication and the discipline that alone can cure it...For what Augustine says, in simplest terms, is this: Human beings cannot be trusted to govern themselves because our very nature—indeed, *all* of nature—has become corrupt as the result of Adam's sin. In the late fourth century and in the fifth century, Christianity was no longer a suspect and persecuted movement; now it was the religion of emperors obligated to govern a vast and diffuse population Under these circumstances....Augustine's theory of human depravity—and, correspondingly, the political means to control—replaced the previous ideology of human freedom." *Adam, Eve and the Serpent,* 145.

2. Jung, *Symbols of Transformation,* **415.**

3. *Katha Upanishad,* II, iii.,1.

4. *Gospel of Philip,* 70:10, in *The Nag Hammadi Library,* San Francisco, 1977, 142.

5. Gershom Scholem, *Major Trends in Jewish Mysticism,* New York, 1977, 249.

6. Scholem, *Kabbalah,* New York, 1987, 344ff.

7. Especially recommended on this topic is Chaim Wirszubski, *Pico della Mirandola s Encounter with Jewish Mysticism,* Cambridge, Massachusetts, 1989.

8. Aristotle, *Nichomachean Ethics,* Book III, *Complete Works of Aristotle, v.* 2, Princeton, 1985, 1760.

9. Aristotle, *Rhetoric,* Book II, *Complete Works,* 2229.

10. Plato, *Apology,* 29.

11. Plato, *Phaedo,* 63e-64.

12. Carl Jung, *The Structure and Dynamics of the Psyche,* Princeton, 1969, **808.**

13. Ibid., **792.**

14. Ibid., **796~798.**

15. Carl Jung, *Symbols of Transformation,* Princeton, 1976, **644.**

16. Carl Jung, *Two Essays on Analytical Psychology,* New York, 1953, **302.**

17. Carl Jung, *Memories, Dreams, Reflections*, New York 1973, 33-34.

18. Medieval art often represented the cross growing from Adam's grave. Supposedly Adam was buried on Golgotha where Seth planted on his grave a twig from the Tree of Paradise, which grew into Christ's cross, the "Tree of Death."

19. Thanatos was not actually a mythological figure but is found in ancient folklore. He was not worshiped as a god and was described as "the only god who loves not gifts." *Oxford Classical Dictionary*, Oxford, 1978, "Thanatos," 1050.

20. Didron, *Christian Iconography*, New York, 1968, v.II, "The Iconography of Death," 153ff.

21. Emile Mâle, *Religious Art,* v.III, Princeton, 1986, 318.

22. Daniel Defoe, *A Journal of the Plague Year*, 1665, New York 1968, 87.

23. Generally speaking, these artists found their themes in areas where Helleno-Latin polytheism had flourished, a situation which was particularly conducive to the development of horrible images about death and about the afterworld. Didron, *Christian Iconography*, v.II, 156.

24. The drama preceded the works of art. Paintings of the Dance Macabre first appear in the fifteenth century. At this time the dead were shown not as skeletons, but as dried up corpses which was thought to be a more terrifying image. Emile Mâle, Religious Art, v.II, 330-334.

25. The association of Saturn with time has to do with a the similarity of the Greek word for time, Kairos, and Kronos, the Roman Saturn. Writers of the fourth and fifth centuries emphasized the temporal significance of Saturn/Kronos. The sickle, originally meant to signify agriculture or an instrument of castration, came to be explained as time which ultimately destroys. See Irwin Panofsky, *Studies in Iconology*, New York 1962, "Father Time," 69-93.

26. Mircea Eliade, *A History of Religious Idea*s, Chicago, 1978, v.I, 40.

27. *Rig Veda,* 10.18.10.

28. Carl Jung, *The Practice of Psychotherapy,* New York, 1954, **347**.

29. Carl Jung, *Symbols of Transformation,* Princeton, 1976, **658**.

15 / TEMPERANCE

Archetype of Mediation

It will be observed that in the *Jungian Tarot* this card differs from the more common design which shows a figure pouring liquid from one vessel into another. And although the "mediation" of fire and water is pictured here for philosophical reasons, it is completely true to the original symbolism of Temperance personified. In Carolingian times, when the iconography of the cardinal Virtues was established, *Temperantia* held a torch in one hand and poured water from a jug with the other. The meaning was very basic, as Julianus Pomerius explained about the water:

"Ignem libinosae voluptatis extinguit" (it extinguishes the fire of unbridled passion).

Sometime during the eleventh century the admonition against physical passion disappeared, and a new message was delivered by a figure carrying a cup and a bottle. Here again no high philosophy was intended. The idea was simply that drinking less is a virtue—a comment on the rather astonishing amount of alcohol consumed by the average person in the medieval period.

During the twelfth century, in a climate of considerable experimentation with the symbolism of the Virtues, Temperance was occasionally represented bearing a spray of blossom as well as two vessels.[1] Such changes in the iconography of the Virtues are of more than passing interest because they clearly provide evidence about the origins of tarot. The significance of the Virtues to the earliest tarot, and the fact that they take the Italian form, indicates that although playing cards in general may have their origins in France, the tarot is an original Italian device.[2]

Alchemy

More than one interpreter of tarot has seen the alchemical *hierosgamos,* the mystic marriage of opposites, in this card. And in fact as the act of mediation between fire and water *Temperance* represents a pivotal principle of Jungian psychology. Jung believed that the alchemists were writing about a psychological experience, a personal and inner process of transformation which they symbolized as the turning of lead into gold. The claim is, of course, made by some that the alchemist is able to manufacture actual gold, which an objective observer must allow may or may not be the case.[3] But historians of religion tend to support Jung's views. Mircea Eliade asserts that

Alchemy would not have become an autonomous discipline merely on the basis of attempts to counterfeit or imitate gold. There is an increasing consensus among researchers that the alchemists were actually disinterested in producing gold, and that their statements had the effect of obfuscating their true purpose.

Alchemy's claims about artificial laboratory transmutation appear to have evolved from ancient myths about an Earth Mother who bears minerals as embryos in her womb. Thus, the primary concern of Greco-Egyptian Alchemy was "the life of matter." The experience of the death and resurrection of matter (as was presumably conveyed by the Greco-Oriental Mysteries) became the transmutation, the *opus magnum* of the Alchemists which produced the Philosopher's Stone (the mineral gift of the Earth Mother).

Arabic and Western Alchemy describe four or five essential phases through which matter must pass to create this Stone.[4] First is the *nigredo* (blackening), then the *albedo* (the whitening), then the *citrinatas* (the yellowing), and finally the *rubedo* (reddening). Some scholars have explained this as an archetypal pattern of initiation appearing in mythologies as the passion, death, and resurrection of the god. The alchemist passes through the same transformation in recognition of the true nature of the Self, and the immortality achieved is symbolized by the incorruptible metal —gold.[5]

Jung draws many principles from the idea that Alchemy is an initiatory discipline which attempts to quantify the relationship between the conscious and the unconscious. He teaches that its stages are conditions in the process of reuniting dualities resulting from the (creation) separation of each person's individual consciousness from a greater totality.

What is shown in the card of *Temperance* is that which brings about the merger of opposites. The figure of a woman here is actually the metaphorical Philosopher's Stone itself. For, like *The Magician,* the Philosopher's Stone is that which creates and that which is created. It is the united qualities of original opposites which reintegrates its "parents." Indeed, as Jung says, the "midpoint" is the Stone, the mediator which unites the opposites."[6] This union brings about an initial darkness and confusion *(nigredo)* which eventually gives way to a light of understanding in the soul (the *albedo).* "The black or unconscious state that resulted from the union of opposites reaches the nadir and a change sets in...the ever deeper descent into the unconscious suddenly becomes illumination from above."[7]

In all of this, Jung warns emphatically that such descriptions "have no meaning unless they are understood in a profoundly psychological sense."[8] And in an exceptionally direct statement about the nature of the personality consciousness, he refers to "the process of becoming conscious, whereby an original unity is split into two irreconcilable halves." He concludes that "There can be no consciousness without this act of discrimination, nor can the resultant duality be reunified without the extinction of the consciousness."[9]

On the other hand, Jung makes clear that it is not possible to explain what this reunification of opposites really means. He states that: "The psychological union of opposites is an intuitive idea....It is not an 'explanatory' hypothesis for something, that by definition, transcends our powers of conception. For, when we say that conscious and unconscious unite, we are saying in effect that this is inconceivable. The unconscious is unconscious and therefore can neither be grasped nor conceived. The union of opposites is a transconscious process and in principle not amenable to scientific explanation."[10] Accepting this, it is not a far leap to Jung's comment in *Psychology and Religion* that in fact, "there being no duality, pluralism is untrue. There are no opposites."[11] The transformation brought about by the action of Fire and Water, as well as the reintegration of these archetypal opposites by that which they produce, is ultimately only a matter of perception. Initiation is a process of mind working upon mind in which the process that Jung called "active imagination" is the key.

Active Imagination: The Act of Mediation

"Active imagination," (a term which Jung first used in 1935),[12] is defined by the psychologist as simply "a means to bringing unconscious contents to consciousness."[13] It is the act of mediating the opposites of conscious and unconscious. And although Jung may claim credit for the invention of a new technique, a process of inner vision and of dialogue with that vision is integral to all mystical systems. Of course, this is usually couched in very obtuse and symbolic language, such as that found in the Gnostic fragments discovered at Nag Hammadi.

But in some documents the teaching is quite explicit. In, for example, *The Didache* or *Teaching of the Twelve Apostles,* one of the oldest known Christian books, the devout person is advised to "seek out daily the company of the saints so that you might find refreshment in their words,"[14] which may be interpreted to mean: visualize, imagine, consort with their images.

Similar procedures of inner watching are found in the documents of Jewish mysticism. Such practices, decribed by Aryeh Kaplan in *Meditation and Kabbalah,*[15] were carried out with a profoundly devotional formality that appears to have influenced the ritual and meditative practices of late nineteenth-century English and French occultists.

The Hermetic Order of the Golden Dawn and other secret fraternities had exercises called "rising on the planes," in which the aspirant employed traditional Hebrew names to invoke the gods (aspects of the One), the Archangels, the Angels, and various other spiritual presences. For an inner voyage with a tarot card, a student was instructed to invoke these divine presences, and then to sit quietly staring at a card, with eyes closed, and in imagination to step into the card.[16] The same basic procedure of becoming an actor on an inner stage was, despite the embellishments of some byzantine ritual requirements, identical to the procedure recommended by Carl Jung.

But there are two main differences between Jung's "active imagination" and the meditative practices universally taught in both East and West. First, Jung's method has none of the excess baggage of a belief system; no special dress, sanctified space, or invocation is required. And second, Jung's stimuli are very nonspecific. Whereas a Catholic mystic's focus of attention and prayers to the Virgin Mary might lead him to converse with her in his mind (what Jung would certainly define as a conversation with the Anima), Jung's nonspecific point of departure could lead almost anywhere.

What Jung has done is to extract the psychological essence of traditional meditative practice. His principles of active imagination are widely applicable, as is his observation about the nature of human invention in such exercises. "I am convinced," he said, "that we cannot do much in the way of conscious invention; we overestimate the power of intention and the will."[17] And although he concedes that a fantasy is a more or less personal invention, he instructs that the images which appear through active imagination have a life and logic of their own—assuming that one's conscious reason does not interfere.[18]

Jung claims that the whole riddle of life and death may be solved through the correct use of fantasy which is "preeminently, the creative activity from which the answers to all answerable questions come." It is fantasy, he says, "which fashions the bridge between the irreconcilable claims of subject and object, introversion and extraversion."[19] And he adds that "since by active imagination all the material is produced in a conscious state of mind, the material is far more rounded out than the dreams with their precarious language. And it contains much more than dreams do."[20]

The Method

Following Jung's system of practice, active imagination involves watching the flow of interior images and becoming a participant in that flow. It begins by focusing on some dream image or on a random visual impression and then watching what happens to that image. One observes the fantasy's spontaneous changes—like a kaleidoscope—from one image or idea or landscape to another. In this it is important that observation be completely objective and noncritical.[21] Most of all it is essential that nothing from outside, no cues from the waking consciousness, contaminate any spontaneous event. The unconscious must be given a free hand for this psychological process, which brings results equivalent to the magical transformation of the alchemists,[22] to be effective. And pursuant to Alchemy, Jung goes so far as to refer to the initial fantasy, chosen as a point of meditative departure, as the *prima materia.*[23] He notes also that the "Old Masters" identified the terrible *nigredo,* which follows, with *melancholia.*[24]

The exercise of fantasy is, of course, easier for some people than for others. Artists, for example, will find mind-fantasy production more natural than will others. But teachers in these areas suggest that people are well advised to follow their own direction. It is said that those who are visually inclined should proceed on the expectation that an inner image will appear, while audio-verbal types should concentrate on hearing inner words[25] Thus, as a matter of practical experience it may be found that by stressing the most comfortable "inner sense," the others will take care of themselves. Generally, those who experience difficulty in seeing and in hearing within an inner landscape will find that by pursuing a sense of touch, vision, and hearing follow easily.

The Problems

The most serious work begins with focus on the root causes of the Anima and Animus (initially addressing the personal unconscious—the "Shadow") an experience which, Jung warned, can be very painful and difficult for "the encounter with Anima and Animus means conflict and brings us against the hard dilemmas in which nature has placed us." [26] The pain and darkness of the encounter with the contrasexual component stems partially from the *incest dilemma,* [27] a principle of considerable importance to Jungian thought. The psychologist says that every person has an inner drive toward wholeness, and instinctually seeks the inner, bisexual, First Man. He explains that "Whenever this instinct for wholeness appears, it begins by disguising itself under the symbolism of incest, for, unless he seeks it in himself, a man's nearest feminine counterpart is to be found in his mother, sister, or daughter." [28]

One striking, and often pathological, effect of the encounter with Anima or Animus is that, if a person identifies with the attributes of these archetypes before their nature is really understood and assimilated, serious and involuntary personality changes may result. The ego may be affected either positively or negatively. Like a form of megalomania, it may become so overbloated that the normal ego-personality is overwhelmed. There may also be the opposite effect where the ego is virtually annihilated, or even an alternation of the two states. One way or the other, the process of integrating materials into the conscious mind that were unconscious and projected (rather than perceived directly) always has a powerful effect on the ego.[29]

Active Participation

After an initial encounter with Anima or Animus and the jolt of interaction with contents of the personal unconscious, fantasy materials from the impersonal unconscious (involving essentially stepped-down collective symbols) begin to appear. These deeper fantasies seem arbitrary and unstructured, but as Jung insists "they pursue definite unconscious lines of direction which converge upon a definite goal."[30] Repeated meditation along the same lines makes it possible to establish consistent patterns in "advanced" fantasies along the way of a process which Jung had no hesitancy in calling an "initiation."[31] Undoubtedly, the most important milepost of inner development is a recognition that the "fantasy" is a real psychic event. In other words, one begins to understand that imagination can produce something that is every bit as real as the daily experiences of the physical environment.

This stage of development, however, happens only as the result of real participation in the fantasy life, rather than by simply watching from the sidelines. "If," Jung said, "you recognize your own involvement, you yourself must enter into the process with your personal reactions, just as if you were one of the fantasy figures, or rather, as if the drama being enacted before your eyes were real. It is a psychic fact that this fantasy is happening, and it is as real as you—as a psychic entity—are real."[32] At this point, once a person begins to deal with the universal, rather than the personal, *regression* into the presexual condition, which Jung described in such cryptic terms, becomes a possibility.

Notes: *Temperance*

1. Adolph Katzenellenbogen, *Allegories of the Virtues and Vices in Medieval Art,* Liechtenstein, 1977, 55.

2. The French and Italian Virtues are very different. In fifteenth century France (the age of the *Visconti Sforza Tarot*) Temperance was curiously shown holding a clock in one hand and a bridle and bit or a pair of spectacles in the other. Generally, the theme of the Virtues was rare in the fourteenth and fifteenth centuries and was very loosely interpreted. Such was not the case in Italy where as early as the fourteenth century the Virtues began to be included on tombs, and where the Virtues were recognized by some very clear and specific aspects. In the case of *Temperance*, the figure carried a vase in each hand, pouring water into wine.

3. Although the tendency today is to view alchemical transmutation as an entirely psychological process, there remain those who insist that actual gold can be created as a sort of by-product of the inner "vibratory" changes of the Alchemist himself. One such advocate of this point of view is "Frater Albertus," author of *The Alchemist's Handbook,* subtitled "A Manual for Practical Laboratory Alchemy," Salt Lake City, 1974. Perhaps the best book ever written by a contemporary alchemist is *Herbal Alchemy* by Phillip Hurley. This is a very rare typewritten book of 100 pages, privately published in 1977.

4. There are innumerable variants in the alchemical literature, which tends to be confusing. However, the basic progression of four or five stages underlies virtually all known systems.

5. Mircea Eliade, *A History of Religions Ideas,* v.II, 303-305.

6. Carl Jung, *Alchemical Studies,* Princeton, 1976, **131.**

7. Carl Jung, *The Practice of Psychotherapy,* New York, 1954, **493**.

8. Carl Jung, *Alchemical Studies,* Princeton, 1976, **131.**

9. Ibid, **456.**

10. Carl Jung, *Mysterium Coniunctionis,* Princeton, 1976, **542.**

11. Carl Jung, *Psychology and Religion: West and East,* Princeton, 1977, **798.**

12. Carl Jung, *Psychological Types,* Princeton, 1977, **722n.**

13. Carl Jung, *The Structure and Dynamics of the Psyche,* Princeton, 1969, **599.**

14. *The Apostolic Fathers,* v.III "The Didache and Barnabas," trans. and commentary by Robert A. Kraft, 151.

15. Aryeh Kaplan, *Meditation and Kabbalah,* New York 1982, passim.

16. The exercise of the "Tattvas" was preliminary to that with tarot cards. This was described as an encounter of the four elements in anthropomorphic guise, i.e., as salamanders, undines, sylphs, and gnomes. In an inner landscape, the student carried on conversations with these beings. Israel Regardie, *The Golden Dawn*, v.IV, 11-46.

17. Carl Jung, *The Symbolic Life*, Princeton, 1980, **398.**

18. Ibid., **397.**

19. Carl Jung, *Two Essays on Analytical Psychology*, New York, 1953, **78.**

20. Jung, *The Symbolic Life*, **400.** Jung says that the same results as active imagination may be created by painting a picture: "Here too a product is created which is influenced by both conscious and unconscious, embodying the striving of the unconscious for the light and the striving of the conscious for substance." *The Structure and Dynamics of the Psyche*, **168.**

21. Carl Jung, *The Archetypes and the Collective Unconscious*, Princeton, 1977, **319.**

22. Jung, *Mysterium Coniunctionis*, **749.**

23. Ibid., **753.**

24. Ibid., **446.**

25. Jung, *Structure and Dynamics*, **170.**

26. Carl Jung, *The Practice of Psychotherapy*, New York, 1954, **470.**

27. Jung was certainly stimulated in his thoughts about incest by Freud's work on the subject, although he felt that Freud's clinical conclusions about incest were unconvincing. Jung viewed the problems of incest as representing far more than merely a sexual (and cultural) phenomenon. See *The Basic Writings of Sigmund Freud*, New York 1938 [The following page references are to this compendium:] Freud published his well-known discussions of Oedipus in his early book *The Interpretation of Dreams*, 309. His important essay describing the "incest barrier" appears in *The Transformation of Puberty*, 616-617 and note. An essay to which Jung must have devoted considerable attention was *The Savage's Dread of Incest*, 807-820. Freud was drawn to this study because, speaking of aboriginals and others, "their psychic life assumes a particular interest for us because, he said, we can recognize in their psychic life a well-preserved early stage of our own development."

28. Jung, *Practice of Psychotherapy*, **471.**

29. Ibid, **472.**

30. Jung Two *Essays,* **384.**

31. Ibid., **384.**

32. Jung warns emphatically that "If this crucial operation is not carried out, all the changes are left to the flow of images, and you yourself remain unchanged." *Mysterium Coniunctionis,* **753.** Jung expands upon this idea considerably, and warns against the creation of a fictitious personality rather then acting out the fantasy as oneself, which prevents real participation and this gain. See *Mysterium Coniunctionis,* **457-553,** "The Conjunction."

16 / THE DEVIL

Archetype of Shadow

The Devil is a creation of Christianity that combines aspects of many mythological personalities. The idea of a Devil traces back to the dark beginnings of mankind and to animistic conceptions of nature involving good and evil spirits. The ground was laid for a Devil when some good spirits were perceived as overtaken or subordinate to the evil ones.

The first actual Devil seems to have appeared in India as *Mara,* the tempter of the Buddha, and later in Persia as the god *Ahriman.* Historically, the Christian Devil is usually explained through the influence of Persian *dualism,* a philosophy which says that good and evil came from two separate and independent sources. It was the prophet of Ahura-Mazda *Zarathustra* (called *Zoroaster* by the Greeks) who, in a later version of the myth, taught that the evil spirit Ahriman was not created by Ahura, and that although Ahura was the greatest power, the two, being uncreated, existed independently and represented two completely contradictory principles.[1]

During the Babylonian captivity of the Jews they came to know a form of Ahriman to whom the Zoroastrian kings had attributed attributes of their own Devil. This figure became the loose model for the Jewish *Satan* (a word which in Hebrew means "adversary"), first encountered in the Old Testament book of *Job*.[2] But this personification of "evil" was not dualist, which is to say that it did not exist separately from good. As Satan first appears in scripture, he is a servant of God who is entirely hostile to man. He is the angel who accuses and demands punishment on behalf of God,[3] rather than the ultimate opponent. There was, at the time of Christ, widespread belief in an Evil One bringing disease and mental possession, but this was essentially an independent demon; it was hardly a figure which could challenge the authority of God.

The earliest period of Christianity, the age of transition between the Old and New Testaments, was one of intellectual ferment and of ideological intercourse between many seemingly disparate philosophies. The rapid development of Christianity at this time had been fueled by Jewish belief that a messiah would appear, linked with the promise of salvation which Eliade has called "the novelty and principle characteristic of Hellenistic religions."[4] It was certainly in the tradition of Greek syncretism that the Christian Gnostics drew upon a variety of Eastern sources, their ideal of fulfillment being much like that of Buddhism, and their teaching about an evil spirit, like that of the Persians, having a separate existence.[5]

The Syrian Gnostics, to whom Irenaeus referred as serpent worshippers, or *Ophites,* taught that the Demiurge who created the world was evil, and that the Serpent who promised knowledge was the messenger of the true God.[6] Thus the Ophites and other Gnostic groups helped to establish the groundwork for a Devil who opposed Christ in the battle for men's souls.

Christianity was unique in that it brought to the fore the question of metaphysical opposites by its reaction to the high point of dualist philosophy, the religion formed by Mani, a Persian born in 216 C.E. Manichaenism was an extremely influential Gnostic movement which was so strong a challenge to Christianity that its ideas about the independent roots of evil had to be quickly countered.[7] In Christian theology God was the only source of creation, but the question had to be asked: "How could any creation of God be evil?"

The answer of the early theologians was among the most important tenets of the emerging Catholic faith, the doctrine of the *privatio boni.* The Church now taught that all being was good, and that evil, which did not actually exist, was brought into being by mankind: *omne bonum a Deo, omne malum ab homine.* This idea, together with that of original sin, formed the cornerstone of a completely new point of view about the human condition.[8] The Devil, through this new reasoning, is a perverted, mirror image of the Divinity, which exists only insofar as man attempts to put himself in the place of God.[9]

Jung was fascinated with the problem of evil, and concentrated especially on paradoxes such as the blame of Judas in the death of Christ—for had Judas not betrayed Christ, there could have been no crucifixion, and consequently no Christianity as we know it. Following the same sort of logic, Jung argues that good and evil are opposites in a pair, and that one

cannot exist without the other. "Evil," he says "is the necessary opposite of good, without which there would be no good
either. It is impossible even to think evil out of existence."[10]
Jung felt that the influence of Persian dualism has been overstressed, and that the real reason for the Christian development
of a Devil was that conception of God as the *summum bonum*
meant nothing unless there was a contrasting *infimum malum.*[11]

And some of Jung's most obscure symbolism becomes clear
when it is understood that maintaining the structure of the Christian Trinity is the Devil who is *the fourth of the mystical quaternity.*[12] And because the Devil is also the archetype of Shadow,
Shadow is another name for the fourth of the quaternity, a point
which has serious and practical implications in the quest for
Self-knowledge. The Jungian Trinity is *Father; Mother; and
Son.* The Son is the True Self, whereas Shadow, is the fourth,
the personal unconscious which falsely accepts the notion that
it has a separate existence.

Iconography of the Devil

The Devil in medieval art combines the characteristics of
many different personalities,[13] including the Phoenician god of
the flies, Beelzebub *(Baal-Zebub),* and various pagan European gods. His identification with the vile and evil Northern
European giants served especially to separate the Devil of Christianity from the very aloof Satan of Hebrew tradition. [14]

In late fourteenth-century art the Devil held a key position
as the opponent of Christ for the soul of everyman. The Devil
and his hierarchy of demons were no mere abstraction to medieval man. He was, rather, a powerful and ubiquitous presence from which only the Church could save them. The concept was simplistic and detached from later interpretations

stressing notions of evil, materialism, and sensuality.

Unfortunately *The Devil* card is missing from the *Visconti Sforza* deck,[15] and modern recreations are competent but speculative. Assuming the tarot cards to have originated in the late fourteenth century, the earliest *Devil* would certainly have followed the style of the period, having an entirely human form with the grotesque head of an animal, and with other faces and figures attached to the body at various points such as the shoulders and groin.

The Oriental (as well as Byzantine) form of Devil was a monstrous animal, whereas that of the West appeared in human form. Images of the Devil in thirteenth and four-teenth-century Italy and France tended to fancifully combine man and animal. It was not until the Early Renaissance of the fifteenth century that Italian artists showed the Devil under the ancient Roman guise of faun or satyr, an image which became more or less standard. The Devil appeared with cloven hooves, hairy animal legs, hairy skin, and horns.[16] It is upon this classically-inspired satyr-Devil type that modern commentators have based their interpretations of the Devil as sexual force and have related it to the grossest materiality of the astrological sign Capricorn.

The Archetype of Shadow

"Shadow" refers to a complex of the personality's most inferior and negative traits, unpleasant qualities which people want to deny.[17] As Jung explains it, "The Shadow personifies everything that the subject refuses to acknowledge about himself and yet is always thrusting itself upon him directly or indirectly...for instance, inferior traits of character and other incompatible tendencies."[18] And he equates this inferior personality with *animal instinct,*[19] describing it as the dark half of each person's sense of separate being.

"The Self," he says, "is the hypothetical summation of an indescribable totality, one half of which is constituted by ego-consciousness, the other by the Shadow."[20] This Shadow aspect of Self is commensurate with what Freud called the "personal unconscious,"[21] a principle on which he did not expand as did Jung. It was Jung who first postulated a specific relationship of the personal to the collective, and who proposed one of the most significant theories of modern psychology in saying that: "Whereas the contents of the personal unconscious are acquired during the individual's lifetime, the contents of the collective unconscious are invariably contents that are present from the beginning."[22]

The archetype of Shadow is of special importance in that it forms a bridge to experience of the personal aspects of Anima, and thus to contact with the largely impersonal denizens of the collective unconscious.[23] It is understood that the painful encounter with Shadow must precede the even more dangerous and difficult encounter of Anima, that fascinating and complex archetype which stands directly behind Shadow.[24] And Jung set a rank order of experience in saying that "If the encounter with the Shadow is the 'apprentice piece' in the individual's development, then that of the Anima is the 'master piece.' The relation with the Anima is again a test of courage, an ordeal by fire for the spiritual and moral forces of man."[25] And this experience is anything but dispassionate. One cannot dispassionately think about these archetypes and categorize them intellectually because they are "complexes of experience that come upon us like fate, and their effects are felt in our most personal life."[26]

The Anti-Christ and the Bondage of Matter

One of the most admirable qualities of Jungian philosophy is the extent to which it allows expression of the inexpressible by reference to corresponding symbols. A student may approach the system through the symbolic language of analytical psychology, or through almost any mystical pantheon. But of course, since Jung was a Christian, he framed his ideas most convincingly in the terms of that system of belief. To Christians the Devil is the Anti-Christ who represents the weight of the material world from which Christ confers deliverance. Whereas Satan offers wealth and power in this life, Christ promises greater wealth in a spiritual world to come.[27] As "prince of this world," the Devil rules the darkness of *sublunary* matter (the ebb and flow of the personal unconscious). And although he is excluded from the Trinity, he is, as the counterpart of Christ, the *sine qua non* of the drama of redemption— meaning Self-knowledge.[28]

To balance Christ with the Devil is to make a statement about the nature of reality. Implicit is Jung's assertion that what one receives through sense perception is not the true reality. Jung stressed that the first step in enlightenment is an appreciation that the images in the mind are real. To invoke a landscape through active imagination, and to see oneself functioning within that framework, may be to experience something of greater reality than that of the normal waking consciousness. In philosophical terms, which have been generally accepted for tarot interpretation, the devil is that which binds mankind to the external vision and to the sensory condition. On the other hand it is well-recognized that the idea of matter as inherently evil is a doctrine to which many theologians, such as Teillard de Chardin, do not subscribe.

The Mechanism of Integration

From the standpoint of initiation (recognition of the true nature of Self), the archetype of Shadow is the key. The process of individuation, as Jung calls it, begins as the repressed materials of Shadow are brought forcibly into consciousness, so that a tension of opposites (which Jung says is essential for forward movement) is created. This is a very natural process for, as Jung states, "all consciousness, perhaps without being aware of it, seeks its unconscious opposite....Life is born only of the spark of opposites."[29]

Jung repeats over and over again that integration of the Shadow and realization of the personal unconscious is the first step in an "analytic" process, and that until the Shadow is recognized and dealt with, it is absolutely impossible to interact directly with, and through, the Anima or the Animus.[30]

But realistically this is something which very few will ever experience because most people are unconscious and wholly uncritical. Most live in a condition of self-deception, believing incredibly, as Jung said, that they abide in a permanent state of goodness.[31] Nor, in fact, might the average person wish for the encounter of Shadow, which is an extremely unpleasant experience. To encounter the Shadow is to face directly the darkest and most frightening aspects of the personality, primitive instincts which civilization has taught are unacceptable. Yet those who make the effort discover that, little by little, as they are able to look at their own Shadow, the problem of the nature of Self begins to be solved.

In practical terms, this emotional inner journey begins with the invocation of the personal unconscious using techniques of inner visualization (active imagination).[32] Serious exercises will inevitably unleash a storm of feelings, the source of which may not be even suspected. And, in one of his most brilliant and provocative statements Jung insists that *"emotion...is not an activity of the individual, but something that happens to him."*[33]

Whatever its origin, a person may be overwhelmed by the emotional power released by the crash of day, the waking consciousness, into night, the collective unconscious. When these opposites of extreme intensity collide, they may cause "a disorientation and darkening of consciousness which can assume threatening proportions, as in the initial stage of a psychosis."[34]

In alchemical symbolism this is the *nigredo,* or blackening. But as Jung explains, light is implicit in the darkness, for "to confront a person with his Shadow is to show him his own Light. Once he has experienced a few times what it is like to stand judgingly between the opposites, one begins to understand that is meant by the Self. Anyone who perceives his Shadow and his Light simultaneously sees himself from two sides and thus gets in the middle."[35]

And he underscores that fact that the "mystic marriage" transcends reason and cannot be in any way explained: "Union of opposites is," he says, "equivalent to unconsciousness, so far as human logic goes, for consciousness presupposes a differentiation into subject and object and a relation between them. Where there is no 'other,' or it does not yet exist, all possibility of consciousness ceases."[36]

Notes: *The Devil*

1. Paul Carus, *The History of the Devil and The Idea of Evil,* New York, 1969, 53. Ahriman and Ahura-Mazda were not poles of a dualism in Zoroaster's original teachings. Ahura-Mazda was itself good as well as the creator of the bad.

2. Maximillian Rudwin, *The Devil in Legend and Literature,* La Salle, Illinois, 1973, 2-3.

3. The Patristic Fathers, including John Chrysostom and Thomas Aquinas explain the Job story as a parable, thus sidestepping the question of The Old Testament's representation of the Devil. See: Edouard Dhormé, A *Commentary on the Book of Job,* New York 1984 (original French version, 1926).

4. Mircea Eliade, A *History of Religious Ideas,* Chicago, 1978, v.II, 277.

5. The dualist conception developed by Christianity had a model in *The Book of Enoch.*

6. Carus, 137-141.

7. Eliade, A *History of Religious Ideas,* v.II, 384-389.

8. Jung comments on this question in *Mysterium Coniunctionis,* Princeton, 1976, **86.**

9. In Dante's *Divine Comedy* the Devil is described as the opposite of God. He is in ice rather than in the warmth of flames; he has three faces as both God and Devil were often represented in medieval art—the one being the Divine Trinity, and the other being its evil reflection. *Inferno, XXXIV.*

10. Carl Jung, *The Archetypes and the Collective Unconscious,* Princeton, 1977, **567.**

11. Carl Jung, *Psychology and Religion: West and East,* Princeton, 1977, **470.**

12. Ibid., 103-104.

13. An excellent article describing various influences on the Devil image in medieval art is to be found in *Christian Iconography* by Alphonse Napoleon Didron, reprint New York, 1965, 109-152.

14. Rudwin, 3. See Also Carus, 241-261

15. Stuart Kaplan, *Encyclopedia of Tarot,* New York, 1978, v.I, 71; Stamford, 1986, v.II, 25, 172.

16. Didron, v.II, 134.

17. Carl Jung, *Two Essays on Analytical Psychology,* New York, 1953,

103 note.

18. Jung, *Archetypes,* 513. Although the archetype of Shadow is considered to be primarily negative in terms of the tarot *Devil,* Jung points out that this is not always the case: "If it has been believed hitherto that the human Shadow is the source of all evil, it can now be ascertained, on closer investigation that the unconscious man, that is, his Shadow, does not consist only of morally reprehensible tendencies, but also displays a number of good qualities, such as normal instincts, appropriate reactions, realistic insights, creative impulses, etc. "*Aion,* Princeton, 1978, **423.**

19. Jung, *Aion,* **370.**

20. Carl Jung, *Mysterium Coniunctionis,* Princeton, 1976, **129**n.

21. Jung, *Archetypes,* **513.**

22. Jung, *Aion,* **13**

23. Jung, *Mysterium,* **129**n.

24. Jung, *Archetypes,* **485.**

25. Ibid., **61.**

26. Ibid., **62.**

27. In this regard one may note that a host of commentators over the centuries have criticized the incongruity of a Catholic Church which has stressed spiritual values while at the same tune amassing great wealth and material possessions. The Church's temporal empire was built originally upon that rather extraordinary fraud known as the "donation of Constantine." Under the rule of the fourth-century Pope Sylvester, a minor church official named Christophorus forged a document claiming that Constantine had actually given all of Italy to the successors of Peter. When in the eighth century, being attacked by Lombards, Pope Steven II, an old man, made a perilous winter journey over the Alps to ask for the help of the Frankish King. The gullible Franks were persuaded that the spurious document was true, and they invaded Italy, drove out the invading Lombards—as well as the Byzantines—and established the Bishop of Rome as the true Pope and ruler over a vast and wealthy kingdom. There appears to have been a very intricate conspiracy on the part of later popes to maintain belief in this fraud. E.R. Chamberlin, *The Bad Popes,* New York 1986, 14-17. See also *Cambridge Medieval History,* v.II, Cambridge 1967, 586ff.

28. Jung, *Mysterium,* **238.**

29. Jung, *Two Essays,* **78.** Pursuant to the idea of regression, Jung

comments that "Freud's theory of incest describes certain fantasies that accompany regression of libido and are especially characteristic of the personal unconscious as found in hysterical patients. Up to a point they are infantile sexual fantasies which show very clearly just where the hysterical attitude is defective and why it is so incongruous. They reveal the Shadow." Carl Jung, *Symbols of Transformation,* Princeton, 1976, **654**.

30. Jung, *Aion,* **42.** 1978, **843**.

31. Carl Jung, *Civilization in Transition,* Princeton, 1978, **843**.

32. Jung, *Archetypes,* **44**.

33. Jung, *Aion,* **15.**

34. Jung, *Civilization in Transition,* **814**.

35. Ibid., **872.**

36. Jung, *Aion,* **301.**

17 / THE TOWER

Archetype of Father as Protector/Avenger

It is interesting to see how, in the history of art, many themes from the Old Testament[1] are given extended meaning by Christian interpreters. The iconography of *tower* is a good example. The best-known biblical tower is that of Babel, but the Bible contains countless references to a more general tower which is symbolic of great strength

Besides the Bible, the most important pseudo-epigraphic source of ideas about a symbolic tower is the *Book of Enoch*. In that work Enoch is shown a vision of a divine tower which overlooks all of Heaven and Earth. Then he is shown a tower being built by blind sheep, which is destroyed by fire.[2] But the sheep try to rebuild the fallen house: "And again they began to place before the tower a table, with every impure and unclean kind of bread upon it." And again, of course, the blind sheep, who aspired to build a tower like that of God, are destroyed. Thus, *Enoch* establishes that there are two towers. The first is the true tower of God, and the second is that false tower of man described in Genesis as the Tower of Babel.

The key early Christian reference to a tower appears in a work of the second century of the Christian era, the *Shepherd of Hermas,* a book which, although little known today, was the most popular of the Christian Church for three hundred years. The book tells how a great tower of square stones was built upon the waters by six young men. And it tells how some were saved while others were thrown from the tower and perished.

This is explained to Hermas by a woman who confronts him in a vision (presumably the Virgin Mary). She says: "The tower which you are building is myself, the Church." The six young men "are the holy angels of God who were first created and to whom the Lord handed over his whole creation...those square white stones which fitted exactly into each other are apostles, bishops, teachers, and deacons....As to those who were cut down and thrown far away from the tower....They are the sons of iniquity, and they believed in hypocrisy and wickedness and did not depart from them."[3]

There is no reference to false, man-made, towers but the idea is implicit. For if the true tower of God is the Church herself, then all other towers must be built by Satan (whose evil, medieval theologians declared, results from the imperfections of mankind).

Another medieval tradition of a true Tower of God, is that of the tower as grave and as tabernacle. During the first Christian centuries and through much of the Middle Ages, there was a popular legend that Christ was placed in an upright grave which was either cut out of rock, or was a detached tower.[4] This protective grave-tower form greatly influenced the development of the medieval altar Tabernacles *(Ciboria),* shrines for the Host. And the ritual by which such tabernacles are consecrated refers to them as "new graves for Christ's body."[5]

The Tower of Babel

The legend of the Tower of Babel was unquestionably based upon beliefs surrounding the earliest type of step pyramid, the *ziggurat*, such as that at the Temple of Marduk in Babylonia. The Bible story referred to Babylonian religious practice, for the ziggurat was conceived to be a form intermediate between earth and Heaven. When the priest climbed it, he was ritually and symbolically in Heaven.[6]

The Bible tells how after the flood the descendants of Noah settled in Babylonia (Babel) where they determined to build a tower that would reach up and conquer the heavens. But God, seeing that men with a common goal and language could foolishly challenge his own authority, confused their languages and scattered them around the earth.[7] In the Bible, God neither destroys the tower nor throws men from it. The builders simply stop their work and disperse.

The Tower and its Theology

The tarot iconography generally accepted today shows a tall structure being struck by lightning with two or three figures being thrown from the top. But this is a later version of the card. The earliest known *Tower* (in the absence of that card in the *Visconti-Sforza* deck) is a card from the Gringonneur deck of 1392[8] showing a tower crumbling and being destroyed by flames, to which was later added the title "La Maison de Dieu." The obvious question here is why would God destroy his own house? The answer is found in the distinction of *Enoch* between true and false towers: "La Maison de Dieu" was a part of the Satan theology: As the Devil appears to be like God, so this house is not built by God at all, but by human builders who claim to be like God. The flames destroy not the real house of God, but a false one.[9]

To reiterate, the traditionally accepted *Tower* is assumed to be a compound image,[10] the biblical Tower of Babel embellished by reference to other sources. It appears that the image of destruction of the false tower by fire (and later by lightning) is taken from the book of *Enoch,* and that the figures being thrown from the top refer to the vision of the true tower of God in *The Shepherd of Hermas.*

Celestial Fire, Thunder, and Lightning

Whereas the first tarot images seem to mirror popular culture, the fifteenth and sixteenth century's rediscovery of classicism brought some new ideas to the cards. And the ease with which various pantheons of antique gods and goddesses were incorporated into this medieval device tends to reinforce the argument that their substance and order is truly archetypal, and that they may legitimately be used to address some basic qualities of the (unconscious) human condition. As aspects of the Father archetype, the gods may be considered to be interchangeable psychological currency. The Greek god of thunder and lightning corresponds perfectly with the fiery Hebrew God of the Old Testament, or with some of the earliest sky gods.

Primitive man saw thunder and lightning as the work of such

a sky god who was usually worshipped as Father of gods and of men. The best known of these gods is the Greek *Zeus* (whose very name means *sky).* He was the weather god of thunder and rain, but he was also the protector of law and of morals.[11] His thunderbolt protects and purifies; it is also the fire of fertility, of crops, and of initiation. This connection of purification and initiation by thunderbolt is very ancient.[12]

Zeus was equal to *Jupiter* in the Roman pantheon and to *Thor* (Donar), god of thunder, in the Nordic lands. Thunder was thought to be created as Thor rolled his chariot on the vault of Heaven. And when lightning struck it was said that Thor had cast his hammer from on high, and that it never missed its mark. The stone hammer of Thor was named *Mjolnir* which meant "the destroyer." It was a magic object which not only fought the enemy, but which, like the thunderbolt of Zeus, also conferred solemn consecration.

Among the Teutonic peoples the god of thunder was Woden (called Odin in the North). Woden was the master of the *wode,* or "fury." Woden was the god of war and of intelligence whose advance in battle suddenly struck his enemies deaf, blind, and impotent.[13]

In all cultures, the sky god has a number of responsibilities after the fact of creation. First, he is the archetypal protector of his "children," meaning that he must preserve and protect the order and integrity of what he has created. But the lightning bolt which creates (seen as "Divine Fire" in the Jungian version) is also that which destroys. This is a key principle of *The Tower.* In fact, as in the myth of Woden, all of the gods themselves eventually fall in battle, the earth falls into the ocean, the sky crumbles, and all life disappears. But Yggdrasil has preserved one human pair from which a whole new humanity emerges.[14] Thus, as is the implication of *The Tower,* the destruction/creation cycle continues.

The Warring Father

The archetype of the Father who makes war is a separated-out aspect of the sky god, the best known of which is Mars, the Roman god second only to Jupiter. The cult of Mars was based on that of Ares, a god of no special popularity whose cult appears to have been limited to Thebes and perhaps Athens.[15]

The Warring Father (a compound vision of all gods of war and of thunder) of the Jungian Tarot personifies those forces which produces the lightning that destroys the Tower. And although the traditional "Tower Struck by Lightning" shows no such figure, the presence of the Father is understood as one asks the question: "Where does the lightning come from, and by what will does it strike the tower?"

That creation and destruction go hand in hand was not lost on those medieval generals who approached war as one of the fine arts. During the fourteenth through sixteenth centuries, when the tarot was being developed, war was considered inevitable if not essential. Only by constantly being prepared for war, it was argued, could a ruler maintain the peace. As Nicolo Machiavelli instructed his Prince, Lorenzo de' Medici, war is "the primary concern of a prince" who "ought never therefore, to have out of his thoughts this subject of war."[16]

The Tower, although largely allegorical, was certainly a reminder of the reality of violent conflict and destruction which surrounded men at this period in history. At a personal level, it was a reminder of the impermanence of all man-made structures.

Clouds Above the Tower

Over the centuries, *The Tower* has been said variously to mean the fall of Atlantis, the wrath of God against Sodom and Gomorrah, the destruction of the Temple, the collapse of the Catholic Church, the fall of Lucifer, and the sacrifice of the individual ego to a higher principle.[17] One imaginative writer has gone so far as to suggest that the tower-struck-by-lightning theme entered tarot vocabulary through Arthurian legend.[18]

As was proposed in an earlier chapter, there are two reasons for such wide speculation on the symbolism of this and of other cards. First, over time ideas which were very common in the fourteenth century ceased to be a part of the popular culture, and commentators could only guess at their original meaning. Second, the connection of tarot with the occult by eighteenth-century dilettantes (who proclaimed themselves initiates of a largely-invented secret tradition), cast the tarot in the public mind as a mysterious and romantic repository of secret knowledge.

Those ideas farthest removed from the intentions of the simple medieval artists who created tarot were developed by English and French occultists of the late nineteenth and early twentieth-centuries. Thus some very creative men and women truly invented the modern tarot by attaching the cards to the Hermetic Kabbalah, an occult philosophy which grew out of the Italian Renaissance. Through a complicated system of correspondences of numbers and of Hebrew letters, *The Tower* was equated with speech, with the male sex organ, and with the very creation of the universe.[19]

This diversity of interpretation, while it demonstrates the ability of these images to challenge intellectually, tends again to underscore the facility with which the archetypal card images may be applied to any visual and ideological pantheon. Modern theories, including the correspondence of tarot and Kabbalah, are philosophically (though certainly not historically) valid, and serve to amplify the utility of the cards as devices illustrating patterns of the collective unconscious.[20]

Activity of the Archetype

The Father represented in *The Tower* is a behavioral archetype which, on the surface, may appear to be of only minor significance in Jung's scheme of things. However the Father who destroys may also be considered to be the unseen and divine purpose behind all human trials. So *The Tower* is an archetype of disaster and of the brutal trials imposed upon Job which so interested Jung.[21]

In commenting on that story, Jung discusses immense powers of destruction being handed over to man, and the necessity for the "healing" intervention of the divinity, who helps mankind to resist the use of these destructive powers.[22] And the heavenly fire which descends is "liberating." Jung points out that it "is a symbol also used by Paracelsus and the alchemists for the same thing....Lightning signifies a sudden, unexpected, and overpowering change of psychic condition."[23] Symbolically, lightning is related to the phallus, as well as to the snake and its "illuminating, vivifying, fertilizing, transforming and healing function."[24]

The sword carried by the Father in this card means solar power and Jung notes that "a sword goes out from the mouth of Christ in the Apocalypse, namely the provocative fire, speech, or the spermatic Word."[25] In the swiftness of its activity and in its reference to both creation and destruction the sword has many of the same attributes as does lightning. And psychologically, it can mean intuition, insight, and even initiation.

From this modern perspective, *The Tower* represents an inner turmoil—appreciating, of course, that the fourteenth-century artist, who saw every ill wind as imposed from above,[26] would have explained the image quite differently. Yet whether a psychological or an environmental condition, the card is agreed to stand for some terrible misfortune which happens suddenly and without warning. It is a brutal and uncompromising destructive event which ultimately brings about renewal. In Astrology, it is the sword of the fiery and warring Mars, who rules the Zodiac sign of Aries that announces spring. So the idea that something new will emerge from a tearing down of one thing (the assertion that the process of anabolism and catabolism is universal) is implicit in *The Tower*.

Notes: *The Tower*

1. Artists, especially monastic ones, were exposed to a considerable amount of secondary literature to which one might look as a source for themes. However Mâle points out that not much art was drawn from apocryphal traditions. "For the Middle Ages, "he said, "the text of The Bible was almost always enough and satisfied interest." See: Emile Mâle, *Religious Art in France, The Thirteenth Century,* Princeton 1984, 211.

2. *Enoch,* LXXXVIII.101.

3. *Pastor of Hermas,* The Ante-Nicene Fathers,v.II, Grand Rapids, 1986 13-15.

4. Hrjo Hirn, *The Sacred Shrine,* Boston, 1957 (Original, Sweden, 1909), 161.

5. Ibid., 161-162.

6. Mircea Eliade, *A History of Religious Ideas,* v.I., Chicago, 1978, 170.

7. This explanation of the origin of languages is one of a class of stories which attempted to explain the roots of social forms to a very primitive society. See: *Dictionary the Bible,* Ed. James Hastings, New York 1963, "Tongues, Confusion of," 1007-1009.

8. Illustrated in Stuart Kaplan *The Encyclopedia of Tarot,* v.I, New York, 1978, 115.

9. In some descriptions The Tower is called *La Casa del Diavolo.* Moakley offers the theory that this card relates to the mouth of Hell frequently found on the medieval religious stage. Gertrude Moakley, *The Tarot Cards Painted by Bonifacio Bembo,* New York, 1966, 99.

10. From the period of *Hermas* into the late Middle Ages symbolism attached to the tower was considerably amplified. In tenth-century France there was reference to a Tower of Philosophy built from the seven Liberal Arts. (Katzenellenbogen, *Allegories of the Virtues and Vices in Medieval Art,* 72 note 3). And through the visions of St. Hildegard of Bingen (1098-1179) earlier conceptions about the Virtues carrying stones to the tower of the Church were revived (Katzenellenbogen, *Allegories,* 42-43).

11. He was equated by the Stoic philosophers with *fire*, their highest principle which is at once the creative reason that developed the universe. *Oxford Classical Dictionary,* "Zeus," 1146-1147.

12. Eliade, *Patterns in Comparative Religion,* New York, 1974, 78. All major pantheons have some equivalent form. Among the Celts it

was the Sky God *Ararnas,* god of storms and lightning. Other such skygods include the Baltic *Percanas* (meaning "lightning," the proto-Slavic *Perun,* as well as the early Indian god of hurricanes, *Parjanya,* whose cult gave rise to that of the most popular of the Vedic gods, *Indra.* Eliade, *Pattems,* 82-83.

13. *Larousse Encyclopedia of Mythology,* New York, 1968, 253-254.

14. Eliade, *History of Religious Ideas,* II, 169.

15. *Oxford Classical Dictionary,* Oxford, 1978, 103-104.

16. Nicolo Machiavelli, *The Prince,* London, 1940, Trans. W.K. Marriot from 1513 original, 111-112.

17. Richard Cavendish, *The Tarot,* New York, 1975, 123-124.

18. Stuart Kaplan, *Encyclopedia of Tarot,* Stamford, 1986, v.II., 174.

19. The intermediate device for attaching meanings to the tarot cards was the Kabbalstic Tree of Life. A tarot card was related to a specific Path on the Tree, to which a Hebrew letter was also assigned. See: Robert Wang, *The Qabalistic Tarot,* New York, *1983, passim.*

20. A problem of interpretation has existed because there has been so little scholarly attention given to the roots of tarot imagery, and because commentators, especially those of the nineteenth century, have tended to promulgate their own personal biases as absolute facts. The historical issues have been further clouded by occultists claiming that their information about the tarot is a special truth received psychically.

21. Carl Jung, *Psychology and Religion: West and East,* Princeton, 1977, "Answer to Job," **560-758.**

22. Ibid., **745.**

23. Carl Jung, *The Archetypes and the Collective Unconscious,* Princeton, 1977, **533.**

24. Ibid., 558.

25. Carl Jung, *Symbols of Transformation,* Princeton, 1976, **557.**

26. This was particularly evident during the black plague of the mid-fourteenth century, diagnosed by the distinguished medical faculty of the University of Paris as the result of a conjunction of Saturn, Mars, and Jupiter at 1:00 P.M. on March 20, 1345 which supposedly corrupted the atmosphere.

18 / THE STAR

Archetype of Sol Invisibilis

The cards which follow, *The Star, The Moon*, and *The Sun* were originally linked. The Sun, the Moon, and all of the planets were called *Stars*[1] and represented the influences of the skies on man's destiny. In the original tarot, they were (like the Virtues and the Liberal Arts) shown as female figures holding their respective attributes.

The figure was not the Star itself but was a personification of the intelligence which directed the course of all heavenly bodies. Presumably this single Star, first after the Sun and the Moon, was a reference to the "Morning Star."[2] And although the tarot is a secular device, no medieval artist could have completely distanced himself from the Christian symbolism of the Star which guided the wise men to the manger at Bethlehem. So the tarot *Star*, which generally encompassed all of the Stars beyond the Sun and Moon, meant not only the astrological forces which controlled the destinies of humanity; it was also a provider of divine guidance by which one might choose a correct action.

Of course the tradition of astrology is antithetical to Christian dogma. As Hippolytus wrote in his *Refutation of All Heresies:* The heretics "think to deceive as many of these that devote themselves over sedulously to the astrologers, from thence striving to construct a system of religion."[3] But interest was never quite lost in Astrology, and that "science" existed side by side with Christian doctrine for centuries. Those tarot cards which represent a fatalist philosophy, the *Wheel of Fortune, The Star, The Sun* and *The Moon*, were more a part of the popular culture than of the official church culture of the Middle Ages.

Evolution of *The Star* in Tarot

In the earliest known card, that of the *Visconti-Sforza* deck, a woman holds a Star in her right hand. In later cards, as in the fifteenth-century *D'Este* deck,[4] the Star is shown in the sky with two astrologers beneath it. In that deck the Sun and the Moon are also removed from the hand of a symbolic female and have been put into the sky above.

Whatever form it took in early versions, *The Star* remained a reference to Astrology and to the heavenly forces behind human lives. The same essential meaning is implicit in the later, and rather curious, invention of a card with a nude woman beneath one large star surrounded by smaller ones, who is pouring out water from two vases. This nude figure, a classical influence in second generation tarot design, undoubtedly bears some thematic relationship to the figure of *Temperance* who pours from one vase into another.

The woman represents that which is poured down upon the earth by the Stars. She, as in the earliest tarot *Star*, personifies the intelligence by which this happens. And insofar as the woman actually manipulates the vessels of "experience," she is a version of *Fortuna*.

There is no evidence that, even by the seventeenth century, *The Star* embodied any of the complicated philosophies attributed to it in the eighteenth and nineteenth centuries.

In twentieth-century Jungian terms, however, the gold and silver vessels from which water is being poured show *The Star* as the source of both conscious and unconscious, the "first among all Stars," which includes the symbolic Sun and Moon (another reference to conscious and unconscious).

The Star Gods

The most important star to the Egyptians, that which regulated the annual cycles, was Sothis (Sirius). This was at first represented as a female divinity, but was eventually assimilated with the goddess Satis. And in virtually all places where a Star appears, it is a regulator of the rising and falling of light, of tides, or of seasons.

The best known of the "Star gods" are those of the Greeks, the morning star, *Phosphorus* (associated with Lucifer and with Venus), and the evening Star,[5] *Hesperus*.[6] In art, both are sometimes represented as a boy carrying a burning torch, an image not too distant from that of a woman carrying a shining Star.

And in fact, the personification of Sun, Moon, and stars is archetypal in its universality. In a culture so far removed in time from Greece as the ancient Indians of California, the Sun, Moon, and Stars were described as having the form of men and of women who disappeared every evening into the western ocean and who reappeared in the east after having swum across the ocean all night long.[7]

In the broad sweep of religions perhaps the most interesting Star (and that most in accord with a psychoanalytic interpretation of the tarot card) appears in the pantheon of some early nomadic peoples. Certain tribes believed that the sky is a tent, and that the Stars are the "windows of the world." In the middle of this tent-sky is the *Pole Star* which holds up the sky like a stake, and which has variously been called the "Sky Nail" and the "Pillar of the World."[8]

The story is simplistic. But the idea of the "heavens," which is in fact the upper reaches of the human conception of reality, being held in place by a star, is quite consistent with the idea of *sol invisibilis*. In philosophical terms the Invisible Sun, the Inner Star, is that on which the vision of reality is based. It is, theoretically, like the "Sky Nail" from which all else hangs, or the Pillar on which the whole world depends.

The Stars and Man's Destiny

Until as recently as the late nineteenth century, it was thought that representations of the heavens, such as the circular " Zodiac of Dendera," from the Temple of Dendera, proved that astrology originated in Egypt.[9] But, in fact, the Egyptians borrowed their twelve signs from the Babylonians. And although Babylonian astrological literature does not appear until the seventh century B.C.E., it is probable that a system of Astrology, linked with stories of the creation, goes back as far as 2300 B.C.E.

Ancient astronomers in Mesopotamia were the first to observe the movement of the heavenly bodies and to attempt to find some mathematical order in these movements. And as these early scientists learned to predict the regular appearance of certain celestial phenomenon, so an emerging system of Astrology attempted to demonstrate the ways in which the interrelationships of the Stars affected human destiny. It was, in fact, astrologers whose pursuit of a special Star supposedly led them to the manger at Bethlehem.

From the temples of Mesopotamia ideas about Astrology spread into Egypt,[10] where they became systematized over the centuries, culminating in works by Ptolemy, such as the *Tetrabiblios,* where one finds no distinction between Astronomy and Astrology. The motions of the Stars are objectively observed, but their activities are assumed to affect the lives of men.[11]

After Alexander, Astrology became of considerable importance to the Greeks and later to the Romans, where it profoundly affected the actions and decisions of all society from the peasants to the Roman emperors themselves. It is the "classical" astrological iconography which was carried into the Middle Ages. As a general rule, one which maybe of use in identifying the period of origin of a tarot card, it may be said that personified representations of Zodiac themes and of Sun, Moon, and Star, were clothed until the rise of Humanism in the fifteenth century, at which point the nude figure became the norm.

Jung and Astrology

A chapter about *The Star* is an appropriate place to consider the great attraction of Carl Jung, and his followers today, to

Astrology. As a psychologist, he was interested in systems which established categories of personality and of behavior. He notes that "From earliest times attempts have been made to classify individuals according to types and so to bring order into the chaos." And he points out that from ideas about the Zodiac the Greeks developed the medical classification of four temperament groups: phlegmatic, sanguine, choleric, and melancholic, which remained in vogue for seventeen hundred years.[12]

Astrology was one of Jung's passionate interests but, as a scientist, he felt compelled to test the validity of the data which it provided. He did so by comparing the charts of 180 married couples (360 total horoscopes) and by subjecting them to a careful statistical analysis in search of relationships in the paired charts.

Jung was disappointed, for his results were unfavorable to Astrology. The facts suggested that it was not possible to state with certainty that Astrology "works," although in many instances the data showed a correlation between horoscope and life which was greater than chance. Jung finally concluded that because psychic phenomena are involved, statistical evaluation may not by itself give an accurate picture.[13]

The Inner Star

It is demonstrably true that anyone can close their eyes and "see" a light which is as intense as any that might be experienced in the physical environment. This Inner Light, which is the raw material of dreams and of active imagination, has been a concern of metaphysical philosophers for centuries. It has been variously called *Sol Invisibilis,* "the spark of the soul," *the Image Dei,* and simply "The Star."

In a lengthy essay entitled "The Two Sources of Knowledge: The Light of Nature and the Light of Revelation," Jung refers to alchemical ideas of Paracelsus[14] about a *"Lumen Naturae* which illuminates consciousness."[15] To Paracelsus the Light of Nature shines forth from the *Astrum,* the Inner Star in man. And he teaches that "as in the Star lieth the whole Natural Light, and from it man taketh the same like food from the earth into which he is born, so too must he be born into the Star."[16] So this Inner Light is the essence of life, and Jung clearly agrees with the conclusion of Paracelsus that "nothing can be in man unless it has been given to him by the Light of Nature, and what is in the Light of Nature has been brought by the Stars." Thus, to discover the source of the Inner Light, is to discover the true meaning of life and of the Self.

Jung explains that the Inner Star is a psychic center "that corresponds psychologically with that of the Self"[7] and discusses at some length the various symbols which are attached to this Star. He refers particularly to *Mercurius* (often identified with the Moon and with Venus/Morning Star) who "heralds, as the Morning Star does, only much more directly, the coming of the light."[18]

Jung tries to resolve the alchemical and Christian symbols by saying that Jesus, who supposedly described himself as the Morning Star *(Revelation,* 22:16), could be called the Archetype of Consciousness, whereas Mercurius is the Archetype of the Unconscious.[19] Both Christ and Mercurius have been related to the Logos, the "word" of renewal, the seed of promise which is like the light of the Star. But the figure eight (which on its side is the *Lemniscate,* symbol of infinity), and the eight-pointed tarot Star refer particularly to Mercurius. The number eight is the number of speech (word) and thus of "magic," which depends upon "words of power."

By reference to the works of Paracelsus, Jung demonstrates

the source of the "magic" of Alchemy. It happens by *imaginatio,* which he translates to mean "meditating." This "is the active power of the *astrum* or *corpus coeleste sive supracoeleste,* that is, of the higher man within. "Here," he asserts, "we encounter the psychic force in Alchemy: the artifex accompanies his chemical work with a simultaneous mental operation that is provided by means of the imagination."[20]

In fact imagination has played a far greater role in the meditation techniques of well-known Christian figures than has been generally understood. A particular case is that of Ignatius Loyola whose *Spiritual Exercises* are now recognized as having originally been intense mystical exercises of active imagination.[21]

The Christian tradition hints at this in that the Star has been called "Christ offering knowledge of himself to those who pursue the Inner Light." And Alice Bailey, one of the early modern syncretists of Eastern and Western thought, says much the same thing: "Through perfectly concentrated meditation on the light in the head comes the vision of the Masters who have attained.[22] In Eastern literature, the Upanishads especially refer to an experience of the inner light by which the self reaches its highest form, the *Atman,* and by which it encounters the immortal, the *Brahman.*[23]

In the alchemical tradition which so influenced Jung's perspective on the human condition, light, gold, and Sun are equivalents. And the relationship of the archetypal Inner Sun to the outer holds the greatest of secrets: "Now the Sun is not alone in the firmament outside of all other creatures, but it is much more in the center of all creatures but shut up, but the external Sun is as a figure of Christ, in that it unlocks in us the enclosed Sun."[24]

Summation

Because the inner light of *The Star* is so pivotal to the philosophy of revelation developed by Jung, it seems important to briefly review and clarify the principles which have been attached to it. It cannot be overstressed that this Inner Light is not symbolic. It is completely real and is experienced in one way or another by everyone. The symbols which have been described here are the answers variously given to some basic questions: What is this light inside my head and where does it come from? And where is my "Self" within my head? Philosophers such as Jung reached the conclusion that this light is the inexplicable and divine link between all persons, that the perception of Self is embodied in it, and that to know the nature and source of this light is to know the Self (described as Mercurius, Christ, the Sun, etc.).

In principle, therefore, illumination is the result of contemplation (conscious and unconscious) of the Inner Light. This act of contemplation, by which the mystic seeker advances, involves the modeling of the Inner Light through active imagination, which ultimately reveals the nature of the Light itself.

Notes: *The Star*

1. In his *Timaeus,* Plato refers to "The Sun and Moon and five other Stars." And he establishes their order: "First there was the Moon in the orbit nearest the earth, and the next the Sun, in the second orbit above the earth; then came theMorning Star." *Timaeus,* 38.c-d. Also, in the last line of his *Divine Comedy,* Dante writes of "love, which moves the Sun and other Stars," showing the persistence of that point of view into the late Middle Ages.

2. The Morning Star has been generally related to Venus.

3. Hippolytus, *The Refutation of All Heresies,* The Ante-Nicene Fathers, v. V, Michigan, 1986, 44.

4. Stuart Kaplan, *Encyclopedia of Tarot,* New York, 1978, v.I, 117-118.

5. *Oxford Classical Dictionary,* Oxford, 1978, "Phosphorus," 828. The name Phosphorus was also attributed to Artemis and to Hecate.

6. *Oxford Classical Dictionary,* "Hesperus," 511. Hesperus was early considered to be the son of Astraeus, and later the son or brother of Atlas. He was the father of Hesperus and the Grandfather of the Hesperides.

7. *Larousse Encyclopedia of Mythology,* New York, 1968, 436.

8. Mircea Eliade, *Shamanism,* Princeton, 1974, 26-261.

9. E. A. Wallis Budge, *The Gods of the Egyptians,* New York, 1969, v.II, 312-313.

10. *Oxford Classical Dictionary,* "Astrology," 133-134.

11. Ptolemy, *Tetrabiblios,* North Hollywood, 1976. Passim.

12. Carl Jung, *Psychological Types,* Princeton, 1977, **933.**

13. Carl Jung, *The Structure and Dynamics of the Psyche,* Princeton, 1969. **872-946.** An Astrological Experiment," is section two of Jung's well-known article (1951, revised *1955)* "Synchronicity An Acausal Connecting Principle."

14. Jung obviously felt considerable attachment to Paracelsus who was, like himself, an innovative physician who believed that true healing was a spiritual process.

15. Jung, *Structure and Dynamics,* **388-393**

16. Ibid., **390.**

17. Carl Jung, *Alchemical Studies,* Princeton, 1976, **188.**

18. Ibid., **273.**

19. Ibid., **299.**

20. Ibid., **173.**

21. See Antonio T. De Nicolas, *Powers of Imagining: lgnatius de Loyola,* Albany, 1986. Passim.

22. Alice A. Bailey, *A Treatise on Cosmic Fire,* New York, 1973.

23. Mircea Eliade, *A History of Religious Ideas,* Chicago, 1978, v.I, 241.

24. Herbert Silberer, *Hidden Symbolism in Alchemy and the Occult Arts,* New York, 1974, 319. This book, originally published in 1917, was among the first modern works to discuss Alchemy as a process of inner discovery.

19 / THE MOON

Archetype of the Deadly Mother

As was the case with *The Star*, in tarot the Moon was originally shown in the hand of a woman.[1] *The Star, The Moon*, and *The Sun* were all part of a simple iconographic scheme of the heavens, much like the accepted artistic re-presentations of the Virtues and Vices. But in later decks the Moon and other Stars were placed in the sky—often above the figures of astrologers or others who were subject to the influence of the planets.

Relatively soon after the introduction of tarot, the support-ing human cast disappeared or became at least secondary.[2] In the seventeenth century, the norm was a Moon above twin tow-ers, with heraldic dogs protecting a path upon which a crayfish climbs. Thus the simple theme of the Moon as one of the Stars controlling man's destiny, was replaced by a complex set of symbolic images which modern writers on tarot interpret psy-chologically.

The Moon like *The Tower*, is a card in which, in the *Jungian Tarot*, a central archetypal figure has been introduced. And as the male figure of *The Tower* is Ares (the Roman Mars), so the figure of the woman, here with arms outstretched to show that she is the goddess of crossroads, is Hecate.

The Phases of the Moon

The Greek writer Hesiod was the first to give serious atten-tion to Hecate (she was not mentioned at all by Homer). In his *Theogony* he described her as essentially benevolent to man-kind and, curiously, as the goddess whom "Zeus, son of Kronos, honored above all others, granting her magnificent privileges: a share of both the earth and the undraining sea...she is the most honored by the immortal gods."[3] There was no sugges-tion of the sinister qualities with which she was identified in later times.

Over the centuries Hecate came to be associated with strange events and with the world of ghosts, and thus she was wor-shipped as the goddess of those crossroads which were believed by many cultures to be haunted. Her cult evolved into one of magic, of sorcery, and of the underworld. In classical Greek times she was shown with three bodies, and even appeared on one Greek vase lighting the way from Hades for Persephone.[4]

In tarot, the three phases of woman (Maiden, Mother, and Hag) are seen as *The High Priestess, The Empress* and *The Moon*. These cards are generally equivalent, in mythology, to Artemis, Selene, and Hecate. Of course, in the ancient world, the connection of these deities was a very loose one; it was later commentators who claimed that their individual activities could be equated with a specific phase of the life cycle of woman or of the moon.

Nevertheless, Hecate's qualities are infinitely darker than those of the other two. She is the Crone, the Wicked Witch, the true Mother of the Underworld.[5] She is, as Jung points out, the huntress of the night, as opposed to Artemis, who is the huntress of the day. But the cult of Hecate is the more complex, for insofar as she is the Mother of Death, she is also a goddess of birth.[6] Jung finds this idea imbedded in the symbolism of the roads which cross; to him they symbolize the union of opposites at which the mother is always present. But he emphasizes that where the roads divide there is a separation.[7] The philosophical implication is that it is the Mother who creates the separation of the individual from the collective, and it is she who brings about the ultimate return; she activates both birth and death.[8]

The dichotomous nature of the Moon-figure is inherent in the Maiden who is an essential participant in the mystic marriage of Alchemy. "The bride," Jung says, "is not only lovely and innocent, but also witch-like and terrible, like the side of Selene that is related to Hecate. Like her, Luna is 'all seeing,' an 'all knowing' eye. Like Hecate she sends madness, epilepsy, and other sicknesses. Her special field is love magic, and magic in general in which the New Moon, the Full Moon, and the Moon's darkness play a great part."[9]

Lilith, Queen of the Underworld

Among all the legends of an Evil Mother, the most complete (from the standpoint of Jungian interpretation) is that of Lilith, a murky figure who emerged from Babylonian-Assyrian superstition into a legend of the Hebrew culture so important that it lasted well into the eighth century C.E. Although mentioned only briefly in the Bible,[10] as a "night monster," she is described in the *Talmud,* in the *Koran,* and in wide variety of noncanonical literature.

In the earliest legend Lilith was a demoness who stole small children and carried them off into the desert.[11] But she was later known as the first wife of Adam, whom she was said to have abandoned for the world of evil spirits after, as some legends insist, she had borne to him a host of demons.

Interpreting the text of Genesis, Talmudic tradition suggests that Lilith and Adam were created simultaneously and joined together, both being called *Adam.* After many quarrels, and obvious incompatibilities, Lilith supposedly pronounced the *shemhamaphoresh* (the unpronounceable Divine Name of God), which caused her to grow wings, and to fly out of Eden. And when God replaced Lilith with Eve, he created her out of one of Adam's ribs so that there could be no doubt of her independence as was the problem for the first wife.

The philosophical balance of good and evil was reached when Samael, chief of the fallen angels, fell in love with Lilith and they settled in *Gehenna.* According to the Apocalypse of St. John, it was Samael (Satan) who, disguised as a snake, tempted Eve to disobey her creator, and brought about the fall of Adam and herself. Another tradition says that it was Lilith herself who, as a snake, caused the downfall of the hated rival.

In any event, there was now a mythological quaternity. The Good Mother was opposed by an opposite, and equally powerful, Bad Mother; the Good Father was opposed by the Evil Father. As there was a King and Queen of Heaven, so there was a King and Queen of Hell.

The Terrible Mother and The Hero

Jung devotes considerable attention to the relationship of the Hero-Son to the Mother and to the incest drive. "It confronts us," he says, "in the guise of the Terrible Mother, and is indeed the mother of innumerable evils."[12] Jung expands on this in his essay "The Dual Mother." "The Hero," he says, "is the ideal masculine type: leaving the Mother, the source of life, behind him, he is driven by an unconscious desire to find her again, to return to her womb. Every obstacle that rises in his path and hampers his ascent wears the shadowy features of the Terrible Mother, who saps his strength with the poison of secret doubt and retrospective longing; and in every conquest he wins back again the smiling, loving and life-giving Mother."[13]

This is one way of expressing the ancient idea of Hecate leading the candidate into the mysteries. And if she is considered to be the goddess of both death and of birth, her secrets must be called the key possession of the enlightened philosopher.

The idea of the Crone who leads the White Knight to a great treasure, or of the alchemist's attempt to make gold from lead, can be expressed in psychological terms. The urgent necessity for understanding one's own behavior and its motivation, is a philosophical precept of *The Moon* which is the path of the darkest phantoms of the mind. To face head-on the shrouded recesses of the individual mind is difficult enough. But to "regress" into the darkest fears and most painful caverns of mankind's collective experience is a true descent into Hell—a journey requiring the courage of the Hero.

Such an experience is truly archetypal, but its details are culturally-determined. Through religious and mythological teaching, a culture provides the individual with a set of expectations about that which will be encountered on another "plane" (such as Charon in his boat on the river Styx). The Jewish mystic is unlikely to have an inner conversation with the Virgin Mary, but might hear the voice of a prophet. And the fact that the unconscious tends to fulfill the expectations of the regressing conscious mind is a subtle trap. Indeed, the search for the universal Grail is initially confined (if not impeded) by what one believes to be the structure of "Heaven," of "Hell," or any other significant braces supporting the pantheon of one's belief system.

Nevertheless, those qualities represented by *The Moon* are cross-cultural. There are two primary experiential archetypes involved. The first is the Archetype of Fear, blind, irrational, overwhelming terror which has the potential to completely destroy the Hero if he allows it to control him. And second, there is the Archetype of Illusion. Fear and illusion work together here, for the aspirant of the mysteries must discover that the most frightening things on this path are not real.

Birth and Death

The Moon and *Death* touch upon the same ideas, but from completely different viewpoints. The card of *Death* represents an impersonal, inevitable, and natural transition in which the thoughts and feelings of the individual are insignificant. But as *The Moon* describes death, it is a very frightening personal specter. As Jung says: "The image of the consuming change

that dissolves the phenomenal world of individual psychic existence originates in the unconscious and appears before the
conscious mind in dreams and shadowy premonitions. And the
more unwilling the latter is to heed this intimation, the more
frightening become the symbols by which it makes itself
known."[14] So the "path" of *The Moon* involves dark, murky,
and threatening presences. The snake is an especially powerful symbol here, one which most people find repellent.

Insofar as this is also a card of physical birth,[15] that birth is
painful and difficult. But in Jungian terms, this is a spiritual
rebirth; the Hero descending into the dark cave in search of
treasure is metaphorical. "The treasure which the Hero fetches
from the dark cavern is *life:* it is himself, new-born from the
dark maternal cave of the unconscious."[16]

The Terrible Mother-Moon is the symbolic gateway to and
from the material condition; she is the waxing and waning force
behind separate human existence. Yet she must be differentiated from the Great Mother who is *The Empress.* The
illusion-creating Moon is not the ultimate giver or taker of life,
but she is responsible for the mistaken perception that birth
and death are realities.

The Terrible Mother weaves a spell and then challenges her
Hero son to break it—which is also to say that in the process of
the individual's Self-discovery, this Mother is anything but
indifferent. In the encounter of the rational conscious mind with
the irrational unconscious, there is a continual interplay between subject and object (the perception of a separate "I" and
"you') which Jung represented at one level as Mother and Son.

The Descent into Hell

Hecate's introduction of the candidate to the denizens of the perilous underworld is an archetypal process described in many ways by different cultures. Experience of the heavens requires that one have first experienced the underworld of personal fear and self doubt, and then the greater and more terrible psychic imprints of mankind's collective nightmares. Thus Virgil brought Dante to the lowest depths of Hell before raising him to the divine heights.

According to the cult of Hecate, the aspirant must descend 365 steps (referring to the course of the sun during the year) into the cavern of death and rebirth which is the kingdom of the Terrible Mother. He is required to pass by her frightful dogs which guard the gates of Hell.[17] These dogs of Hecate are symbolically equivalent to the snake which is at once a symbol of death and a guardian of the great treasure buried in the earth (meaning within the unconscious). But to Jung the dog is more than just a guardian. "Because of its rich symbolic content," he explains, "the dog is an apt synonym for the transforming substance."[18]

A further modern interpretation of the card is that it shows primitive life forms evolving from the depths of the ocean. This idea is loosely extrapolated from the third generation of tarot's development of a *Moon* card with a crustacean moving from the water onto the land and up the path between the two menacing dogs. Psychologically, this is the emergence of the differentiated consciousness out of the dark waters of the unconscious.

But again this complex interpretation is contemporary. There can be no doubt that the seventeenth-century artist created a card with the simplest of intentions. The form emerging from the water was probably a crab, symbol of the astrological sign of Cancer which, especially as cardinal water, is ruled by the Moon. And the dogs, rather than being the hounds of hell, are probably those of the Moon goddess Diana who, as the huntress, was a very popular theme in art at this time.

The Alchemical Connection

It should be self-evident that the divisions established by tarot are extremely useful but not absolute. The cards, like the states of consciousness which they represent flow into one another. Thus, aspects of a given stage of medieval Alchemy are described by more than one card. In the case of the *nigredo,* the blackness of soul from which gold will eventually emerge, both *The Devil* and *The Moon* take part. This is the kind of conclusion that results from applying Jung's ideas about spiritual Alchemy to the cards.

Of course, Carl Jung was not the first to suggest that Alchemy should be interpreted as the process of turning the leaden darkness of the normal waking consciousness into spiritual gold. It was a book, anonymously published by Mrs. Mary Anne Atwood in 1850, entitled *Hermetic Philosophy and Alchemy: A Suggestive Enquiry into the Hermetic Mystery,* that formed a bridge between the seventeenth-century alchemists and the twentieth-century psychologists.[19]

In her methodology Mrs. Atwood was Jung's precursor. By comparing schools of religion and of philosophy, she attempted to extract principles of universal truth and to develop a methodology for approaching an inner reality. Such being the case, it is interesting that Jung dismissed her work so lightly, calling it "a thoroughly medieval production garnished with would-be theosophical explanations as a sop to the syncretism of the new age."[20]

Notes: *The Moon*

1. The Moon was commonly associated with the Virgin Mary, who was also *Stella Mans,* the Star of the Sea. The fact that there is not the slightest reference to Mary here underscores the secular nature of the tarot.

2. The separate Sun, Moon, and Star above was probably a late fourteenth century French innovation on an original Italian design. The classical tradition of Virtues and Vices was never particularly strong in France, which accounts for a high degree of creative innovation with these subjects to be found in late medieval French manuscript painting.

3. Hesiod, *Theogony,* Oxford, 1988, 411ff. Since no other author describes this goddess with such reverential enthusiasm it must be assumed that Hesiod was reflecting a strong local cult.

4. *The Oxford Classical Dictionary,* Oxford, 1978, "Hecate," 490-491.

5. The Greek cults of Artemis and Selene drew upon that of Hecate. Artemis was originally a goddess of the earth, especially of dense forests, and a huntress like her Roman counterpart. In Greek myth it was Selene who drove the Moon chariot. *Oxford Classical Dictionary,* Oxford, 1978, "Artemis,",136, "Diana," 337, "Serene," 970.

6. Carl Jung, *Symbols of Transformation,* Princeton, 1978, **577.**

7. Ibid., **577.**

8. This is a modern argument. Despite Hesiod's effusive tribute to the goddess Hecate, there is no indication that the province of this deity was ever quite so broad in its scope.

9. Carl Jung, *Mysterium Coniunctionis,* Princeton, 1976, **24.**

10. *Isaiah,* 34:14.

11. The Hebrew word *lilith* comes from the Hebrew *lay'la,* and the Assyrian *leila* meaning simply *night.* Initially Lilith was not a specific person, but was a "daughter of the night," which implied any evil power of darkness. Rudwin, *The Devil in Legend and Literature,* La Salle, Illinois, 1959, 95ff. Rudwin's chapter, "The Legend of Lilith" is an excellent general survey of her legend.

12. Jung, *Symbols of Transformation,* **254.**

13. Ibid., **611.**

14. Jung, *Symbols of Transformation,* **681.** The psychologist amplifies this comment with a small joke. "Life,"he says, "is a disease with a bad prognosis because its outcome is always fatal." *Psychology and Religion,* **842.**

15. Jung identifies Hecate as goddess of birth as well as of death by con-
sidering one to be a reversal of the other. In Greek Mythology, however, Hecate was not a goddess of childbirth.

16. Jung, *Symbols of Transformation,* **580.**

17. Ibid., 577.

18. Jung, *Mysterium,* **174n**.

19. M.A. Atwood, *Hermetic Philosophy and Alchemy: A Suggestive Enquiry into "The Hermetic Mystery" with a dissertation on the more celebrated of the alchemical philosophers,* New York, 1960. Mary Anne South, whose married name was Atwood, was the daughter of Thomas South, a gentleman of leisure and a scholar of comparative religions. Mary Anne Atwood was his student and was herself an excellent scholar of Latin and Greek, lff. A historical perspective of Atwood's work is also found in C.A. Burland, *The Arts of the Alchemists,* New York, 1968,

20 / THE SUN

Archetype of the Child

The daily appearance and disappearance of the Sun has evoked more speculation and myth creation than any other natural phenomenon. Primitive man reasoned that this was a light of God which defied the laws of nature, for since ancient sages accepted the Biblical concept of a flat earth, they were quite baffled by the Sun's reappearance in the East each morning.[1]

It was an assumption of the earliest anthropologists that Sun worship was a thread common to all ancient societies. But by the late nineteenth century scholars had concluded that Sun worship was actually rather unusual. It was really only popular in Egypt, in Asia, in primitive Europe, and to some extent in the ancient Americas.[2] But the Sun archetype gained strength as Western society from the late antique period to the present—linked Jesus Christ with Apollo/Sun, as an affirmation of the tendency which Eliade grandly called the "solarization" of supreme beings.

The ancient Greeks were certainly not worshippers of the Sun although they had a critical interest in the movements of the heavens. Plato made it clear that the Sun itself was not considered a divinity; he related to it as a Star and as a bringer of light. In his *Timaeus,* he associates the creation of the Sun, moon, and other "Stars" to the creation of *time,* which, he says, appeared at the moment of creation of the heavens.[3] And he points out that "whatever is created, is of necessity corporeal, and also visible and tangible."[4] Moreover, in the *Republic* he explains that the Sun is not vision itself, but is that which by its light makes vision possible, an idea which he relates to the soul, saying that: "When it is firmly affixed on the domain where truth and reality shine resplendent it apprehends and knows them."[5]

The Divine Child

The Child-Sun motif is pivotal to Jungian philosophy. It is a point of connection between the individual and the collective which is, first and foremost, a principle of the collective unconscious. "The archetype," Jung says, "is always an image belonging to the whole human race, and not merely to the individual." It "represents the pre-conscious, childhood aspect of the collective psyche."[6]

The Child symbolizes the emerging Self-recognition described by Jung as being born out of the womb of the unconscious, begotten out of the depths of human nature, or rather out of living Nature herself. It is a personification of vital forces quite outside the limited range of our conscious mind; of ways and possibilities of which our one-sided conscious mind knows nothing.[7]

Jung certainly appreciated that the average reader would have difficulty following his arguments. He thus goes to some lengths to clarify that "the Child" must be understood as symbolic of a complex but well-ordered and complete pattern of ideas. "The mythological idea of the child," he stressed, "is emphatically not a copy of the empirical child, but a *symbol* clearly recognizable as such: it is a wonder-child, a divine child, begotten, born, and brought up in quite extraordinary circumstances, and not—this is the point—a human child." And he amplifies this point by insisting that "The same is true of the 'Father' and 'Mother' archetypes which, mythologically speaking, are equally irrational symbols"[8]

In one of Jung's most important essays, "The Psychology of the Child Archetype,"[9] he summarizes the considerable symbolism surrounding the Child, who is the *Son* and the *Sun* of growing Self-awareness. And since the primary goal of Jungian psychology is "individuation," *The Sun* is a pivotal card in the *Jungian Tarot* deck.

In the most simple of terms, the Child symbolizes the early phases of Self-discovery. Its relationship to the nurturing Mother and to the protective Father is critical because the "parents" are the opposite forces from whose power the Child is seeking release. Thus Jung explains that the child means something evolving toward independence.[10]

Aspects of the Child Archetype

The fact that such a remarkably broad and confusing collection of symbols exists around this archetype, suggests that the experience in question is beyond language and thought *per se.*

The Child archetype appears under many guises. It is the hermaphroditic *filius sapientiae,* the reborn Mercurius; it is the dwarf and elf of mythology which personifies the hidden forces of nature; it is the *puer aeternus;* it is the child god, and it is the young Hero."[12] It is this child which paves the way for future change of personality. In the individuation process, it antici- pates the figure that comes from the synthesis of conscious and unconscious elements in the personality. It is therefore a symbol which unites the opposites, a mediator, a bringer of healing, that is, one who makes whole.[13] This unification, this perfection is *the quaternity.* It is also the circle and the spheri- cal sun.

Insofar as the Child of *The Sun* card is the young *Magician*, he has a dual role. He is at once the young Hero who goes in search of spiritual gold, and he is the gold itself. And Jung is speaking in the context of its encounter in active meditation and in dreams when he notes that "seen as a special instance of 'the treasure hard to attain' motif, the child motif is extremely variable and assumes all manner of shapes, such as the jewel, the pearl, the chalice, the golden egg, the quaternity, the golden ball, and so on."[14]

The Child's Birth

The birth of the Child is understood to be the birth of a new kind of awareness. The birth of this so-called "divine Child" comes about as one reconciles tension between the opposites which are "Father" and "Mother." Their attributes—meaning conscious and unconscious—are brought together in the Child who is the Inner Man, the True Self.

The birth of the Child, the rejection of a separate ego, is a deeply disturbing experience to the personality of necessity overwhelmed by a new sense of reality. This is what Jung means when he says that "nothing in the world welcomes this new birth" It is terrible and unsettling experience from which one cannot retreat. Nothing whatsoever in the life process can prepare a person for the overwhelming power of this revolutionary perception which is a key step towards Self-realization.[15] The birth of the symbolic Child brings one to a primitive condition where there is an unconscious link of man and the universe. Jung said, cryptically, that that it is "a phase of non-differentiation...which is both man and universe, and yet neither."[16] And he offers what seems to be both a warning, and a record of his own experience when he says that "Abandonment, exposure, danger, etc., are all elaborations of the 'Child's' insignificant beginnings and of its mysterious and miraculous birth."[17] The "danger" has to do with the perilous situation into which the Child is born—that peril being to the personality consciousness which, perceiving itself to be separate, encounters the contents of the collective unconscious. Here some distinction must be made between the birth of the Child and of the Hero, two aspects of the "rising Sun" of consciousness symbolism.

The birth of the Child is a redemptive second birth which heralds the beginning of the quest to be carried out by the young Hero. The birth of the Hero-to-be (a Christ or a Buddha) takes place under the most extraordinary circumstances. The Hero is not born like an ordinary mortal because, rather, his birth "is a rebirth from the mother-wife."[18] This is to explain why the Hero is said to have two mothers, and is often described as being brought up by a foster mother. Even in canonical Christianity there is reference to a dual birth, the "rebirth" effected by baptism.[19] But esoteric Christianity contains some very specific references to Christ having dual mothers. In the *Gospel of Thomas* (as the text has been reconstructed,) Jesus says, "My mother gave me falsehood, but my true mother gave me life."[20] This can be interpreted to mean that first there is the physical birth into a condition of unreality, and then there is a rebirth by which the individual comes into contact with the Mother who is the ultimate unconscious condition from which the perception of separate existence issues.

The Young Hero

Jung teaches that the human figure is the most excellent of the symbols of the libido, which can be seen as Demon or as Hero. And he relates the adventures of the Hero, who passes from joy to sorrow, to the Sun which at one point is blazing in the sky, but which must eventually descends into darkness, only to arise with renewed brightness. This rising and falling of the Sun is used as a metaphor for the very course of man's existence. Man is born, lives, dies,and is reborn over and over again in his children.[21]

The Hero is the magical Child "growing up." He is the experience-collecting aspect of the Self who, like Dante with his teacher, first descends into the depths of Hell (the horrors of undifferentiated feeling and thought) and then ascends into Heaven where he becomes the light itself.

Jung explains that to overcome the monster of darkness is the whole point of our life journey. The triumph of consciousness over the unconscious is the ultimate goal, and the actions of the "Child," the early steps toward enlightenment, foreshadow a future over the darkness.[22]

This idea is inextricably interwoven into the fabric of Christianity. Saint Jerome, for example, speaks of baptism (which confers rebirth) as a mystery of light. The illumination of the Easter Sun is conferred by this ritual, an idea expanded upon in numerous sermons by the patristic fathers.[23]

Ra, Horus, and Christ as the Sun

It is no surprise to find that, when interpreted in psychological and metaphorical terms, ancient Egyptian religion suggests some remarkable parallels with Gnostic Christianity, with Alchemy considered to be a process of spiritual enlightenment, and with the modern principles of Jungian psychology. The comparison demands that one ask a difficult question: Is the modern psychology of the spiritually evolving individual describing the same process addressed by the ancient mystery religions? Did the initiates of such religions understand the pantheons of their gods in a very different and personal way than did the ordinary devotees of the cult? In other words, is the language of Jungian psychology describing an experience of revelation as old as mankind, as Jung repeatedly asserts? Is there really such a thing as Huxley called the *Perennial Philosophy*? The answer cannot be an unqualified yes because there is no way to know exactly what the ancient sages experienced. Nevertheless, some useful insights into the question emerge as one compares, in Jungian terms, the attributes of Christ with those of gods from earlier religious pantheons.

Ra,[24] Egyptian god of the Sun and of everything else, was an androgynous (like *The Magician*) creator who emerged out of the primordial watery mass, Nu. He was the Father of the Gods, whose evolutions are the history of creation itself.[25] Ra, who was potentially all gods, originally came into being out of Nu as the beetle god, Khepera.[26]

It is Ra as Khepera who first brings forth male and female

from himself by an act of masturbation. In an ancient text the god says that: "I had union with my hand, and I embraced my shadow in a love embrace; I poured seed into my own mouth, and I sent forth from myself issue in the form of the gods Shu and Tefnut."[27] Thus Ra was, like the alchemical Mercurius, the unified creator of the dualities which mankind is born to resolve.[28] Psychologically, the Sun god Ra is analogous to the emerging Self-consciousness which begins to work its way backward (Jung's *"regression"*) through the dualities which it has created, to the amorphous (watery/unconscious) condition from which it originally emerged.

And the trials of Ra (whose primary responsibility is the overthrowing of the wicked serpent Apep) are those of the Hero, who must descend into the dangerous underworld before he can emerge, Finally victorious, into the light. As the Sun, he is subject to the regulation of *Maat* (see the chapter on *Justice*) who causes him to rise into the heavens each day, and then to descend into the perilous underworld at night. There he must successfully fight against Apep before he can rise again in the East.[29]

The course of the Sun is a passage from the Child to the Old Man—recalling Jung's observation that the Child and the Old Man are an archetypal pair. The Child is the Sun rising in the East while the Old Man is the Sun setting in the West. The young Christ is often described in this way by the earliest Christian documents, such as the *Acts of Thomas.* After being baptized, Christ is said to have appeared to his apostles, like the sun symbolized in ancient art, as a youth holding a lighted torch "so that their lamps became dim at the approach of the light thereof."[30]

The Child who is himself the rising Sun of the tarot card is commensurate with the young Christ; with Ra, a god also often shown as a child; and with *Horus* (called *Harpocrates* by the Greeks), the child god who represented the earliest rays of the rising Sun.[31] So the Child as rising Sun is a powerful archetype linking paganism and early Christianity.

Actually, it took several centuries for the Christ mythology to be totally extricated from ancient Sun worship. As late as 275 C.E. an emperor declared the Sun god to be the highest divinity of the empire,[32] although thirty-seven years later Christianity was recognized as the official state religion by Constantine. But even Constantine himself confused Christianity with Sun worship.[33] And although the Epiphany (commemorating the coming of the Persian astrologers to Jesus at Bethlehem, but understood as the celebration of a god's birth)[34] was originally celebrated on January 6, by the fourth century Christmas began to be celebrated on December 25, day of the pagan festival of *solis invicti,* the "birthday" of the Sun triumphant.[35]

Rahner points out that this was understandable because the early Christians thought naturally in terms of solar symbolism and were only too ready to enliven this teaching with the imagery of Christ himself as the Sun.[36] "The Christian," he said, "had begun to think of Christ rising under the figure of the rising Sun and his death under that of a sunset."[37]

Notes: *The Sun*

1. Robert Graves, *Hebrew Myths,* New York, 1964, 38, n 1.

2. Mircea Eliade, *Patterns in Comparative Religion,* New York, 1974, 124.

3. Plato, *Timaeus,* 38.b-c.

4. Plato, *Timaeus,* 31.b.

5. Plato, *Republic,* VI, 508.

6. Carl Jung, *The Archetypes and the Collective Unconscious,* Princeton, 1977, **273.**

7. Ibid., **289.**

8. Ibid., **273.**

9. Ibid., **259-305.**

10. Ibid., **290.**

11. Bisexuality is implicit in the Child/Self and "As civilization develops, the bisexual primordial being turns into a symbol of the unity of personality, a symbol of the Self where the war of opposites finds peace." *Ibid,* **294.**

12. Ibid., **268.**

13. Ibid., **278.**

14. Ibid., **270.**

15. Ibid., **286.**

16. Ibid., **290.**

17. Ibid., **285.**

18. Carl Jung, *Symbols of Transformation,* Princeton, 1976, **494.**

19. Jung points out *(Symbols of Transformation,* **494**) that the death of Christ on the cross may be understood as a "baptism" in the redemptive sense—it was "a rebirth through the second mother, symbolized by the tree of death."

20: *The Gospel of Thomas,* translation *The Nag Hamadi Library,* New York 1977, 128, line 101.

21. Jung, *Symbols of Transformation,* **251.**

22. Jung, *Archetypes,* **284.**

23. Hugo Rahner, *Greek Myths and Christian Mysteries,* London, 1963.

24. The meaning of this title appears to have been "operative and creative power," something like "creator." E. A. Wallis Budge, *The Gods of the Egyptians,* New York, 1979, v.I, 322. The cult of Ra was flourish-

ing at Heliopolis in about 3350 B.C.E. Budge points out that although sun worship had been a part of the Egyptian culture since earliest times, the worship of Ra and that of Osiris came into serious conflict. He explains that Heliopolis had a very mixed population, being a stopping place for travellers from Arabia and from Syria into Egypt, and that Heliopolis mixed Egyptian and Western Asiatic doctrines which were resisted by the Egyptians. Budge. v.I, 334-335.

25. In this regard he is like the Kabbalistic *Chokmah,* an idea which impresses itself on *Binah* and ultimately produces a "child." See also Budge, vi, 308.

26. Budge, v.I, 294.

27. Ibid, 297.

28. Mercurius is analogous to *The Magician* if considered to be the universal creator. *The Sun* is Mercurius/*Magician* in manifestation; expressed in another way, the Son is the Father on a lower arc.

In the Fifth Dynasty a female counterpart, *Rat* was assigned to Ra. Her titles included "Lady of Heaven," "Mistress of the gods," and "Mistress of Heliopolis" Budge v. I, 328.

29. Apep was the greatest and most wicked of all forces. Originally Apep was the thick darkness which surrounded the Nu, and through which the Sun had to pass before it could rise for the first time. The frequent mention of Apep in *The Book of the Dead* is as a mortal enemy who is the opposite of the qualities of "rightness" characterized by the *Maat* which so guided Ra.

30. *Acts of Thomas,* in Montague James, *The Apocryphal New Testament,* 27, Oxford, 1979. 376.

31. Horus was not a single god, but was a company of gods of which *Heru-p-khart* was one of the seven expressions. Budge, *The Gods of the Egyptians,* v.I, 469.

32. It was the Emperor Aurelian who created an image of the sun god of Emesa and declared it to be the Empire's primary divinity. Walter Lowrie, *Art in the Early Church,* New York 1947. 21.

33. Some of his coins bear the Mithraic motto: *Soli invicto comiti.*

34. The "Magi" were not merely wise men from the East. They were priests of Zoroaster who represented the ancient religion of Persia, most recently appearing as Mithraism, the chief rival of Christianity. It appears that the inclusion of the Magi into the formal cycle of sepulchral art was based on a simple likeness to the Three Children in the Fiery

Furnace, one of the most common themes of Catacomb art. Lowrie, *Art in the Early Church,* New York, 1947, 81.

35. Celebration of Epiphany on January 6 was in direct competition with pagan Sun mysteries celebrated on that day. In fact, that date seems to have been chosen specifically to protest the pagan rites.The date is explained as the result of reform introduced by the more accurate Julian calendar into the ancient Egyptian calendar: the change from January 6 to December 25 resulted in a calculation which put the Winter Solstice on January 6. See Hugo Rahner, *Greek Myths and Christian Mystery,* London, 1963, 141.

36. Rahner, 116. Although Rahner meticulously traces the relationship of ancient sun worship to the emerging Christianity, one of his key points is that "The results of the Church's encounter with the Sun-cult of antiquity was nothing less than the dethronement of Helios, n.93.

37. Rahner, 105.

21 / JUDGMENT

Archetype of Rebirth

Following tradition, the *Jungian Tarot* shows two nude figures being called forth from their graves by the trumpet blast of an archangel. This is another of those cards which represent a milestone in the travels of the soul.

Judgment is the only card in the tarot which examines the concept of life after death and the principle that consciousness continues. Answering the question about what happens after death has been the essential role of religions; the earliest societies, including the Babylonian, the Egyptian, and the Hebrew having established a framework upon which later beliefs about Heaven and Hell were based.

The primitive Egyptian imagined a Heaven which was something of a celestial farm, or estate, where all of the work was done by the gods. This was very different from early Hebrew and Mohammedan beliefs at the time which stressed food, drink, and sensual pleasures.[1] *Tuat*, the hell of the Egyptians, was a dark and terrible place filled with snakes. And although the Hebrew abode of the damned, *Gehenna* (which was based upon the Egyptian Tuat) lacked such serpents,[2] it was no less terrifying. The Hebrew Heaven and Hell are of special interest to the student of Kabbalistic symbolism because of their complex system of interwoven opposites; the seven palaces of Gehenna are a negative counterpart to the seven palaces of Heaven, like the opposing Sephiroth and Klippoth.[3]

There was passed down from the ancient world an underlying belief that life continued after death, and that a judgment of man's behavior in life was inevitable. This idea was of particular significance in the late fourteenth century when the tarot originated. At that time the plague has made death all too commonplace and the Christian promise of resurrection was the only solace presented to the doomed sinner. Thus the earliest *Judgment* card carried an implicit message of Christian salvation and of resurrection. It was a card of hope and of faith that on the day of judgment the righteous man would be rewarded.

The *Jungian Tarot* card does not show the day of "Last Judgment." Rather it illustrates a judgment of the individual's life on earth—what Egyptian religion conceived as the weighing of the soul. It is, nevertheless, impossible to separate the personal from the collective insofar as the drama of the personality under scrutiny for its past deeds is the microcosmic reflection of the same drama which unfolds on the stage of the collective unconscious.

The day of Last Judgment, administered by Christ seated in

majesty among the saints and his angels, has never been a part of tarot, although what the tarot does show is something of a scaled down version of that theme.

In the *Visconti-Sforza Tarot*, God the Father presides over the resurrection of a man and a woman (presumably Francesco Sforza and his wife Bianca Maria).On each side of him is an angel who trumpets a call to judgment before the Lord.[4] The emphasis here is on resurrection rather than on judgment, a hopeful Italian perspective which has been passed down to the modern tarot decks.[5]

The Day of Jahweh

Mention of a day of judgment for all mankind, at which time this era ends and a new one begins, is first found in the Old Testament book of *Amos*, written in the eighth century B.C.E.[6] It is a story of gloom and doom proclaiming that: "There shall be wailing in every street, and in all open places cries of woe. The farmer shall be called to mourning and those skilled in the dirge to wailing; there shall be lamentation in every vineyard; for I will pass through the midst of you, says the Lord." Amos speaks of the Day of Jaweh as one of utter darkness in which the sins of Israel would be judged and punished.

Later Old Testament writers expanded upon this theme, and the Day of Jahweh was increasingly anticipated as a turning point in history where the Israelites would be redeemed. And it was the prophet Isaiah who expressed the idea that this would be the greatest day of judgment in which all of the earthly and celestial foes of Jahweh would be vanquished, and he would establish his eternal rule over the universe.[7] It was a time when, Isaiah said, "The Lord God will wipe away the tears from every face"[8]

Concepts about resurrection are very different in the Old and in the New Testaments. In Hebrew scriptures very few references to a resurrection occur. The Hebrew religion actually rejected some of the ancient beliefs about cyclic death and rebirth of the body associated with agriculture, and generally substituted a belief in an immortal soul and the principle that the physical body is of no ultimate significance.

The Judgment of Christ

Judaism established that one day God would destroy all that has been, that he would judge all men, and that he would sit forever in unchallenged majesty. It created the intellectual foundation for a Christian myth of the resurrection of the God whose Kingdom was to come and who was to preside over mankind at a final day of judgment.[9] This was the basis of the New Testament day of last judgment at which Christ was to preside, and at which those he judged to be worthy would live beside him in heaven while those judged unworthy would receive the ultimate sentence: eternal banishment from his presence.[10] Medieval artists were inspired by Bible passages such as that of the Gospel of Matthew,[11] warning that "at the end of time the Son of Man will send out his angels, who will gather out of his kingdom whatever makes men stumble, and all whose deeds are evil, and these will be thrown into the burning furnace, the place of wailing and of grinding of teeth. And then the righteous will shine as brightly as the sun in the kingdom of their Father."

That there was no escape, and that kings and peasants were judged equally, was stressed in the stone carvings of the cathedrals. Above the main doorway of the church there was usually an intricately carved scene of Christ separating the saved from the damned (the implicit message being, also, that the Church was the way of ultimate salvation). And although this picture showed the end of the world, it was a stern warning to all passing beneath it that their time of personal judgment would come soon. Thus there was, effectively, no distinction between the ultimate fate of mankind and of the lowly individual "sinner."

The resurrection of the God was the model for that of the individual, who might suffer death and be personally reborn if he had lived properly. So, to reiterate, there are two forms of judgment. There is the judgment of the individual at death, and there is the Last Judgment. Obviously, the theme of the individual judgment draws upon the ubiquitous medieval symbols of the Last Judgment.

In this regard Scholem points out that the Jewish Kabbalists recognized a contradiction in having two judgments on man's fate —one after death and the other after resurrection. Thus some early Kabbalists concluded the on the final day of judgment God would pass judgment not on the individual, but upon nations.

Resurrection of the Ancient Gods

The theme of a god's death and subsequent resurrection was very common in the ancient world. It is an archetypal pattern having to do with crops and agriculture, couched originally in ancient legends such as those about an Earth Mother who arouses her Son from the sleep of death. This sequence of death and resurrection, ultimately played out as the seasons of the year, is repeated daily in the rise and setting of the sun.

A great many ideas picked up by Christianity, and by the Western occult tradition, trace back to the Egyptians and to

other early societies. But the correspondence between the stories of Christ and of the Egyptian resurrected god, Osiris, is
particularly striking. The resurrection of Osiris was as essential a theme to Egyptian religion as was the resurrection of
Christ to Christianity. There are many variations on the god's
story. In the most common version Osiris, son of the sky goddess and the earth god, became King of Egypt. After having
greatly improved the lives of his subjects by showing them
how to till the earth, to sow and to reap crops, he put his wife
Isis in charge and left his country, travelling across the world
to teach all of this to others.

During this time the evil Typhon resolved to kill Osiris upon
his return. He created a beautiful chest, the size of the body of
Osiris, which he offered to give to the person who could most
comfortably fit into it. When Osiris was tricked into lying in
the coffin, it was nailed shut and he suffocated to death. Typhon
and his co-conspirators put the casket into the Nile. Eventually
the chest came into the care of Isis, and it became an object of
worship. As the story goes, the jealous Typhon found the box
and cut Osiris' body into fourteen pieces which he scattered
across the kingdom. However Isis found the parts and restored
the body of Osiris, after which Osiris himself returned from
the other world.[13]

An important parallel between Christ and Osiris is that both
are judge of the dead after resurrection.[14] There is a simple logic
here: Since it was obvious that not everyone was worthy of life
immortal, only one who had himself proven perfection, and
who had transcended death, could be a judge.[15] And resurrection of the god (the proof of his immortality) necessarily precedes his role as judge of the worth of the deceased.

As has been discussed (see chapter 12, *Justice*), the iconography of the *weighing of souls* by the archangel Michael is
taken directly from Egyptian mythology. And critical to the

Egyptian concept of resurrection was an internal spirit duplicate called the *Ka,* something which Alice Bailey and others
have called the "etheric double."[16] The Egyptians believed that
this Ka was born with a man and survived him after death. But
it did not leave the body, and it was maintained by offerings
made to it in the tomb."

In Egyptian art Osiris is seen in the long hall of judgment
with the two goddesses of truth, and with Thoth in the form of
an ape, seated before a pair of scales on which the heart will be
weighed against the feather of *Maat.*[18]

The Greeks had their own versions of the Osiris myths,
including that of Orpheus, who descends into the underworld
and then returns.[19] But most important was the cult of Dionysus,
the divine Child who symbolized resurrection. In the Phrygian
cult of that god he was asleep or bound in winter, and was
awake in summer, being a god of fertility, and probably of
vegetation.[20] In other areas Dionysus was worshipped as a god
of wine, but despite regional variations his cult was predominantly one of the underworld.[21]

The Symbolic Resurrection

Late in his career Jung explained to a correspondent, who
asked the psychologist why he had never commented on the
theme of resurrection, that he had avoided writing on this complex issue because the topic required more knowledge than he
had. Yet he asserted that resurrection was perhaps the most
"important item in the myth of the biography of Christ."[22] Jung
felt that "the fact of the resurrection is historically doubtful,"
but that "spiritual reality could not be demonstrated to the un-
educated and rather primitive population in any other way but
by crude and tangible 'miracles' or stories of such kind."[23]

Ultimately Jung discussed resurrection in terms of the *continuity of consciousness*. He wrote that "since we are psychic beings and not entirely dependent upon space and time, we can easily understand the central importance of the resurrection idea: we are not completely subjected to the powers of annihilation because our psychic totality reaches beyond the barrier of space and time. Through the progressive interaction of the unconscious we have a reasonable chance to make experiences of an archetypal nature providing us with the feeling of continuity before and after our existence."[24] And so, from a Jungian perspective, the Judgment Day when all of the "enemies of God" are vanquished can be interpreted to mean the absorption of all potential opposites into the One.

This union of opposites and the rebirth of consciousness has often been symbolized by phases of the Moon. The Moon sometimes plays an important part in initiations where the candidate ritually dies and is reborn as his "True Self."[25] This is very much the same as Christian baptism which, as John Chrysostom taught, represents the total scheme of death, burial, life, and resurrection.[26] Symbolic death and resurrection is a part of virtually all initiation schemes.[27] On the other hand, there have been many belief systems espousing the principle that the actual physical body will be resurrected.

Life After Life

It was at the age of twelve, in 1887, that Carl Jung began to have experiences which confronted him with the possibility of reincarnation. In his autobiography, *Memories, Dreams, Reflections,* he describes a long walk returning from school when he suddenly felt " the overwhelming impression of having just emerged from a dense cloud." "At this moment," he said, "I came upon myself."

Shortly afterwards, Jung felt the extraordinary confusion that he was actually two persons. One was the schoolboy of his current life, and the other was a "high authority, a man not to be trifled with." He was "an old man who lived in the eighteenth century, wore buckled shoes and a white wig and went driving in a fly with high, concave rear wheels between which the box was suspended on springs and leather straps." He never actually stated that he believed this old man to be an earlier incarnation of himself, but related three separate instances in which he felt an innate relationship with an earlier period. Of this he said: "I cannot describe what was happening in me or what it was that affected me so strongly....I could not explain this identity with the eighteenth century."[28]

Striving for an appearance of scientific objectivity, Jung clearly wished to avoid any specific statement about a belief in reincarnation. But the psychologist presents the "facts" of his own experience in such a way that the reader can only assume that he accepted some principle of rebirth.

Notes: *Judgment*

1. E. A. Wallis Budge, *The Gods of the Egyptians,* New York, 1969, v.l,165-166.

2. The structure of Hell relates to the geographical terrain of the two areas. Predynastic Egypt was filled with snakes of all kinds around which a mythology of fear developed. In Palestine and Syria, however, snakes were never very plentiful.

3. Budge v.I, 274-275.

4. Gertrude Moakley, *The Tarot Cards Painted by Bonifacio Bembo,* New York 1966, 110.

5. Generally Italian artists took the theme of Judgment and Last Judgment, more lightly than did their French counterparts. The somewhat nonchalant resurrection of the *Viscount-Sforza Judgment* is in stark contrast to the gruesome scenes carved into some French cathedrals.

6. *Amos,* 5:18. Although this is the first known written reference to a Day of Judgment, the idea certainly existed some time before this.

7. James Hastings, ed. *Dictionary of the Bible,* New York, 1963., "Day of the Lord," 203. See also: "Judgment," 542.

8. *Isaiah,* 25:8.

9. *Dictionary of the Bible,* ed. James Hastings, "Resurrection," New York, 1963, 843-846.

10. The absence of any specifically Christian image can only be interpreted as a specific affirmation of the Tarot's secular intent. Presumably, reference to Christ, Mary, or to other biblical figures in a common game would have been considered blasphemy.

11. *Matthew,* 13 :40-43.

12. Gershom Scholem, *Kabbalah,* New York 1974, 336.

13. E.A. Wallis Budge, *Osiris,* New Hyde Park, 1961, 1-8.

14. It happened very slowly that an early cult of ancestors was replaced by the cult of Osiris who became the final judge of the dead. The Osiris cult is understandably quite ancient, but there is no known representation of it earlier than the Eighteenth Dynasty. Budge, *Osiris,* 315.

15. Pursuant to the use of the resurrection theme to symbolize spiritual rebirth ("individuation") it should be noted that the Egyptians believed it quite possible for a person to attain attributes of divinity, and to function on Earth and in Heaven at the same time. Budge, *Gods of the Egyptians* v.I, 162.

16. Alice A. Bailey, A *Treatise on Cosmic Fire*, Albany, 1973, 77-133.

17. Budge, *Gods of the Egyptians,* v.I, 163.

18. Budge, *Osiris,* 315-316.

19. Orphism was an eclectic movement of the sixth century, B.C.

20. *Oxford Classical Dictionary,* Oxford, 1978, "Dionysus," 352.

21. *Oxford Classical Dictionary,* 353.

22. Carl Jung, *The Symbolic Life,* Princeton, 1980, **1559.**

23. Jung, *Symbolic Life,* **1562-1564.**

24. Ibid., **1572.**

25. Mircea Eliade, *Patterns in Comparative Religion,* New York, 1974, 175.

26. Ibid., 197.

27. Mircea Eliade *Shamanism: Archaic Techniques of Ecstasy,*

22 / THE WORLD

Archetype of Persona

The earliest known tarot deck includes a prototype of what was later to be called *The World* or sometimes *The Universe*. Two *putti* hold a sphere in the center of which is a castle floating between sky and water. It is likely that this card represents not the whole earth, but the principality over which the Sforza ruled, the Milanese court and countryside shown in the tarot cards. This is, of course, an iconography far removed from that the dancing female, called *Le Monde*, which appeared in eighteenth-century French tarot.

It is likely that the modern version evolved from an image of Christ encircled by a *mandorla.*[1] In support of this thesis one scholar cites a French deck from the mid-seventeenth century by Jacques Vievil. In *The World* card of that deck, a haloed and classically-nude Christ stands at the center of a mandorla around which are the symbols of the four evangelists: man, eagle, lion, and ox. Later decks appear to have transformed the image of Christ into that of a nude woman dancing in a mandorla surrounded by four animals which are today sometimes interpreted as the four elements.

Definitions of "Self" in Western Mysticism

One of the clear points of agreement among the diverse philosophical sects which make up the "mystery tradition" is the idea that each person has a "Higher Self" generally unknown or obscured to the waking consciousness. The goal of the mysteries is the opening up of this higher consciousness and the recognition that what had previously been known as the focus of consciousness does not exist *per se,* but is a projection of the Higher Self.

The principle is expressed in the ancient Indian concept of *Atman,* the Divine Essence in a human being. The Atman is related to the *Brahman,* which is the Ultimate Divine, the First Cause. It is through spiritual exercises and meditations that this True Self is known and the "Inner Light" is experienced. "Light" in this regard, is equated with inner being and with Spirit. According to one Vedic text "the Sun is the life or the Atman—*the Self—of all things.*"[2]

The True Self, the Inner Sun, is commensurate with the *soul* described by Kabbalistic cosmology. *Tiphareth* (solar Logos) is the area of the Tree of Life to which this Self is related and which is obscure to the lower waking consciousness rooted in *Yesod* (the Moon). The aim of the Kabbalist is, as the thirteenth-century mystic Abraham ben Samuel Abulafia asserted, "to unseal the soul, to untie the knots which bind it,"[3] meaning a perception of the True Self of Tiphareth, whatever that Self may be called.

Such ideas are imbedded in the earliest Hermetic Qabalah of the sixteenth century, in Rosicrucianism, and in the occult movement of the late nineteenth century. During that period, the idea of the Atman attracted special interest due to England's incursions into India and to curiosity about Eastern culture. Movements such as Blavatsky's Theosophy espoused the Eastern point of view that all of life is a mere illusion and that one has the capacity to awaken from the mortal "dream" into a greater reality.[4] These Western advocates of Eastern thought, including Blavatsky and Alice Bailey, have been criticized for their grandiose claims of infallibility by way either of their own "initiation into the greater mysteries," or of "inner plane" contacts with "Masters." There is no question that late nineteenth-century romanticism fostered a great deal of theatrical charlatanism. But at the philosophical heart of what has been called "the occult revival" were principles which have had a profound effect on Western culture.

It is particularly interesting to discover the ways in which Jungian philosophy parallels the essential principles of the modern occult movement. In the lessons of the *Hermetic Order of the Golden Dawn* (arguably the fraternity most influential to twentieth-century occult thought) it is stated that the True Self "in the ordinary man can but rarely act through the spiritual consciousness, seeing that for it to do so the king of the Physical Body, that is the Lower Will, must rise from his Throne to acknowledge his superior."[5] In other words, the personality must acknowledge that it exists only by reference to a greater principle. Moreover, the Golden Dawn's lessons refer to an idea very similar to Jung's postulate of the "collective unconscious." This is the "automatic consciousness."

Those aspiring to knowledge of the True Self should, it was advised, act purposefully to "prevent the Lower Will and Human Consciousness from falling into and usurping the place of the Automatic Consciousness."[6] Theoretically this automatic consciousness is highly structured and relates to the various levels of the Kabbalistic Tree of Life. One approaches it through a defined system of active imagination referred to as "skrying" or "rising on the planes."

Later writers in the Hermetic Kabbalist tradition, such as Dion Fortune, while rejecting the Eastern methodologies fostered by Theosophy,[7] strongly affirm the reality of a Higher Self as the object of all mystical investigation. Fortune says that: "The four Sephiroth below Tiphareth represent the personality or lower self; the four Sephiroth above Tiphareth are the Individuality, or Higher Self, and Kether is the Divine Spark, or nucleus of manifestation."[8]

Jung's Principle of the Persona

In all of Jung's writing two essays, worked and reworked over his entire life, contain the core of his philosophy. Published as volume seven of his collected works, *Two Essays on Analytical Psychology* is Jung's primary statement about the relationship of the personality to the collective unconscious.[9] It was in 1912 that Jung began to publish his then somewhat tentative principles of archetypes and of the collective unconscious, essays which he completely rethought forty years later.

As descriptions of the process of Self-discovery these essays are historically unique. They purport to explain, in psychological terms, exactly what happens when the waking consciousness, in which a belief of separateness and of individuality is based, begins to interact with the collective unconscious.

Jung chose the term *Persona*—the mask worn by actors in the ancient theater—to mean a "personal" self which does not exist in the way that most people believe. The Persona, with which most people identify, is "that compromise role in which we parade before the community."[10] Jung wrote that "when we analyze the Persona we strip off the mask and discover that what seemed to be individual is at bottom collective"[11] In other words, what we understand as the personality is only a mask hiding the collective psyche. The Persona is not, in itself, real. Rather it is described by Jung as a "compromise between individual and society." It has the qualities expected of a person by a given society.

Jung asserts that it is because the Persona is cut off from the collective psyche that one can believe it to be something individual. What the mask of Persona covers is the collective psyche; it pretends to itself and to others that it is individual, although it is really a part of the collective psyche.[12] So the Persona is a point of compromise between the true individuality and society. On the one hand it makes an impression on others; and on the other hand it conceals the true nature of the individual. He makes the point that society compels one to play the part of his Persona, or be considered weird and unacceptable.

Self-Realization

There are two basic aims of the process of "individuation." The first is to free the real Self from what Jung calls the "false wrappings of the Persona; the second is freedom from the power of those primordial images of the collective unconscious."[13] This is, at base, a process of discrimination whereby the Self determines *what it is not.*

"Just as for the purpose of individuation, or Self-realization, it is essential for a man to distinguish between what he is and how he appears to himself and to others, so it is also necessary for the same purpose that he should become conscious of his invisible system of relations to the unconscious, and especially of the Anima, so as to be able to distinguish himself from her."[14] Jung explains that the Anima reinforces the hold of the Persona. "I am," he said, "of the opinion that it is absolutely essential for a certain type of modern man to recognize his distinction not only from the Persona, but from the Anima as well."[15]

Plainly and straightforwardly stated, Persona is opposed by dark and complicated Anima which "continually thwarts the good intentions of the conscious mind, by contriving a private life that stands in sorry contrast to the dazzling Persona."[16]

Jung points out that the True Self (the Individuality) is both conscious and unconscious. And he says that although we can easily see ourselves as a Persona, it is beyond the abilities of our imagination to appreciate what is meant by the "Self." Nor can one reach so much as an approximate idea of the Self because it comprises so much unconscious material.[17]

The Dissolution of Personality

The winning of Self-knowledge requires that the personality be dissolved back into the collective as well as a dissolution of what Jung called "projections," meaning ideas and conclusions formed about others which may or may not be correct.[18]

The process means a total giving up of what one believes to be the Self —which is without doubt the most terrible thing that one could be called upon to do. It requires the purposeful invocation of what Saint John of the Cross called a "dark night of the soul." But the desire to return to the womb of consciousness is an innate one. As Jung affirmed: "the dissolution of the Persona in the collective psyche is a direct invitation to wed oneself with the abyss and blot out all memory in that embrace. This piece of mysticism is characteristic of all better men, and is just as innate in every individual as the 'longing for the mother,'the nostalgia for the source from which we spring."[19]

In his *Two Essays* Jung attempts to explain how it happens that the ego-self begins to open up to the collective unconscious.[20] The first step is to approach the personal unconscious through nonjudgmental creative visualization. In this way the materials of the collective unconscious begin to pour into the conscious mind which becomes increasingly open to the patterns of the True Self.[21]

But as a new world of consciousness begins to flower, the wealth of possibilities in the collective psyche is at first confusing and blinding. "With the disintegration of the Persona there is a release of involuntary fantasy, which is apparently nothing else than the specific activity of the collective psyche. This activity brings up contents whose existence one had never dreamed of before. But as the influence of the collective unconscious[22] increases, so the conscious mind loses its power of leadership." The process of discovery of "all the richness of mythological thought and feeling," may be overwhelming, and may present a genuine danger to psychological stability.[23]

The resultant dissolution of the perception of separateness can be devastating and frightening because there is an intermediate point of development where one does not know who he is.[24] This is not a pleasant experience—"it always feels like the end of the world, as though everything had tumbled back into original chaos."[25] "It will readily be understood that this condition is insupportable, and one ought to put an end to it as promptly as possible, for it bears too close an analogy to mental derangement. The most common form of madness is...characterized precisely by the fact that the unconscions mind almost entirely suppresses the function of the conscious mind and supplants it."[26] And, "in a similar but not quite identical manner the unconscious is pushed into consciousness when the Persona is dissolved in the collective psyche."[27]

As the Persona is dissolved, the ideal response would be critical understanding, but that does not necessarily happen. One person may identify with the collective unconscious, having a heightened sense of self-confidence, and an attitude of arrogance; the feeling of "godlikeness" happens. He may in dreams, as Jung says, seem to fly through space, or feel that "he is the Earth, the Sun, or a Star, or that he is of an immense size or is extremely small, or that he is dead, etc."[28] Another person may be so overwhelmed when faced with the contents of the unconscious that he loses all self-confidence and submits himself to the power of unconscious, becoming mentally ill, eccentric, and infantile. He may isolate himself, or he may simply deny the experience and restore the Persona.

Jung's Summation

In an appendix to his *Structure of the Unconscious,* entitled "Identification with the Collective Psyche," Jung offers a profound key to his psychological theory of revelation: "Access to the collective psyche," he says, "produces a renewal of life in the individual, whether the sensation resulting from it be agreeable or disagreeable." And he insists that this renewal is quite normal. "This 'mystic phenomenon,' which is a propensity of all mankind, is as innate in every one of us as is the 'desire for the Mother,' the longing to return to the source from whence we came."

And Jung explains that each man or woman may be the mythic hero because, "It is precisely the best and the strongest among men, the heros, who give way to their regressive nostalgia and purposely expose themselves to the danger of being devoured by the monstrous primal cause. But if a man is a hero, he is a hero because, in the final reckoning, he did not let the monster devour him, but subdued it—not once but many times. It is in the achievement of victory over the collective psyche that the true value lies; and this is the meaning of the conquest of the treasure, of the invisible weapon, the magic talisman—in short, of all those desirable goods that the myths tell of."[29]

Notes: *The World*

1. Stuart R. Kaplan, *The Encyclopedia of Tarot,* v.II, New York, 1986, 178-181.

2. Mircea Eliade, *A History of Religious Ideas,* v.I, 241-243.

3. Gershom Scholem, *Major Trends in Jewish Mysticism,* New York, 1977, 126.

4. Interest in Theosophy and other such movements of the time have been explained by some historians as a response to fears about a crass materialism brought into society with late nineteenth century industrialization.

5. Israel Regardie, *The Golden Dawn,* v.I, Chicago, 1937, 214.

6. Ibid., 217.

7. Dion Fortune, *The Mystical Qabalah,* London 1951, 10.

8. Ibid., 190.

9. The original articles are "La Structure de l'inconscient," (French translation of 1916 based on the lost German original) and "Neue Bahnen der Psychologie," (original German 1912). These are originals translated in their entirety as an appendix to Carl Jung's *Two Essays on Analytical Psychology,* New York, 1953, **243**ff.

10. Jung, *Two Essays,* **246.**

11. Ibid., **246.**

12. Ibid., **468.**

13. Ibid., **269.**

14. Ibid., **310.**

15. Ibid., **317.**

16. Ibid., **318.**

17. Ibid., **274.**

18. See Marie Louise von Franz, *Projection and Recollection in Jungian Psychology,* Illinois, 1990, 1-19 et passim.

19. Jung, *Two Essays,* **260**.

20. Although Jung often underscores his points using mythological, alchemical, biblical, or materials derived from conferences with patients, these *Two Essays* bear the mark of Jung's personal experience

21. Jung, *Two Essays,* **246.**

22. Ibid., **251.**

23. Ibid., **470.**